Feminisms on Edge

Politics, Discourses and National Identities

Edited by

Karen Atkinson, Sarah Oerton and Gill Plain

Cardiff Academic Press
St Fagans Road, Fairwater,Cardiff CF5 3AE

British Library Cataloguing in Publication Data

A catalogue record for this book is available
from the British Library.

ISBN 1 899025 146

Printed & bound in Great Britain by
Antony Rowe Ltd.

Typeset by Elgan Davies Partnership, Cardiff

Published in Great Britain by
Cardiff Academic Press
St Fagans Road, Fairwater, Cardiff CF5 3AE
2000

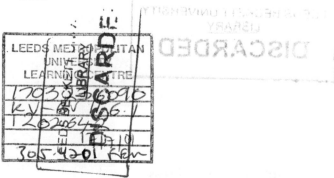

Contents

Acknowledgements

Thanks are due to many people for their help and support over the years it has taken to compile and produce this volume. First and foremost amongst these, however, are our co-organisers from the original conference, Jane Gardner and Pauline Young. Jane and Pauline were instrumental in shaping the 'Feminisms Past, Present and Future' event, and their input and ideas have equally contributed to the conception of this book. During the conference we were also assisted by volunteers from the University of Glamorgan BA in Women's Studies and by many other staff and students at the university who gave generously and unstintingly of their time. We are also indebted to Jackie Jones, who gave us confidence along with her constructive editorial advice, and Jill Gamble, who helped enormously with the preparation of the manuscript. Cardiff Academic Press worked with remarkable speed and efficiency to bring the project to fruition, but the final vote of thanks must go to Professor Douglas Dunn of the School of English at the University of St. Andrews, whose timely intervention made all the difference. Family and friends who have put up with it all know who they are, and just how much we owe them!

edge *n.* **1.** sharpened side of blade of cutting instrument or weapon; sharpness of this (*the knife has no edge*), (fig.) effectiveness; **be on --**, be excited or irritable; **take the -- off**, blunt, weaken, dull (appetite, argument, etc.); **have the -- on**, (colloq.) have an advantage over; **set** person's **teeth on --**, cause him revulsion as from eating sour fruit; **rough** or **sharp -- of** one's **tongue**, reviling....
3. boundary line of region or surface; area close to steep drop (of precipice); **on the -- of**, (fig) almost involved in or affected by.

edge *v.* **1.** sharpen (tool etc., also fig); ... furnish with or *with* border, form border to; insinuate, push, (thing, one*self*) *into, in, out, off,* etc.; ... **2.** *v.i.* advance, esp. gradually and obliquely.

(The Concise Oxford Dictionary of Current English, 1982)

Feminisms on edge: Feminisms advancing – gradually, imperceptibly, marginally. Coming round and over the edge. Boundary, border, lines of inclusion and containment, or of prohibition and exclusion. Beginning and end. Something constituitive yet decentered. Fundamental. Marginal.

Feminisms on edge: Touchy. On the verge, on a precipice, on the instance of change. In transition. Conflictual. Cutting. Sharp. Reactive. Angry.

Feminisms on edge: Conceptual, theoretical, practical, academic, communal, creative, political. Cross-cutting discourses.

Feminisms on edge: A volume of feminist edges. Edge to edge.

Introduction

Karen Atkinson, Sarah Oerton and Gill Plain

Feminisms on Edge arises from our collaborations with the many diverse women who attended the Ninth International Women's Studies Network Association Conference, held at the University of Glamorgan in July 1996. This event aimed to create a space from the constructive interplay of feminist ideas and practices, enabling connections to be made between women working, researching, teaching and learning across the UK and beyond. *Feminisms on Edge* aims to embody both the diversity and the dialogue of the original conference. The plurality of feminism is our focus, and this volume opens up for discussion its multiple definitions and manifestations. In so doing, it represents a critical intervention into current feminist debates and unites inter-disciplinary research both inside and outside the academy. Some contributors have chosen to foreground how feminist concerns have been developed, contested and refigured to date. Others, given current socio-political changes in which discourses of postmodernism and globalism repeatedly surface, have opted to address what the functions, obligations and future directions of feminist projects might be. Taken together, the papers in this volume move through history and across complex boundaries of nation, ethnicity and sexuality to voice women's concerns. They form an illustration of the complexity and sophistication of engagement inherent in cutting-edge feminist debates.

Feminisms on Edge also lays bare the tension long evident in women's studies between a desire for co-operative community and the need for an acknowledgement of difference. Indeed, a significant proportion of the papers collected here argue that unless women's studies as a body of knowledge confesses the impossibility of homogeneity, it will cease to have relevance for the majority of women. Yet what is also apparent within such discussion is that the centring of difference need not necessarily preclude constructive communication. Diversity does not devalue feminism as a political movement, it enhances and empowers it – and the disparate elements that shape contemporary feminism do not have their value in isolation, but rather in debate. Furthermore, feminism is not an amalgam of discrete differences but a movement filled with shifting and unstable boundaries – geographical, political, social and corporeal. And the borders of debate are already destabilised by a discourse that presupposes the possibility of alternative alliances, changing perspectives and different readings. It is to these tensions and shifts that *Feminisms on Edge* attends.

All too often women have been wary of subjecting to critical scrutiny political and academic work undertaken in the name of feminism, but the mark of a mature movement is often its ability to be responsive, even proactive, in the face of criticism. There is a long and sometimes tension-filled history between feminist academics, researchers and activists concerned with wider struggles for power at the societal level (both locally and globally) and those at the internal micro-political level, where the focus is upon women's organisational protocols and practices. From such struggles for power can come new and improved ways of ensuring that feminist issues remain relevant and engaging. Issues relating to how women can understand more about the operation of power and how best to prioritise efforts to bring about necessary change are dealt with in the first four contributions to this volume by **Liz Kelly, Jill Radford and Joan Scanlon; Jane W. Grant; Gail Chester** and **Frances Connelly and Monika Reinfelder.** They all explore potential sites for women's empowerment, showing how power relations inform and are informed by complex nuances that operate at both institutional and grass-roots levels, locally, nationally and internationally.

For **Liz Kelly, Jill Radford and Joan Scanlon** this requires a return to the basic tenets that shaped the women's liberation movement. Their paper charts what they see as the tendencies which have fragmented feminism and identifies ways in which the academy in particular is implicated in the process of rewriting for posterity earlier feminist struggles. They challenge what is rapidly and problematically becoming women's studies orthodoxy by offering an alternative reading of the developments in UK feminist theory and activism from the seventies' women's liberation movement, through the development of academic feminism in the eighties, to the present tensions between postmodernism and global activist feminism in the nineties. The authors dispute academic accounts of the history of the women's liberation movement by looking back on it from a standpoint that recognises the inseparability of theory and activism. They also question particular directions in contemporary women's studies, and the relationship between feminism and poststructuralism. Finally, they present an alternative vision of feminism that fight backs for a key concept, that of women's liberation.

Jane W. Grant also contributes to this focus by putting under the microscope power relations within organisations run by and for women, identifying some of the pitfalls and pleasures of both hierarchy and collectivism in all-women settings. In focusing upon autonomous women's organisations rather than mainstream public or corporate bodies, Grant explores women's capacity to change organisations which they themselves have created. The paper looks particularly at the lessons that can be learnt from the many women's organisations that are undergoing often painful processes of change, whether by moving away from the more traditional structures, or by moving from non-hierarchical to more hierarchical structures. Grant suggests that, contrary to traditional expectations, power can be abused within women's organisations and women can be the perpetrators as well as the victims of such abuse. In her view, the power relations between voluntary boards (or management committees) and staff, and the confusion between governance and management, can lead to feelings of resentment, ambivalence and misunderstanding on all sides. More widely Grant advocates the sometimes radical changes which may be needed to help women's organisations become 'enabling' structures, releasing the potential of all involved, instead of the 'disabling' structures so many have become today. Ultimately she argues that it is such problems of power and governance which prevent many women's organisations from reaching their full potential, not only as vehicles of much needed social welfare but as powerful catalysts of political change.

Lest we should be complacent about the ways in which feminists have sought to bring together theory and action, **Gail Chester** addresses the controversial issue of how and why the collection, storage and retrieval of the history of women's liberation might usefully be achieved by means of electronic technology. She takes as her case study the Essex Road Women's Centre, and argues for a timely consideration of how best women might shape their history in ways which relate openly and honestly the struggles for power which took place there. The history of feminism is not easy to record accurately for many familiar reasons. Many key events were not recorded at the time and the need to catch the different and changing perspectives of the women involved, as well as acknowledging the complexity of why things happened how and when they did, all pose huge problems to the history of women in print. Chester discusses ways in which electronic, interactive multimedia might be used to express many different voices, both to convey the complexities of women's activist histories and to capture as many as possible of the original text and non-text sources for future reference. Finally, she explores how to use state-of-the art electronic technology to deliver an invaluable living political resource to feminists today, including a framework through which women might follow the evolution of ideas in an exciting period of change and outreach for feminism.

In the next contribution, **Frances Connelly and Monika Reinfelder** pick up Chester's concern with the issue of public visibility and describe the efforts to get lesbians and their concerns rendered visible at the Fourth International United Nations World Conference on Women in Beijing in 1996. The authors discuss how, both inside the lesbian tent (T46) and outside at the main conference, commonality overrode the diversity and differences between lesbians world-wide. As a result, the voice of lesbian politics made its mark as, for the first time in history, space was secured at this UN event to discuss and collaborate on issues which could work towards securing full democratic rights for lesbians across the globe. Connelly and Reinfelder comment on how working internationally as a lesbian contrasts with working at a local or national level. One thought-provoking difference between lesbians that surfaced was the basic human right not to face the death penalty (as lesbians in Iran do) and in recalling this, the authors end with the sobering thought that for many lesbians in the world the very articulation of 'difference' and 'differences' is in fact a luxury.

While maintaining a focus on issues of 'difference' and drawing on her own experiences in the UK educational system, **Akuba Quansah** argues that, to date, black lesbian mothers have been rendered invisible in feminist theoretical discourses. This is reflected by how, even in these 'postmodern nineties' when non-oppressive heterogeneity is supposedly in vogue, the dearth of black lesbian voices in social science and humanities literature, and even at feminist-orientated events, is conspicuous. The author provocatively claims that black lesbian mothers are distinctive in not only having to resist white Eurocentric racist ideologies on lesbian motherhood, but in having to contend with a range of other oppressions which articulate white heteropatriarchal materiality.

Discourses of motherhood, albeit from a rather different perspective, are also the key theme of the next contribution by **Steph Lawler**. Here, through an analysis of interviews with white women, the articulated links between 'being a mother', 'loss of the self' and Euro-American definitions of children's needs, are explored. Traditional white Euro-American discourses publicly define a child's growing need for independence to be relationally dependent on the mother's sensitive nurturance of this. In Lawler's study, it was mothers who most used this understanding of childhood who felt themselves as having 'lost a sense of self' as autonomous persons. Some of the middle-class women in Lawler's study who resisted this loss of autonomy did so by adopting the discourse of choice. Yet *choosing* to be a mother was problematic too since non-maternal wants and needs were still subordinated to those of the child. Others discursively 'escaped' from the subject-position of 'mother' at times to become 'daughters', 'lovers', 'friends' or 'sisters', thus inscribing a sense of self that 'broke out' of maternity. Lawler, however, problematises such normative middle class accounts, arguing that without a revisioning of childhood and personhood, no radical revisioning of motherhood can in fact occur.

Considerations of women's bodies as sites of contestation, power and containment figure prominently in the set of contributions that comprise the second half of the volume. Traditional concerns around corporeality tend to ignore difference altogether and as a result, fall back upon unquestioned notions of essential nature(s) rooted in biology or the psyche, or posit an abstract masculine body as the 'norm'. In the process of being inserted into gendered regimes of power and knowledge, women's bodies have been invested with certain properties. As several contributors, notably **Sophie Nield**, **So-Hee Lee** and **Jane Aaron** argue, the association of woman and nation is not an enabling strategy that brings women into the body politic, but rather a disabling corporeal disenfranchisement of women. 'Elevated' to the status of icon, or commodified as object of exchange, the female body becomes a highly visible signifier of national pride. With national honour at stake, it is not surprising that force, be it literal or rhetorical, should be employed to ensure the conformity of women's bodies to their symbolic mould. The more the nation is symbolized in terms of the feminine (whether that be a vulnerable domestic femininity that must be protected, or an adulterous territory awaiting repossession), the greater the impossibility of women finding a site from which to speak. 'Woman' is thus associated with mute space rather than articulate subjectivity and public speech is rendered impossible – particularly in relation to the body that is no longer hers but the nation's.

Sophie Nield discusses how nationalism and ethnicity are played out on the bodies of women in specific ways. In particular, she addresses the emblematisation of nations as female which, it is argued, has been historically rooted in seeing women as aligned with 'nature' and not

4

'culture'. As Nield points out, the allegorical female form is not uncommon. From British towns to nation states, monuments representing 'Justice', 'Virtue', 'Victory' or 'Liberty' demonstrate such iconic imagining which has little served the interests of real women. Together with the 'land-as-female' (as 'mother') these representations functioned to reiterate male agency and female passivity. Subsumed by 'nature', women were seen to be subject to regulation and control. Recently however, as women's voices in public arenas have become more strident, there appears some resistance to abstracting women's bodies in this way. Nield optimistically points to how the Millenium Dome architects' decision to construct a giant female form to overlook 'cultural space' was challenged and subsequently changed.

Continuing the theme of nation and gender, **Cara Aitchison** draws on contemporary theoretical debates of space and place to argue that 'heritage' too is masculinised and structured in ways that largely render women invisible. She calls on feminist analysis to pay attention to 'heritage' not only as a business where few women are employed in positions of power and status, but also as a potent cultural form and process which both constitutes and represents gender along particular lines. To illustrate, Aitchison offers a critical reading of the Scottish university town of Stirling which seized on tourism as one of its major sources of income after the collapse of the industrial economy in the 1980's. As the old orders and terrain started to fragment, in moved a form of cultural capitalism which allowed patriarchal modes of masculinity to masquerade as 'heritage'. As a consequence, Stirling offers nationalistic and militaristic landmarks and monuments, buildings and statues, tourist trails and promotional literature which forefront men's lives and experiences, whilst backgrounding those of women. In analyses of 'heritage' tourism, Aitchison argues, such hegemony needs problematising.

The construction of nation and national identity is also central to the work of **Ranjana Sidhanta Ash**, who provides a valuable overview of South Asian women's writing in Britain. As a researcher Ash is not concerned with establishing a hierarchy, or even particularly in charting a progression, between the three positions of biculturality, hybridity and fusion. Rather she is concerned to illustrate the extent to which these categories are not discrete, nor fixed within a specific temporal period, but instead emerge from each writer's particular location within the diasporic cultural diffusion. This is not, however, to suggest that this body of writing is nothing more than a fragmented collection of personal subjectivities. Irrespective of the categories into which the writing might be seen to fit, Ash detects an ongoing and unifying concern with the wider politics of community and nation. Particularly for the first generation of Asian women moving to Britain, writing is a significant factor in facilitating their interaction with an otherwise alien public sphere. Although the specific political focus may change, South Asian women's writing can be said to be characterised by its continual engagement with an Asian-ness emerging from both myth and reality, and by an outward looking, intensely political perspective.

In the course of her analysis, Ash, like so many of the contributors to

5

this volume, finds herself examining the problematic conceptions of nation and tradition. She too is concerned with the connection between women and nation, but in marked contrast to Sophie Nield's reading of national iconography, she sees the symbolic alignment of the mother and the nation as a stabilising force for women looking to root their identities in a sea of change. However, as Ash's work reveals, gender exists within a complex matrix of identities, intersecting not only with the concept of nationhood, but also with race, ethnicity and sexuality. This matrix forms the subject of **Ling-Yen Chua's** analysis of the New Zealand film, *Desperate Remedies*. Taking an ostensibly transgressive film as her subject, Chua conducts a critical examination of the messages that actually underpin the narrative. Her reading suggests that the film encodes a series of deeply embedded cultural anxieties surrounding the idealised body of the white women and the conception of New Zealand national identity. The heroine Dorothea's engagement in illicit interracial and same-sex liaisons transgresses racial, sexual and national boundaries, and threatens to undermine the stability and authority of the 'pure white' British colony (tellingly called 'Hope' in the film). The fear that such encounters will produce miscegenated offspring who confuse the racial boundaries of 'black' and 'white', or that no offspring may be produced at all, contributes towards a conclusion in which Dorothea, the transgressive female, is expelled from the brave new world of 'Hope'. What is being articulated, argues Chua, is clear: if women's sexuality is not contained and controlled, it constitutes a threat to pakeha New Zealand society. With Dorothea's departure, the danger disappears, and the hegemony of white heterosexual identity is left intact.

The intersection of nationality, sexuality and textuality remains to the fore in **So-Hee Lee's** innovative cross-cultural reading of Margaret Atwood's *The Handmaid's Tale*. Starting from Michel Foucault's problematisation of the idea of author, Lee illustrates how the feminist text can facilitate a questioning of the relationship between gender and national identity – irrespective of the author's actual national location or allegiance. Foucault argues that, 'the author is not an indefinite source of significations which fills a work; the author does not precede the works, he [sic] is a certain functional principle by which, in our culture, one limits, excludes and chooses; in short, by which one impedes the free circulation, the free manipulation, the free composition, decomposition and recomposition of fiction' (Foucault, (1969) in Lodge (ed.) 1988 *Modern Criticism and Theory*, London, Longman, p.209). And it is exactly such a coercive model of textual authority that Lee rejects when she introduces a group of Korean women students to Margaret Atwood's *The Handmaid's Tale*. Lee's paper, then, records the displacement of the western feminist text from its customary interpretative framework. In the Korean classroom, Atwood's novel is both the subject of, and the stimulus for, a series of readings and re-readings of the boundary between history and fiction. Korea's subjection to colonial rule by the Japanese (1910 – 1945) instituted a regime which not only violated the borders of the nation, but also the bodies of its women, in the now notorious practice of military sexual slavery. For Korean students, reading Atwood's Canadian dystopia dissolves the boundaries between imagined future and historical past. The feminist text succeeds here in displacing national boundaries, facilitating the discussion of taboo subjects and forming a new understanding of gendered relations within both historical and contemporary state structures.

Finding a voice – speaking women's subjectivities – is central not only to the work of So-Hee Lee, but also to that of **Jane Aaron** and **Francesca Rhydderch**. While Lee finds Korean women silenced by the traditions of Confucian law and lacking a vocabulary for the articulation of sexuality or feminism, Aaron discovers nineteenth century Welsh women ironically urged to speak about the virtues of their own silence! The paradoxical double bind explored by **Jane Aaron** emerged from the notorious Commission of Enquiry into the State of Education in Wales, published in 1847. On the basis of complete cultural misunderstandings, the report accused Welsh women of licentiousness and want of chastity – faults that were in turn seen to underpin the 'failings' of Welsh education. The Welsh nation was traumatised by the damning conclusions of this document. In a familiar situation whereby the body of the woman becomes a metonym for the wider national body, an attack on Welsh women was immediately translated into an assault upon the Welsh nation and the journal *Y Gymraes* (The Welshwoman) was established to counter this slur. Women were encouraged to speak out in defence of their bodily purity and moral superiority, but in a society that defined women's roles according to the tenets of Calvinist non-conformity, such a demand represented a fundamental impossibility. If nothing becomes a woman more than her silence, how, and from where, can she speak?

Against the backdrop of this paradox Aaron analyses a series of texts by nineteenth century Welsh women that 'obsessively encode the body and sexuality at the same time as they overtly deny their existence'. In a series of fascinating textual readings it becomes clear that the repressive force of both English imperialism and Welsh puritanism were insufficient to wholly contain the inscription of female corporeality. While patriarchal society and, ostensibly, the women themselves, worked to remove the uncomfortable traces of female desire, that desire remained encoded within the interstices and inconsistencies of textual production. Aaron concludes that for many Welsh women: 'the consequences of the trauma of 1847 were an increased alienation from the female body . . . a disfigurement which could not be conceived of as a matter of play, and which took more than one generation to efface'.

Just how pervasive and long term this impact was to be, is illustrated by the next paper in the volume. **Francesca Rhydderch** examines the autobiography of Kate Roberts, a 'legendary' Welsh woman writer, in the light of Roland Barthes' theorisation of the pleasure of the text. In this sense, Rhydderch's project is not unlike that of So-Hee Lee. Both argue for the beneficial effects of cross cultural textual conjunctions – of reading texts in literal or metaphorical landscapes of difference. While Lee's work emerges from a Canadian/Korean axis, Rhydderch is concerned with the critical collision between Welsh conservatism and French radicalism. In the light of Barthes's transgressive injunction to 'disfigure' the mother tongue, however, Robert's ostensibly conservative fictions fracture, revealing a paradoxical resistance to the values seemingly embodied by the archetypal Welsh 'mam'. Yet, importantly, Rhydderch does not see the process of illumination as a one way street, and she stresses that the intersecting narratives of Welsh woman and French man can also be seen to throw light upon the concerns and limitations of the 'master text'. Thus this is not a hierarchical use of Barthes to control or expose Roberts, but rather a critical and mutually illuminating dialogue between two very different discourses.

The final two contributors to the volume, **Gill Jagger** and **Chris Weedon** offer ways forward in terms of thinking anew about some of the perennial problems that have beset the feminist project. **Gill Jagger** argues that in re-thinking the sexed/gendered specificity of bodies, even those feminist agendas that move beyond dualisms and destabilise bodily boundaries have been limited. She calls for new ways of re-thinking the imbrication of the material with the symbolic, the politics of signification and the imaginary (in the Lacanian sense). Recent postmodern turns to the problems of embodiment and the salience of sexual difference, subjectivity and its bodily roots, and change at the level of the symbolic may offer, Jagger argues, a way out of this theoretical impasse. The problem however is one of how to do it, of how to theorise materialisation in ways that allow feminists to re-think corporeality without simply tying bodies to their biology. The author argues that this has important political implications; her aim is to avoid Cartesian frameworks, and dualisms such as mind/body, sex/gender, biology/culture, whilst retaining feminist political and ethical commitments.

The concluding chapter by **Chris Weedon** pertinently focuses upon where 'feminist study' should go in the future. Taking up some of the issues surfacing in previous chapters, she argues that contemporary feminism must address broader concerns, speak to a wider audience and render work more accessible. Yet crucially, this must be accompanied by a more sophisticated engagement with the politics of 'difference' and a more self-reflexive critique of ourselves as socially situated feminists, activists, researchers, teachers and students. In particular, Weedon contends that it is vital that conventional ideas of reason and the reasoning subject are exposed as privileged Western traditions, and that theories and practices are seen as incomplete, partial and interested. Moreover, it is crucial to acknowledge that 'difference' itself can be the product of power relations between women; and that such inequalities are discursively generated. Maintaining the theme of marginalised discourses and identities, the author argues that, above all, feminism needs to listen to those women whose lives are shaped by the power relations of class, race, heterosexism and Eurocentrism in order to further understand and take account of these 'differences'. This conclusion serves as an apt closure for the volume: it is only when different voices are heard and understood in this way that they can become the basis for shared forms of struggle.

Feminism, Feminisms: Fighting back for Women's Liberation

Liz Kelly, Jill Radford and Joan Scanlon

This paper addresses our concerns about the representation of feminist politics and the history of the Women's Liberation Movement as taught and handed on to new generations of women, in academic women's studies. We each have a long history of involvement in women's education, including women's studies in the community and the academy. We have raised some of the issues in this paper in other places (Radford 1994, 1996; Kelly, Burton & Regan, 1996; Kelly and Radford, 1996).

Whilst academic women's studies is only one mode of transmission for feminist knowledge, it has become an increasingly important one. There is still access to feminist ideas through (a decreasing number of) feminist publications, campaigns, community women's studies classes, community and voluntary sector women's groups and organisations, and also, more problematically, sections of the mainstream media. But apart from the latter the other sources of knowledge, at least in England, Wales and Scotland, are either less visible than in previous decades or far more focused on service provision than developing and communicating feminist knowledge. It is this changed context which means that academic women's studies is becoming the primary route of access to knowledge about and potential involvement in the women's movement.

This paper is a consolidation of something we prepared for teaching purposes eight years ago. The motivation behind this was our perception of the need to challenge the authority with which certain insidious exclusions and inclusions were coming to characterise a new generation of women's studies curricula and textbooks. We have frequently revised that early paper in our collective and separate uses of it. Our basic aim was to propose an alternative way of representing the development and current understandings of feminism. From our perspectives as activists as well as academics this approach to history is both more accurate in reflecting the relationship between theory and activism in the 1970s and highlights the ongoing necessity of their interrelationship in the present and future.

In pursuit of these aims we outline trends and practices in contemporary women's studies which concern us, critically examine dominant academic representations of feminism in the 1970s, 1980s and 1990s, and contrast these with an account which owes more to activist perspectives, which is frequently 'written out' of the current orthodoxy. We conclude by reflecting on why the original naming of our movement – the Women's Liberation Movement – has fallen into disuse, and even disrepute.

Troubling trends in contemporary women's studies
Women's studies began in the 1970s in most areas within local communities. Study groups and classes were explicitly initiated as one

9

strand of the wider project of Women's Liberation (see Radford, 1994). Many of those early classes were either study groups which activists used to reflect on practice and develop thinking, or intended as introductions to a movement which aimed at nothing less than fundamental social change. Today in the 1990s we have arrived at a position when even the inclusion of the word 'feminism' in course materials has become controversial. This shift obscures the original oppositional intention of women's studies as far more than a corrective critique of mainstream education, and has positioned women's studies as an aspiring new discipline seeking assimilation and status within the academy.

What facilitated this transformation was the increasing separation of academic women's studies from the Women's Liberation Movement, one aspect of which was the increasing marginalisation of community women's studies. One (possibly unintended) outcome has been a move away from presenting feminist knowledge as provisional, contested ideas to more rigid and definitive scholarship. The early insistence that women were creators of, and contributors to, knowledge has been overlaid by late twentieth century consumerist culture, which far too many of us have accommodated to. The fluidity between knowers and known which characterised women's studies practice is increasingly replaced by traditional models of teachers as holders of knowledge and students as consumers of it.

That much of what at present passes as women's studies is inaccessible has both contributed to and reproduces this shift. The most obvious forms this takes are: the language that has become increasingly fashionable in the academy, which is often unnecessarily complex and excluding, and which obfuscates concepts and theories for which feminism already had a perfectly adequate, well thought-out and lucid terminology; the prohibitively high cost of women's studies classes and texts in an era of qualification hunts and contract culture in higher education; and the decreased involvement of many academic feminists in community and adult education. These shifts are connected to changes in the political and economic realities in Higher and Further Education. But within this there are significant elements of collusion. How often do we, as women's studies teachers, feminist academics, ask ourselves key questions, such as who we are teaching, who we are writing for and why?

One particularly significant aspect of these changes is the ways in which feminism and the Women's Liberation Movement have been reconstructed and certain representations have acquired definitive status. This is especially important since there are fewer 'memory bearing women' in the classroom as students or tutors who can challenge these accounts. In fact the absolutism with which a version of history is presented as 'truth' can and does silence 'memory bearing women' who are present. We are extremely frustrated at hearing repeated stories of women's studies teachers (many of whom should – and do – know better) talking about radical feminism and activism as something which disappeared in the 1970s, or being defined solely in terms of lesbian separatism. After a recent talk one of us was told that for the first time a woman was able to recognise her own history of involvement in the WLM in the 1970s; she had not questioned the teaching on her MA Women's Studies course, since she thought it must be her rather than her teacher who was wrong! This mis-representation of history is frequently achieved by the privileging of a limited number of texts, and the exclusion of many others. Alternatively certain texts are selectively cited, with the implication that this is sufficient to assess a woman's work. The paragraph can be deconstructed, critiqued and this often suffices to discredit entire strands of feminist thought. This process of fragmentation and deconstruction has been accentuated in the 1990s by the growth of anti-feminist theory, post-it theories and the misogyny of queer.

To illustrate these points, we argue that there always have been lively and controversial debates within the Women's Liberation Movement (WLM) at conferences, in newsletters and journals. Books were produced which aired different positions and reflected a range of standpoints. As women's studies made inroads into academia some of these books were selected for reading lists and ordered for libraries; others were not. On the whole texts selected were those which posed the least threat or challenge to the liberal academy of the 1970s; liberal feminism with some token inclusion of marxist/socialist feminism thanks to the existence of a politically sympathetic male presence, then fairly strong or vocal in sociology faculties, which was where most original women's studies courses were based. Excluded were writings by black feminists, lesbians and radical feminists. Many of these early texts, which constitute evidence that the WLM was not entirely exclusionary at the outset, are now out of print (for example, Bambara, 1970; Bunch and Myron, 1975; Redstockings, 1978). Their absence in university libraries serves to confirm the 'total exclusion' story which now predominates in contemporary reflections on the origins of the WLM.

During the 1980s and early 1990s 'authoritative' text books began to appear. These books further summarised the summaries of earlier books, and presented these bowdlerized versions as both definitive and representative of the entire body, or one strand, of feminist theory. Some of these texts have become central to women's studies teaching, with the associated drawback that in the preparation of teaching the original texts are not read, let alone re-read; searching for (or researching) the excluded texts is not considered necessary or even relevant scholarship, nor is such research deemed grant-worthy. The most obvious loss to feminism in this process is the writing out of radical feminism. Frequently the only reference to it is in the form of summaries constructed by an author critical of that politics, possibly accompanied by unrepresentative and out-of-context quotations selected for ease of deconstruction and dismissal.

The costs of this systematic distortion have been high for feminism in Britain. Much that made for the richness of feminism of the 1970s has been lost through the practices of exclusion and partiality. These distortions have resulted in:
- the exclusion of the voices of black feminists, working-class feminists, lesbian feminists, and radical feminists who were active in the 1970s;
- the loss of a significant route to political consciousness through the particular educational process which women's studies was originally intended to provide.

These shifts and practices within women's studies have made a significant contribution to the fracturing of feminist praxis. Constructing exaggerated separations, most particularly the separation of feminism into mutually exclusive strands ('feminisms'), accentuates differences at the expense of the commonalities which enabled women to see themselves as part of the WLM. Such separations are achieved through looking at feminism as a set of (contested) ideas/theories; that previous and current activism belies some of these distinctions resulted in it being marginalised within the available knowledge base. Concurrently the link between theory and process is increasingly lost; where there is no reference to historical context, processes evaporate and theory is rendered meaningless. Alongside these developments an increasingly simplistic, individualised and therapeutic interpretation of 'the personal is political' has replaced the more sophisticated ideas that informed the early WLM (see Kitzinger and Perkins 1993).

From the WLM to feminisms
It is hardly surprising that feminism has given way to feminisms – personalised, diverse and without politics, process, activism. At the same time feminism itself is dismissed as racist, classist and outmoded, and represented by the post-it theorists as 'essentialist' for holding on to unfashionable notions: that women exist; that they are subject to inequality, oppression and violence on a global scale; and that this matters. It is no wonder that *feminism* is feminisms' lost discourse. If this was only about history it would be sad enough, but it is also about what is happening within feminism today. Women's studies plays a role not only in constructing representations of feminism for students, but also, by handing these representations to the media – a powerful and traditionally hostile voice – contributes to representations of feminism consumed by a wider public, a public which includes large numbers of women. Feminism as a politics of resistance is virtually unrecognisable and therefore unavailable to women at a moment in a time when they have been under political attack from a succession of governments and there is a marked absence of a coherent opposition which is willing to defend women's right to choices and autonomy. As a consequence, at a time when the then Tory government was scapegoating single mothers for every conceivable social problem and legitimising attacks on women seeking to end relationships with violent men through mechanisms such as the Family Law Act, resistance was left to a handful of committed feminists, while the majority of women were encouraged to view feminism as irrelevant to their lives.

The sub-title of this chapter is 'fighting back for women's liberation'. In order to do that, however, we have to re-discover some basis for commonality. That basis has to begin with an agreement about the meaning of feminism/the Women's Liberation Movement. With the current emphasis on pluralism(s) it is easy to forget that all plurals are dependent on a prior singular. Our understanding of the term feminism involves a recognition that differences exist between women, both at a personal level in that all women are unique, and, more significantly, in terms of those differences which matter politically. Women's different positioning in terms of major global and local power structures has led to claims that feminism is either **indefinable**, as every woman develops her own feminism – or **impossible** since it is inevitably white, heterosexual, able-bodied and middle-class. This position is only tenable if we negate feminist struggles in the third world and deny struggles within local movements by black, working class, disabled and lesbian feminists. In contrast we propose that Women's Liberation Movements across the world are based on a common perspective which can be summarised as:

- an understanding that women are oppressed and a commitment (collective and individual) to political change, with the intention of ultimately ending women's oppression.

Rather than arguing about the word 'feminism' (which does not directly translate in many languages), we contend that it is the definition which matters. Our definition is intentionally not prescriptive, can accommodate a wide variety of strands or positions, including all those which characterised the British women's movement of the 1970s, 1980s and 1990s:

- it recognises the oppression of women, while leaving open to analysis who or what is responsible; nor does it presume that all women are oppressed in the same ways
- it contains a commitment to progressive struggle towards ending the oppression of women, but does not prescribe specific strategies or directions of struggle
- it leaves room for both analysis and strategy to be discussed and debated by politically committed women in light of their experiences in terms of political, historical, geographical, cultural variations and in the context of specific struggles
- it contains both a gendered understanding of the world and a commitment to activism, what in 1970s western feminism was known as praxis: a recognition of the inseparability of theory and practice.

In the following sections we present an alternative reading or understanding of feminist history and politics, using activism as our starting point, by:

- re-examining the women's liberation movement of the 1970s
- tracing some developments in feminist politics and theory through the 1980s
- contrasting the postmodernist deconstruction of feminism with a vision of activist feminism which is constructed through alliances and coalitions, which can focus on commonalities whilst respecting differences, locally, nationally and internationally.

The early WLM from the perspective of activism

It has become a convention to classify and categorise differences in emphasis within 1970s feminism by representing them in terms of competing fixed positions: liberal, equal rights feminism; socialist feminism and radical feminism. The apparent academic need for this kind of typology leads to a maximizing of political and theoretical differences and a disregard for the processes through which feminists worked together in activist campaigning. Local feminist projects like setting up bookshops, women's studies courses, health projects, feminist support services like Women's Aid, Rape Crisis, newsletters and discussion groups, make a nonsense of this rigid categorisation. In local women's groups, as Jill Radford (1994) has described in one account of the local history of the WLM, these strands in feminism were even less meaningful. When the members of this women's group discussed the typology in *Sweet Freedom*, they spent an entire evening puzzling about where they each fitted. Whilst it may be true that in London differences in emphasis were more pronounced, and as the 1970s developed these strands did become the basis of personal and group identity, this typology is at best a very partial account. It is an account based on metropolitan areas, written by white middle class women, and they have presumed (and others have accepted) that their experience could be universalised. It is not uncommon for political agendas to be set, and political histories written, from the centre rather than the margins, but one would expect feminist teachers to at least note and comment on this and suggest that there may be other stories. The, as yet to be written, histories of organisations like Women's Aid would further illustrate how women from a range of perspectives worked (and in this case continue to work) together – in harmony and conflict – locally, regionally and nationally.

In using the ideas in this paper as a teaching tool, we have given a brief account of the major theoretical tenets of these different strands in feminism, within the wider definition outlined above. In doing this, we point to the individualism of liberal feminism, its use of the language of equal rights, its focus on the public sphere and equal opportunities, and contrasted this with the structural analysis of socialist and radical feminism. We identify how socialist feminism attracted many activists on the left, was rooted in class politics and emphasised the central positioning of capitalism as a power structure in interaction with patriarchy. We note the range of perspectives within socialist feminism, mirroring the plurality of left of labour politics in the 1970s – encompassing varying marxist, maoist and anarchist strands. The primary (but by no means exclusive) focus of socialist feminism was on work issues, women's position within the workplace, the employment market, and the double shift of paid work, domestic labour and child care. In our account of radical feminism we attempt to broaden the narrow definition generally available to students. We therefore explain that the theory which underpins this strand of feminism is focused on the problem of men and masculinity as mediated by the power structures of patriarchy, which creates power hierarchies amongst men as well as between men, women and children. Radical feminism thus takes patriarchy as structuring all social power relations, including capitalism and institutionalised racism (see also Wingfield, 1993). Radical feminist activists focused on issues such as health, education, and violence against women, as well as developing autonomous women's spaces and culture, including women's music, art, and writings, establishing feminist presses such as Onlywomen Press, women's centres and women's communities in rural and city areas.

We extend this traditional account by pointing out that many feminists, particularly outside London, embraced various positions in their thinking and activism. Perhaps a more significant point, however, is the fact that, although feminists from the different perspectives conceptualised issues differently, they frequently worked around them together.

This was evident in the case of workplace campaigns: while equal pay issues were clearly liberal feminist in their focus on legal reform and the notion that equality was a achievable within a capitalist society, they were nonetheless supported by socialist feminists who campaigned for union support for the principle of equal pay. Support for women on strike to achieve equal pay (for example the Grunwicks workers, many of whom were Asian women) came from all stands within the movement. Radical feminists also supported campaigns which were linked to more typical radical feminist concerns like sexual harassment in the workplace.

Similarly, abortion was conceptualised as a women's rights issue by liberals, linked to employment and child care issues in socialist feminist analysis, while for radical feminists it connected to sexuality, women's autonomy and control over our bodies. But all were happy to march under the slogan: 'not the church, not the state, women will decide our fate'. Differences and heated discussions erupted over issues like the presence and role of men on marches, and radical feminists on one occasion frustrated the TUC's determination to lead a march against one of the 1970s attempts to introduce anti-abortion legislation. While theoretical differences produced lively, sometime productive and sometimes anachronistic, debate, feminist process, consensual decision making, non-hierarchical structures, together with the excitement and elation of successful actions, produced a cohesiveness which could hold us together in specific local contexts and particular struggles and campaigns. This is the other side of the oft repeated frustration of this way of working, and the heated debates and painful divisions which were also evident.

While it is true that activist feminism in Britain in the 1970s was predominantly white, it is not true to say that it was predominantly middle class and heterosexual. Many of the women attracted to the WLM in the early years were either already lesbians and/or women from working class backgrounds who had benefited from the post-war extension of education opportunities. Many of the most intense debates at the national women's liberation conferences and those of the National Women's Aid Federation involved issues of differences between women. Moreover, black women were not absent from 1970s activism, although it was not really until the 1980s that a visible black feminist/womanist movement developed. Interestingly class was far more of issue in the early phase of the movement, but never solidified into an identity based strand subsequently.

In place of the dry typologies which present these trends by highlighting their differences and conflict, our suggestion is that an interlinking helix more adequately represents and explains the interrelationship of these various strands in the development of the WLM. This model allows us to think in terms of an issue being identified within one strand of feminism, being picked up by others in different ways which sometimes led them to spiral off in different directions and yet reconnect at certain points in new struggles and alliances. Neither the issues nor the movement were static, but developed in a dynamic history across and within the different strands of feminism.

Continuities and transformations: Feminism in the 1980s

For British feminism, and possibly in some other countries also, the 1980s was a period of continuities and transformations. Continuities existed in relation to the central concerns of feminism and in the building of feminist services, the development of feminist education and in feminist activism, particularly in relation to violence against women. However the 1980s were also a period of transformation. Transformations for example occurred in the wider political context, as the new far right conservatism of Thatcherism grew in strength and created a political backdrop more explicitly hostile to feminism. Transformation also occurred in relation to some institutional responses to feminism and within feminist activism there was a more deliberate concern to create a more inclusive feminism. Identity politics was yet another contradictory development within British feminism of the 1980s. It represented an attempt to acknowledge and address significant differences between women, paying attention to the voices of women who had been previously marginalised. However at the same time it became a source of division between women and the apparent cause of the notorious tendency to hierarchise different forms of oppression.

While these continuities and transformations have had a far reaching effect, our concern in the context of this chapter is with three specific themes: the acceptance of feminism by academia or the making of feminism acceptable to academia, in the development of academic women's studies; the acceptance of feminism by town halls, or its being made acceptable to town halls through the institutionalisation of women's units and women's services; and the development of particular forms of identity politics. On the surface these themes: the assimilation of feminism within the academy, the institutionalisation of feminism via local authority funding and the rise of identity politics, may seem unconnected. But in this chapter we are arguing that these tendencies intersected in the 1980s in critical ways and had contradictory impacts on the Women's Liberation Movement. On the one hand institutional recognition and funding can be seen as a mark of its success and facilitated its further development. On the other hand, as we argue here, these shifts also represented a selective appropriation of women's issues, women's education and services, at the expense of feminist politics.

The establishment of women studies in universities in the 1980s had a major impact on both feminism and the WLM. While clearly a positive development, it also served to create separations between for example academic and community based activist feminism – a source of major tensions in a 1984 Women's Studies Conference in Bradford. It also led to the separations we have already outlined, particularly that theory, or at least the version of feminist theory which found its way into mainstream literature, became separated from activism. Theory constructed and published within the academy was perceived as the only feminist theory that counted, while theory that continued to be developed in women's kitchens and loo queues, or while making placards, writing slogans and songs and writing speeches, or in discussion groups and self-produced feminist publications, was discounted until or unless it was appropriated and reproduced by the academic elite. Feminist practice was increasingly lost within academic women's studies as feminist process gave way to institutional structures and arrangements. This is not to say that some feminists within academia were unable or unwilling, on occasion, to use feminist strategies in institutional networking, teaching and approaches to research, but the overall trend became more accomodatory and less challenging. Part of this trend can be seen in the ways some feminist academics transformed themselves into academic feminists.

At the same time local authority funding had an significant impact on the movement, constructing femocrats by attributing professionalism to some while withholding this status from others. This process of inclusion and exclusion, inevitably privileged those deemed least threatening to the fundholding establishment. While the positive potential of this funding was immense and constituted another transformative factor in various feminist endeavours, its high costs were soon evident as funders exerted controls, and the pressure to deliver feminist services without the politics that produced and sustained them began to take its toll. Feminist groups responded in a range of ways, not always directly linked to their theoretical location. Some, like the London Women's Liberation Newsletter refused to apply for funding and survived until the mid 1980s (Bindel, 1996). Others survived, particularly groups with longer histories, and feminist initiatives like the Fawcett Library found a home within the academy. Some groups, like Rights of Women, were successful in their funding applications and continued to struggle, strategise and negotiate working arrangements with funders (Radford, 1994). Others refused to compromise their principles and, as in the case of London Rape Crisis Centre, lost their funding on several occasions. The acceptance of funding frequently led to pressures to separate out service provision from campaigning and the development of theoretical perspectives. One of the lasting legacies of 1980s 'funding for feminism' has been an increasing sense that women's organisations cannot function without it – a notion that would be anathema to many of the most effective groups in the 1970s.

While issues of class, race and sexuality were the subject of many heated debates within the 1970s women's movement, these were not always dealt with by white, middle class and heterosexual women with as much political insight or sensitivity as they might have been (Radford, 1994). Unresolved tensions around these issues contributed to the rise of identity politics in the mid 1980s. Identity politics developed the concept of 'the personal is political' in relation to race, class and sexuality in quite particular ways. Its initial impetus was politically coherent and strategically necessary, as bell hooks has pointed out:

> Identity politics emerges out of the struggles of . . . exploited groups to have a standpoint on which to critique dominant structures, a position that gives purpose to struggle (1991:180)

Where identity is politically defined, identity politics can be important in enabling an articulation and understanding of how women can be simultaneously in positions of privilege and oppression: privileged for example as middle class, white and heterosexual, while at the same time oppressed as women. Its influence varied across different feminist organisations – in some, like Rights of Women, it led to focused work around lesbian and Black women's issues – such as the Lesbian Custody Project and Black workers groups. We have explored elsewhere (Hester, Kelly and Radford, 1996) the ways in which identity politics encouraged recognition of differences within women's experiences of sexual violence, resulting in the establishment of specialist services (both refuges and in some rape crisis groups) for Black women and women with disabilities. In women's studies it undoubtedly resulted in a widening of what was considered the necessary foundations for study, and this is especially noticeable, and to be welcomed, in the inclusion of Black feminist writing.

However, identity politics as it developed also had a 'down' side (Bindel 1996; Kelly, Regan and Burton 1996; McNeill, 1996) since in some versions identity was thought sufficient to constitute politics. Thus speaking from a particular standpoint in and of itself comprised a political authority and consequently operated to stifle debate. Unresolved tensions emerged in terms of the relationship of identity based groups to feminism and whether identity alone could provide the basis of an oppositional politics. Identities have different meanings and consequences in different contexts. Being Catholic, for example, has a different meaning in the six counties of Northern Ireland than in the Irish Republic or other countries, depending on whether it is a majority or minority religion. Similarly the meaning of being a Catholic has changed dramatically in countries like Poland following the fall of communism. Lesbianism can be defined as a political identity when rooted in feminism and a critique of institutional heterosexuality, but if seen solely in terms of a lifestyle or a sexual preference, it is difficult to see how it can be a basis of a feminist politics, since this encourages a separation from rather than connection with other groups of women. These and other examples demonstrate that it is not identity per se which is the issue, but the relationship between identity, political context and political consciousness.

Reclaiming cultural identity is fraught with ambiguities and contradictions, and depends on how identity is defined in terms of its political possibilities. If identity has no political context, then any form of organising will take place solely on the basis of shared identity. This becomes more difficult to unravel if that identity is constructed through oppression. Reclaiming identity, whilst often represented as a political act in and of itself, contains the seeds of contradiction, since it can result in a vested interest in maintaining identity and difference, rather than challenging the oppression which created and gave meaning to the difference in the first place. One consequence of the construction of hierarchies of oppression and credibility associated with identity politics was a 'credentialism' game, whereby the more oppression points one could claim, the more right one had to speak. In the process histories of involvement in and commitment to activism ceased to 'count' as a relevant standpoint from which to speak. Defensiveness and 'claims making' replaced debate, and all too often action. In the fallout, some white middle-class heterosexual women, with no specific standpoint beyond being a woman, claimed to feel threatened or excluded and moved away from feminism. Some of these women have since made public statements in the mainstream media to the effect that there no longer was a Women's Liberation Movement.

It is no coincidence that the particular focus on identity politics within feminist activism was accompanied by a parallel pursuit, within academic feminism, of a theory which emphasised fragmentation and 'difference'. Nor is it a coincidence that the foregrounding of psychoanalytic and postmodern theory within the academy mirrored the increasing tendency towards individualism and therapism within certain sections of the movement. Moreover the bureaucratization of feminist practice through local authority structures, and the obfuscation of feminist theory through aspirations towards academic acceptability, only further served to distance feminist activism from these more public developments. The established respectability afforded to certain kinds of feminist practice and forms of employment only reinforced the notion that divisions amongst women – and the separation of grass roots activism from theory and policy development – were identity based phenomena, since it was predominantly middle class women who occupied these jobs. In this way the three tendencies, far from being coincidental, served to reinforce each other, often quite directly, and contributed to the manner in which the 'authoritative' or 'authorised' account of 1980s feminism has been promulgated.

Back to the personal: feminism in the 1990s
Our aim in tracing these perspectives through to the 1990s is to enable reflection upon current feminist thinking and theorising, and question whether the dominant form of academic women's studies has lost its connection with feminist politics as we have defined it here. Many women have moved away from feminist politics towards a focus on personal identity issues. For some this was a reaction to the limited possibilities for radical change in Thatcherite Britain. Nonetheless the struggle for political change was replaced by either the pursuit of personal change through therapy and various 'new age' philosophies or the pursuit of individual success via a career. These shifts were often fuelled by the perception that the changes which political consciousness would logically imply did not seem to be realisable in personal practice. Moreover, for some, the disaffection from a materialist feminism derived from the perception that there was no easy correspondence between political conviction and the newly prioritised discourse of sexual desire. These shifts can be traced on the shelves of bookshops, where self-help and self-improvement volumes – sometimes written by long-time (or one time) feminists – occupy more space and prominence than feminist analysis. We also ought to ask whether the disappearance of a concern with class and poverty, of attention to the material reality of most women's lives, reflects the fact that many feminist academics now occupy positions of relative economic privilege.

As feminist academics fought to gain academic respectability and kudos in an increasingly competitive environment, limited time, energy or commitment seemed available for activist work, or even for the production of feminist theory that was relevant outside of self-referental academic debates. A perceptible shift in the primary frame of reference has taken place; for many – but by no means all – feminist academics it is no longer the Women's Liberation Movement but the academy. This has culminated in the detrimental application of the newly fashionable theories of post-structuralism and post-modernism to an increasingly post-it theory of feminism. The shift involved trying to find a place for women in the misogynist theorising of men – gurus in this tradition being mostly dead, white men such as Freud, Foucault, Derrida, hardly renowned for their feminist sympathies. The writings of these individuals, or women's engagement with their ideas, are now far more likely to appear on women's studies curricula than the unapologetic feminism and more accessible ideas of women like Catharine MacKinnon, Cynthia Enloe, Christine Delphy or Cynthia Cockburn.

Post-structuralists took the logic of recognising differences between women (already acknowledged by feminism) to the point of arguing that women no longer exist as a relevant social group, a position which makes feminist politics extremely difficult, if not impossible. The basis for this argument is that, since power is no longer structured through the power relations of the economy, racism or patriarchy, everyone exists in flux, identities are transient and can be transformed at the individual level. Hence the 'View From Nowhere and the Dream of Everywhere' (Susan Bordo, 1990) and as Tanya Modeleski (1991) has so succinctly put it, 'Feminism Without Women'. Much feminist theory is now purely idealist, based on representation, with virtually nothing to say about material reality. Watching TV and going to the cinema, as a deconstructionist activity, has for all too many women replaced a critical analysis of women's oppression and the struggle for women's liberation.

Back to the future

Our concerns in the paper are not simply to critique, but to examine, resist and counter the consequences of particular directions and shifts within women's studies and the Women's Liberation Movement. A central tenet of our argument is that particular accounts of feminism have been prioritised and made acceptable, whilst others, particularly feminist practice in activism, including its capacity to inform and inspire feminist theory, have been neglected. The intentional or unintended exclusion of developments in feminist practice and denial of the continuing relevance of activism, as well as the tendency to universalise highly localised observations, have made it possible to suggest there is no longer a Women's Liberation Movement. Such accounts misrepresent feminist history through their partiality and present a distorted version of feminist politics in the guise of contributions to the construction of academic knowledge, rather than continued resistance in the struggles of women in their daily lives. It is no wonder, then, that we are told that feminism has no relevance to the majority of women in the UK.

As feminist activists and academics, we still locate ourselves within a movement for women's liberation, albeit with considerably more awareness of the enormity of what achieving this might require. Our main concern is the increasing disjunction between feminism in the academy and feminist activism, and the loss of possibility and potential that has resulted. There are smaller and larger things which could be done to counteract this trend which offer benefits to feminists wherever they are located. We offer the following as initial, and interim, suggestions which might bring us closer together within an overarching commitment to women's liberation.

- Women's studies courses ought to take time to present a more complex history of the WLM, and differences and debates with it, than is currently the case. Two key issues here are questioning the 'total exclusion' story of the 1970s WLM, and recognising the continued vibrancy of radical feminism (Bell and Klein, 1996).

- Discussion of 'feminisms' and the problematic meaning of 'feminism' for women in some localities ought to be supplemented with exploration of the term 'women's liberation' – which has enormous potential in linking women's struggles.

- The contemporary relevance of early feminist ideas and analysis should be presented alongside more recent developments, and routes for students to be become involved in activism, working for change, ought to be part of the curriculum

- In exploring issues of difference and epistemology, conversations need to be taking place between theorists and activists, in this way the attempts being made in practice to create a more inclusive women's movement could offset the pessimism of much contemporary theory.

- Since we are in danger of losing much of our own history, research on the history of the WLM in Britain ought to become a priority for students and staff. Sasha Roseneil's (1995) work on Greenham Common is an example of the kind of insightful and challenging work that can be produced; see also Gail Chester's paper in this volume.

- Issues of concern to women outside the academy ought to inform thinking about research priorities, both small scale local studies and larger scale national ones. For example, local women's groups may have intuitions about changing policies and practices, or tensions between the current state of feminist theory and what they are struggling with either within their group or in the work they do with other women, but not have time to pursue them. Some models of this kind of process exist in Britain, but the potential for exploring and developing feminist praxis is immense.

- Global feminism ought to be included as an example of attempts in the 1990s to move beyond traditional typologies or obituaries of feminism. Within this examples of international networking and campaigns ought to be used as examples of global feminism in action. Two examples would be the continental networks which came together to ensure violence against women was defined by the UN as a fundamental violation of women's human rights and the networking between lesbians before and at the Beijing conference (See Frances Connolly and Monika Reinfelder in this volume).

These are just some of the most obvious ways in which we can do ourselves, each other, and the complex history of the women's movement justice. If we fail in this challenge we are likely to contribute to a repetition of previous eras where much of women's activism and thinking was hidden from history. If we participate in so doing we will have also contributed to the loss of faith in our ability to change the world. The alternative is to find ways to fight back for women's liberation.

Notes

[1] Community women's studies and community women's groups are extremely vigourous throughout Ireland, and increasingly so. There a strong link exists between these groups and women's studies a taught in universities. The experiences of Irish women offer an important antidote to the general picture we present in this paper, a source of inspiration and example as to how things could be different.

[2] NWAF was formed in 1974, and included groups throughout the UK. By the end of the 1970s there were four national federations: Northern Irish Women's Aid; Scottish Women's Aid; Welsh Women's Aid; Women's Aid Federation, England.

References

Bell, Diane and Klein, Renate (1996) *Radically Speaking: Feminism Reclaimed* London, Zed Press.

Bindel, Julie (1996) 'Neither an ism nor a chasm: maintaining a radical-feminist agenda in broad based coalitions' in Harne and Miller (eds) *All The Rage*, London, Women's Press.

Bordo, Susan (1990) 'Feminism, postmodernism and gender scepticism' in Linda J Nicolson (ed) *Feminism/Postmodernism*, London, Routledge.

Bunch, Charlotte and Nancy Myron (1975) *Lesbianism and the Women's Liberation Movement*, Baltimore Mass, Diana Press.

Kelly, Liz; Burton, Sheila and Regan, Linda (1996) 'Beyond victim or survivor: sexual violence, identity, feminist theory and practice' in Lisa Adkins and Vicki Merchant (eds) *Sexualising the Social: Power and the Organisation of Sexuality*, London, Macmillan.

Kitzinger, Celia and Perkins, Rachel (1993) *Changing Our Minds: Lesbian Feminism and Psychology*, London, Onlywomen Press.

Kumar, Radha (1993) *The History of Doing: An Illustrated Account of Movements for Women's Rights in India*. 1800-1900, Dehli, Kali for Women Press.

McNeill, Sandra (1996) 'Identity Politics' in Harne and Miller (eds) *All The Rage*, London, Women's Press.

Modeleski, Tanya (1991) *Feminism Without Women: Culture and Criticism in a 'Postfeminist' Age*, New York, Routledge.

Bambara, Toni Cade (ed) (1970) *The Black Woman:An Anthology,* New York, Signet.

Radford, Jill (1994) 'History of the Women's Liberation Movement in Britain: A Reflective Personal Account' in Griffin, Hester, Rai and Roseneil (ed) *Stirring It: Challenges for Feminism,* London, Taylor and Francis.

Radford, Jill (1996) 'Backlash: or new variations on an old exclusionary theme' in Harne and Miller (ed) *All The Rage,* London, Women's Press.

Radford, Jill; Kelly, Liz and Hester, Marianne (eds) (1996) 'Introduction' *Women, Violence and Male Power,* Milton Keynes, Open University Press.

Redstockings Collective (1978) *Feminist Revolution,* Random House.

Roseneil, Sasha (1995) *Disarming the Patriarchy: Feminism and Political Action at Greenham,* Milton Keynes, Open University Press

Wingfield, Rachel (1993) 'The myth of the bad girl': review of "Unleashing Feminism"' *Trouble and Strife* 27.

The Use and Abuse of Power in the Autonomous Women's Movement

Jane W. Grant

This paper is a part of a larger project provisionally entitled 'Enabling Sisterhood: the Governance of Women's Organisations' being undertaken under the aegis of the Centre for Women's Studies at the University of Kent. This larger project draws on archival material gathered through fourteen years of my active participation in the organised women's movement in the UK, case studies drawing on written material produced by women's organisations themselves, together with a series of semi-structured interviews with key players within such organisations. In addition the project draws on material gathered in seminars and workshops, from a focus group of women who have played a key part in the management and governance of a range of organisations, and from a research group with two other researchers which has met regularly over the last two years. The purpose of this research is to discover what determines whether organisations develop 'enabling' or 'disabling' structures and to suggest strategies which encourage the first rather than the second, looking particularly at what happens to organisations going through a process of change. The fuller study will look at both mainstream and feminist organisational theory although this paper draws more heavily on feminist theory.

This paper concentrates on the use and abuse of power but power, of course, does not have to be disabling. Gareth Morgan identifies the 'empowering aspect of power' (and it is ironic how 'power' is so often used as a negative term in feminist discourse while the term 'empowerment' is almost invariably positive) and defines 'potential or transformative power'.(Morgan, 1986:186) Kanter distinguishes between power 'as efficacy (the ability to mobilize resources) rather than domination' (Kanter, 1977:6) and Judi Marshall between 'power with' rather than 'power over' (Marshall, 1984) while Riger's very important paper on the development of feminist organisations makes a similar distinction:

> Distinguishing between power as effectiveness and power as domination, Nancy Hartsock claimed that the women's movement erred in its condemnation of leadership by confusing those who wanted to achieve with those who wanted to control others. Similarly, members of the Chicago Women's Liberation Union argued that what was needed was not an absence of leadership but, rather mechanisms for keeping leadership accountable. (Riger 1994:276)

A great deal has been written about the abuse of power in mainstream organisations and about how women are often the victims of this abuse (Kanter 1991; Mills and Tancred, 1992; Coleman, 1991; The Journal 1991-

93). Alongside an analysis of the potential 'transformational leadership' which women can bring to organisations, (Rosener, 1990) there has been an increasing interest shown in how women too can abuse power when they achieve positions of influence in mainstream organisations (Freely, 1996). The continued obsession with Mrs Thatcher's performance in power is an obvious example of this and of how, instead of challenging the prevailing culture, women are often subverted or co-opted by it. Less has been written about the use and, particularly, the abuse of power within the autonomous women's movement and within organisations which are run predominantly or wholly by and for women.

It is not hard to explain this neglect. A few might share Gillian Coleman's rather depressing assertion that 'there is clearly limited value in feminist research into all-women organisations' (Coleman, 1991:19). But I believe it is more likely to be that the subject is painful rather than because it is considered to be of little value. Because we feel intensely loyal to our organisations we would rather not expose them in public. There are already enough people ready to question or mock the concept of women organising (how many times have each of us been asked 'why not men's organisations'?) for us to wish to give them any additional ammunition. My research has shown again and again how fiercely protective women are of their organisations so that to offer even a balanced critique is seen as potentially very threatening. Much of the argument about the abuse of power in mainstream organisations is postulated on the fact that a 'critical mass' of women breaking the glass ceiling at a sufficiently senior level would be enough to transform the organisation, to feminise the organisational culture. An extension of this argument would find autonomous women's organisations models of good and supportive management, whether self-managed as collectives or with a more hierarchical structure. Indeed an organisational sociologist Joyce Rothschild defines the 'feminine model of organisation' under six characteristics ('valuing members as individual human beings, non-opportunistic, careers defined in terms of service to others, commitment to employee growth, creation of a caring community and power sharing') (Rothschild, 1993:537).

This is certainly true of part of the women's voluntary sector. Many organisations strive, and largely succeed, in being models of good practice - in making the 'process' within the organisation, the way decisions are made, staff are treated, as important as the way services are delivered or campaigns conducted . Parents at Work (formerly the Working Mothers' Association), for instance, does not just advise others on 'family friendly employment practice' but strives very hard, within a restricted budget, to be a family friendly employer themselves. And I was struck very recently by someone who had moved from mainstream to a woman's organisation talking about the 'utter bliss' of working for an organisation run by and for women.

However, in reality women's organisations do not always embrace these characteristics with any more enthusiasm than mainstream organisations. Women's organisations from the traditional to the radical, have too often displayed examples of very bad management, revealing disturbing degrees of envy and over-control, a failure to delegate power, suspicion and distrust between different staff members or, more often, between paid staff and elected or appointed boards, and no commitment to employee growth. Such organisations, far from being transforming, merely replicate the very worst of bad management in the mainstream (or 'malestream') with an added layer of misery because most of those involved feel such deep commitment to the cause or client group which the organisation serves. Commitment, it seems, is no guarantee at all of good management or governance or, as Helen Brown explains in her detailed and invaluable account of three organisations run as collectives, 'the espousal of a value for equality does not, *in itself,* ensure that equality will prevail'. (Brown, 1992:17)

It is clearly painful for feminists to confront what is happening in some of our organisations and to acknowledge that women do not necessarily 'do it better', are not necessarily 'nicer', do not necessarily abuse power less than their male counterparts. But to look hard and critically at what is happening within women's organisations is not in any way to downgrade them but rather to acknowledge that what they are doing is both vitally important (the importance of women's NGOs worldwide was at last fully acknowledged at the UN Conference on Women in Beijing in 1995) and very hard. Helen Brown shows very graphically both how important leadership is in a collective and how hard it is to negotiate 'distributed leadership'. Most women's organisations are also forced to operate in a climate of chronic underfunding. (Bowman and Norton, 1986; Riordan, 1998). My research is born out of a strong and passionate belief in women's organisations as powerful agents of social change and a desire to work towards effective strategies to prevent the abuse of power and promote better management and governance. It should be read alongside work by Margaret Page, and by Siobhan Riordan who argues:

> When talking to women who work with, or have worked with women's organisations, 'power' is a major issue . . . from the experience of women who have gained power, it is no longer possible to pretend that the impulses to dominate, aggress, or exploit others are 'male' urges alone. Women have the ability to abuse power just as much as men I believe that the 'legacy of sisterhood' has created an unrealistic and unnatural expectation of women and their organisations . . . (power-sharing) has become an expectation, that because of their sex, women will automatically share power and decision-making . . . this is not always the case. And when women don't live up to this expectation strong feelings of betrayal, anger and resentment ensue.

> The organisational values of egalitarian social relationships and participatory democracy have become both a reality and a myth in women's organisations. By myth, I mean a widely held belief that women create caring, sharing organisations, because they are women . . . (Riordan, 1996:55-56)

Riordan quotes from Naomi Wolf's book *Fire with Fire* (Wolf, 1993)

27

which is one of several recent books to debate the question of women and power (see Kline, 1993; Miles, 1985).

Undertaking research in such a subject is highly 'sensitive' in many of Renzetti's terms 'where research delves into some deeply personal experience . . . where it impinges on the vested interests of powerful persons or the exercise of coercion or domination . . . where it deals with things sacred to those being studied' (Renzetti and Lee, 1993). In this case, however, it is the 'double sensitivity' of researched and researcher, both of whom have a deeply vested concern for, and interest in, the success and good name of the organised women's movement. This sensitivity can be partly overcome by the 'open acknowledgement by the researcher of her or his assumptions, beliefs, sympathies and biases' and feminist advocacy of the 'use of self-disclosure or reciprocity on the part of the researcher' (Renzetti and Lee, 1993:177-8). In thus 'establishing intersubjectivity', I have certainly been concerned, like the feminists cited by Raquel Kennedy Bergen in the same volume, 'to create research "for" women – that is, research that considers women's experiences and tries to improve their lives – rather than research merely "on" women' (Bergen in Renzetti and Lee, 1993:202). And I have certainly found that women have been extremely willing to talk and very open about their experiences, even when these have been very painful to them. They have also been very willing to engage in a kind of 'action research' which tries to draw lessons and strategies from the experience and involves them in the search for solutions. They are much less willing to be personally cited or to have their organisation identified as experiencing problems and the issue of confidentiality remains a problem.

The parameters of my research have been loosely the period leading up to and following the two UN Conferences on Women – in Nairobi in 1985 and in Beijing in 1995. It was a period with a Conservative government almost throughout, five of those ten years under Mrs Thatcher. It was a period characterised by some as **post**-feminist (see Evans, 1994; Faludi, 1992; Tuttle, 1986). It was a period in which participation in Europe had a profound effect on anti-discrimination legislation in relation to sex in Britain. And it was a period during which the collapse of socialist economies and increased globalisation affected the climate in which *all* organisations operated.

During this time I was very much a participant observer both of individual women's organisations, of the 'alliance politics' of the National Alliance of Women's Organisations (NAWO) with its 220 member organisations, and other infrastructure organisations such as the UK Joint Committee on Women and the European Women's Lobby, and of the international arena around the UN Conference in Beijing. Umbrella bodies present challenges of leadership, management and distribution of power of their own, which Margaret Page has examined very usefully in her study of the networks, alliances and coalitions which formed around Beijing (Page, 1997). For the purposes of this paper I shall concentrate on six categories of organisations (Grant, 1995), although this is very much a working categorisation and is not meant at this stage to be seen as an analytic taxonomy, or imply anything about the prevalence or otherwise of the abuse of power in any category or named organisation.

- *The traditional long-established mass membership organisations* (although almost all face falling and ageing membership so none are as 'mass' as they were) such as the National Federation of Women's Institutes (NFWI), the Townswomen's Guilds (TG), the Mothers' Union (MU) etc. These all operate very much within the status quo and most have an extremely hierarchical structure, although some, like the Mothers' Union, have made strong efforts recently to address this, reducing their Trustee body from around 500 to 22 in an attempt to create more streamlined, less expensive structures. On the whole, however, this category of organisations seems quite resistant to change. Most would probably be reluctant to define themselves as feminist.

- *Organisations providing a service for young women.* Many of these fall into a similar category of those above – long-established, hierarchical, very much within the status quo. However, organisations like the Guide Association and the YWCA have made very strong efforts to make themselves more accountable to the young women they serve (to become responsible *to* rather than responsible *for*) and to make their structures less bureaucratic, more open and more democratic. Both would undoubtedly claim that they have a long way still to go, but both have taken on board the fact that change, to be effective, has to be brave and radical rather than merely cosmetic (e.g. setting up a Junior Council with no power at all will very rapidly be rejected by the young women as pure tokenism), although sadly progress at the Guide Association was disrupted by the peremptory departure of its high profile Chief Executive. More recent organisations like Women and Girls Network, which provides counselling and information for women and girls who have experienced male violence, came more directly out of the feminist movement.

- *Organisations providing a wider service for women*, although often accompanied by advocacy or campaigning on behalf of their client group. Into this category I would put the Maternity Alliance, the childcare organisations, the rape crisis centres, the women's aid movement, women's housing groups, Women in Special Hospitals and the other organisations for women in prison. Most of these organisations would call themselves feminist and most started being run as a collective or at least on non-hierarchical lines. An increasing number (the Maternity Alliance, Housing for Women, No. 59 Greek Street and Southwark Women's Aid) have moved or are moving to a more hierarchical structure.

- *Professional Women's Organisations* which have grown up over the last twenty years, as more and more women join the workplace and are the fastest growing part of the autonomous women's movement. Most operate within the status quo although some are far more elitist and exclusive (e.g. Network) than others (e.g. Women as Role Models – WARM – exists entirely to encourage young women and girls to join the building industry). Although few employ more than one or two paid staff, most are run quite hierarchically. Some would define themselves as feminist, some not.

- *Black and ethnic minority women's groups:* most of which are quite recent and many established with money from the GLC. Some like Akina Mama Wa Afrika faced particular challenges from older women being reluctant to share power with young women, while Southall Black Sisters have always had to operate against a background of strong disapproval from their male community leaders. Some of these groups might prefer to define themselves as 'womanist' rather than feminist and many (although certainly not all) are prepared to challenge the status quo. There is also a growing network of refugee women's groups, such as Tawakal (established in 1991 by and for Somali women) and South Sudan Women Concern set up in 1993. Margaret Page's study of women managers of refugee projects is not specifically about women only groups but much of it is very relevant about the challenges women managers face. (Page, 1998)

- *Pressure or Campaigning Groups:* This category includes groups like the 300 Group, the Women's Environmental Network, Women Against Sexual Harassment (WASH), Wages for Housework, the Campaign Against Pornography and Justice for Women. It also includes the Fawcett Society which, while still very much a long-established organisation with roots back to 1866, has managed to transform itself into a very focused 'cutting edge' campaigning organisation with a rapidly growing membership, many of them young women. Almost all of these groups would define themselves as overtly feminist and in the business of challenging the status quo, and most are, at least in theory, run on non-hierarchical lines.

At the same time there are long-established hierarchical organisations like the Fawcett Society striving, with effort and some pain, to democratise and open up their structure, if not abandoning hierarchy altogether. It seems that if contemporary women's organisations are to be equipped to cope with the challenges they face they need to be able to avoid the famous so-called 'tyranny of structurelessness' of organisations run as collectives which Jo Freeman defined, (Freeman, 1984) and which, she claims, conceals an informal structure within which elite members are able to wield unchallenged, and unchallengeable, power. But they also need to avoid the contrasting tyranny of rigid rules and regulations, a 'culture of dependency and conformity' which Mary Stott describes so vividly in her study of the Townswomen's Guilds (Stott, 1978) and which applies equally to other traditional organisations. If the women's movement could only draw the best from both traditions – the strength and efficacy of appropriate structures with the power of democratic consensus building – it would be greatly strengthened.

Types of use and abuse of power
There is no space here to do more than sketch out some of the main categories of abusive power relations which occur and recur in women's organisations. Many of them are mirror images of each other.

- *The 'Queen bee syndrome' of 'organisation woman'* so well described by Mary Stott. This usually, although not invariably, applies to the elected members in more traditional type organisations rather than to the paid staff members. Stott's book describes some very distinguished, almost legendary, paid General Secretaries of the past but the norm seems to have been for these organisations to increasingly emphasise the voluntary contribution of members at the expense of staff and to find it extremely difficult to delegate power to their chief executives (and it is significant how often this post is designated as General Secretary – with its implication of purely administrative responsibility – rather than director or CEO). However the full-time unpaid 'organisation woman' is, of course, becoming increasingly rare.
- This leads on to the whole vexed relationship between elected Boards and paid staff and the way in which many Boards are suspicious of evidence of leadership in paid positions, preferring senior staff to 'run' the organisation rather than in any way 'lead' it. This is the case even when organisations are large and complex and urgently in need of skilled leadership and management. Evidence of good, high profile leadership is often met not with approbation but with remarks like 'Who does she think she is?'

When I was at NAWO I used occasionally to attend the lunches arranged for General Secretaries of the large women's organisations. I have never met a group of professional women who felt less professional satisfaction in their work. Several gave priority to organising opportunities for training and development for the staff they were managing but were given no such opportunities themselves (some were not even officially 'allowed' to attend these lunches). Far from being given chances to develop, several were facing attempts to have their job description and their whole position eroded (in the words of one, 'whittled away under our feet'). The only one who admitted to finding her job reasonably satisfactory gave as her reason the fact that she had learnt to 'manipulate' her chair rather than be manipulated. Hilary Williams, the high profile Chief Executive of the Guide Association who **did** manage to get her title changed from General Secretary to CEO and, before her premature departure, helped to lead the organisation through quite a dramatic process of change, spoke with feeling of how she had to go through three committees to employ a part-time secretary and of how the Association 'needs but does not want me' and how 'members are all, staff are nothing'. There was recently a spate of precipitous departures of apparently well-respected chief executives of women's organisations amidst distress and acrimony. While it is hard to tell how many of these are examples of bullying and unfair dismissal, they are certainly examples of bad management or recruitment

It is hard to analyse the reason behind this particular abuse of power. Part of it may be the fact that, in the case of more traditional organisations, most Boards are still made up of women who have not been in recent paid employment and are thus uneasy with professional staff and sometimes even resentful that they are being paid for services which they give freely (coupled with an insensitivity on the part of professional staff who can make members feel patronised). It may also be an internalised inability to acknowledge success and excellence in other women because of an upbringing that discouraged it in oneself. Susie Orbach and Luise Eichenbaum have analysed the complexities of love, envy and competition in women's friendships, emotions which are often carried over into their organisations. (Orbach & Eichenbaum, 1994) But power over staff is not abused only in traditional organisations. Shirley Nelson of the National Women's Network identified the problems of sole workers in small organisations who often find themselves subject to constant criticism from their Management Committees without corresponding support or validation. WISH (Women in Special Hospitals) in 1992 experienced acute problems over leadership which seemed to stem from a new committee who could not manage or support women of calibre and, because they felt out of their depth, adopted a very controlling and autocratic management style. This led to a regime which was experienced as very cruel and attacking, with accusations made against the co-directors which they took as both professional and personal criticisms. The two co-directors only stayed with the organisation because they were able to support each other and felt so closely identified with the future of the organisation (which, as with many founder members or groups 'felt like a cherished baby they had given birth to being cut in half'). In the end, after intense pain on all sides, the Chair and some of the Committee left and things slowly settled down. In order to avoid any repetition, WISH instituted workshops in the roles and responsibilities of staff and committees and keeps this work very much alive through the induction of new members, supervision structure etc. Having survived, the organisation was able, holding to its original principles and aims, to establish an environment which was nurturing to **all** (staff, trustees and women patients) and to lay the foundation to develop a thriving and growing three branch organisation. WISH's Annual General Meeting held in Broadmoor Hospital in November 1996 was a very strong testimony to the current strength of the organisation.

But such abuse is not, of course, unique to women in the voluntary sector. Kanter cites stereotypic views of women bosses as 'mean and bossy' *from women* as much as men and concludes:

> Stereotypes persist even in the face of evidence negating them. The *real* extent of bossiness among women in authority in organizations may have little to do with the persistence of the stereotype, but this particular portrait has one very important characteristic: *It is a perfect picture of people who are powerless. Powerlessness tends to produce those very characteristics attributed to women bosses.* (Kanter 1977:202)

It is the particular abuse of power *by those who have been powerless* which seems to distinguish organisations run by women from mainstream organisations or those run by men.

- *The challenge of the 'founder director'.* This is a very common phenomenon in the women's voluntary sector with many organisations started by strong, often charismatic, women with great drive and sense of vision. Protection from the abuse of power in this case works two ways: the need to protect the protagonist from the sort of envy and spite experienced by the founders of WISH quoted above, *and* the need to protect the organisation from the founder who runs it like her personal kingdom, will not delegate, will not leave, will not allow others to take over and develop the vision which she sees as uniquely hers, and will not appreciate that the skills needed to set up an organisation are not necessarily those needed to develop it. Riger analyses the situation with clarity:

Founders who are used to controlling their organizations may find a more rule-bound, less subjective style of management anathema. They may be reluctant to step aside because of a proprietary interest in the organisation. The reluctance of founders to institutionalize leadership by establishing procedures and policies which do not require their personal judgement has been labelled the 'founder's trap'. Ironically, just as the organization attracts more clients or external funding, the founder's personal style of management may become inappropriate because of the expansion in organizational size. Especially when they have taken risks or made sacrifices to get the organization off the ground, founders may resent their sudden obsolescence and resist change. A critical challenge in this situation is to loosen the founder's control of the organization. In some cases this means the founders will depart; Suzanne Staggenborg identifies a long list of social movement founders, feminist and otherwise, who chose to leave or were rejected from organizations that they had begun. (Riger, 1994:285)

The situation described here is from the USA but most would recognise it as substantially true of the UK. One of the latest of a long line of examples (ranging from Chiswick Women's Aid, the Women's Press, Everywoman etc) is the Women's Art Library. The situation is none the less sad (both for individuals and organisations) for often being necessary or inevitable. The organised women's movement needs to be able to honour its founding foremothers while building in safeguards to ensure they cannot retain a stranglehold on their organisations *in perpetuo* if this becomes damaging. What are needed are structures which do not stifle personality but also hold it accountable.

- *The abuse of power based on diversity of race, class . religion, sexuality or age etc.* The problems and conflicts associated with the first two have been well documented in the literature of the women's liberation movement (see Phillips, 1987). More recently, Razia Aiz explored the complexities of the oppressive nature of 'difference invested with power' which she argues black women experience in women's organisations (Aziz, 1992). Abuse of power based on age is often even

33

more complex. We have seen the difficulty younger women can find managing older, well-established, women in the example from WISH above. Iannello in *Decisions without Hierarchy* describes how an informal hierarchy can mean older members are 'in a very real sense ignored', with even younger members admitting that 'the organisation as a whole discriminates against the older members' (Iannello, 1992).

But of course it more often works the other way. My own research shows that young women experience most traditional organisations as almost completely excluding (Grant 1995). In this category the abuse of power can appear very benign, even ambiguous, but be none the less damaging. Gilligan quotes David McClelland's research that 'while men represent powerful activity as assertion and aggression, women in contrast portray acts of nurturance as acts of strength' (Gilligan, 1993:167-8). And Riger describes the accepted ideal of the feminist leader as nurturing mother, and how 'when she does not live up to this ideal, irrational and intense criticism may befall her' (Riger, 1994:276). But it is my experience that this role is even being questioned as an ideal. One organisation working with young women, for instance, accepts that its role is not to mother the young women it serves, to replace a patriarchy with a matriarchy.

The foregoing is not, of course, an exhaustive list. Apart from the 'Queen bee syndrome' (of which Mary Stott's book *Organisation Woman* remains an exemplary analysis), such abuses of power can be found in any type of organisation.

Strategies for coping with these abuses of power

My research is not yet at a stage where I would feel comfortable suggesting definitive strategies (although high-quality training for staff and committees and built-in conflict resolution and power-sharing mechanisms which are in place well before any conflict can develop seem to be increasingly obvious) but much has been written which is extremely useful and illuminating. Not all of this is feminist theory, or even written by women. Charles Handy, for instance, is extremely useful on the different way in which power is wielded in voluntary organisations, about democracy and issues like the difference between trust and control (Handy, 1988). John Carver's (Carver, 1990 et al) distinction between governance (the province of 'Boards' or 'Management Committees', terms which tend to be used interchangeably according to preference) and management (the responsibility of the CEO) is extremely pertinent and would, if adhered to, prevent a great deal of potential for conflict in women's, as in other voluntary organisations .

However, what has been written by women, from within the women's movement is obviously especially relevant. There has been an increased interest in the structure or governance of women's organisations and it was, linked with politics, one of the thirteen themes under which workshops were arranged at the NGO Forum running alongside the UN Conference on Women in Beijing in September 1995. Before that, in 1988, the radical international group DAWN (Development Alternatives with Women for a New Era) had, in their book, *Development Crises and Alternative Visions:*

Third World Women's Perspective created a heading called 'Empowering Ourselves through Organisations: Types and Methods'. It analyses six types of organisation (traditional, service orientated, affiliated to a political party, worker-based, those that have flourished during the Decade for Women, grassroots related to a specific project and research organizations). It points out very helpfully that: 'It is important to draw on existing organizational strengths while working out ways to overcome weaknesses and conflict'. (Sen and Grown, 1988:89). It is quite realistic about these 'weaknesses and conflicts' (which they see as coming often from 'class or other biases') but upbeat about the possibility of devising strategies for overcoming them:

> Empowerment of organizations, individuals and movements has certain requisites. These include resources (finance, knowledge, technology), skills training and leadership formation on the one side; and democratic processes, dialogue, participation in policy and decision making, and techniques for conflict resolution on the other. Flexibility of membership requirements can also be helpful. (Sen and Grown, 1988:89).

They go on to ask 'Why is it that many women have found it difficult to delegate organizational authority?' and conclude 'Our mistrust must stimulate us, however, to devise innovative ways of sharing responsibilities so that we do not reinforce existing relationships of domination. And we must develop structures which keep leaders accountable and responsive to the voices and needs of the membership.' (Sen and Grown, 1988:94). Finally they deal with the challenge of power direct:

> A final issue is our ability and willingness to share power within our organizations. Related to this is the question of our styles of conflict management and resolution . . . democratization of organizations and widening of their membership base is essential since it distributes power and diffuses hierarchy . . . explicit assertion and commitment to an ethic that rejects personal aggrandizement, and a firm stance in that direction should be built into the organization from the beginning. (Sen and Grown, 1988:95).

Although this is written from a Third World perspective it is highly relevant to women's groups in this country who are, as we have seen, grappling with all these problems.

I have found Riordan's concept of the need to overcome the 'power illiteracy' and the 'myth of sisterhood' which many women bring into organisations very illuminating (Riordan 1996). I have also found Rothschild's 'Feminine Model of Organisation', especially the points about commitment to employee growth and power sharing, very useful and also Helen Brown's comments about the relationship between values and action and the need for participants to constantly renegotiate this (Brown, 1992:53). Brown is also very useful about the vexed question of how to deal with difference, conflict or diversity: 'Dissension and difference were taken seriously and explored for the possibility of compromise or accommodation.' (Brown, 1992:116). On the same theme of strategies for dealing with conflict and/or diversity I have found very helpful both the work of Cynthia Coburn at City University and the work in progress papers from the Stone Centre, Wellesley College, Boston, USA, whose 'model of mutuality' allows 'building connections trhough difference'. For the Stone Center theorists 'such mutually empathic connection is the basis of relational growth and healing. Intensity of feeling and powerful conflict are frequently part of this process'. (Coll, Cook-Nobles and Surrey, 1993:9)

The willingness to deal honestly and openly with diversity and conflict, as well as the previously identified need to balance the strength and efficacy of appropriate structures with the power of democratic decision making, could enhance the efficacy of women's organisations and forms the basis of my on-going research.

Notes

[1] I use the term 'autonomous women's movement' to encompass 'not-for-profit' organisations which are run overwhelmingly *by* women, *for* women (or girls), with women in all the key leadership positions. It does not imply they are necessarily 'women only' or feminist in orientation.

[2] Interview with Clodagh Corcoran, Press Officer of the National Childbirth Trust 22.5.96.

[3] See 1994 *The Submission of the Mothers' Union to the Archbishops' Commission on the Organisation of the Church of England*, The Mothers' Union.

[4] Although many local authorities in London do continue to support women's organisations financially, and the London Boroughs Grant Scheme gives support to organisations operating in more than one Borough, this in no way matches the funding that was available from the Labour controlled GLC in the first half of the 1980s. The other metropolitan county councils abolished at the same time as the GLC were also generous to women's organisations and their successor bodies have equally found it hard to match this generosity (See Bowman and Norton, 1986 and Riordan 1998).

[5] Interviews with Hilary Williams, 2 February 1995 and 5 June 1996.

[6] Interview with Shirley Nelson, 15 February 1995.

[7] Interview with Jennifer McCabe and Prue Stevenson, 17 October 1994 and with Jennifer McCabe, 2 July and December 7 1996.

References

1991-1993, *The Journal: Women in Organisations and Management*, issues 1-7, Newcastle: Research Training Initiatives.

Aziz, R. 1992, 'A Few Thoughts on Difference and Unity', *Report on London Women's Forum*, Women's Resource Centre.

Bowman, M. & Norton, M., 1986, *Raising Money for Women*, London: Bedford Square Press.

Brown, H., 1992, *Women Organising*, London: Routledge.

Carver, J., 1990, *Boards that make a Difference: A New Design for Leadership in Nonprofit and Public Organisations*, Jossey Bass.

Coleman, G., 1991, *Investigating Organisations: A Feminist Approach*, Bristol: School for Advanced Urban Studies.

Coll C. G., Cook-Nobels, R., and Surrey, J., 1993, *Building Connections through Diversity*, Boston: The Stone Center.

Evans, M. (ed), 1994, *The Women Question (Second Edition)*, London: Sage Publications.

Faludi, S., 1992, *Backlash: The Undeclared War Against Women*, London: Chatto & Windus.

Freely, M., 10 June 1996, 'Monster raving loony bosses', *Guardian*.

Freeman, J., 1984, *The Tyranny of Structurelessness*, London: Dark Star Press and Rebel Press.

Gilligan, C., 1984, *In a Different Voice: Psychological Theory and Women's Development*, Harvard University Press.

Grant, J., 1995 1984, *Where have all the women gone? The experience of women aged between 18-34 in women's organisations*, London: DEMOS.

Handy, C., 1998, *Understanding Voluntary Organisations*, London: Penguin.

Iannello, K. P., 1992, *Decisions without Hierarchy; Feminist Interventions in Organization Theory and Practice*, London: Routledge Chapman & Hall.

Kanter, R. M. 1977, *Men and Women of the Corporation*, New York: Basic Books Inc.

Kline, N; 1993, *Women and Power: How far can we go?*, London, BBC Books.

Marshall, J., 1984, *Women Manager; travellers in a male world*, Chichester: John Wiley & Sons.

Miles, R. 1985, *Women and Power*, London, Futura.

Mills, A. J., & Tancred, P., 1992, *Gendering Organisational Analysis*, London: Sage Publications.

Morgan, G., 1986, *Images of Organisation*, London, Sage Publications.

Page, M: 1997, *Women in Beijing One Year on: Networks, Alliances, Coalitions*, Community Development Foundation. – 1998 Compassionate leadership: A Question of Gender? The Experience of women managers of refugee projects (unpublished paper).

Phillips, A., 1987, *Divided Loyalties: Dilemmas of Sex and Class*, London: Virago.

Renzetti, C. M. & Lee, R. H.(eds), 1993, *Researching Sensitive Topics*, London, Sage Publications.

Riordan, S., 1996, *Women's Organisations in the UK Voluntary Sector: A Framework for Future Research*, Centre for Institutional Studies, University of East London.

Riordan, S., 1998, 'Organisations of the Women's Movement – Countering

Invisibility', in Pharoah C. & Smerdon M. (eds) *Dimensions of the Voluntary Sector: Facts, Figures and Analysis*, Kent: Charities Aid Foundation.

Riger, S., 1994, 'Challenges of Success: Stages of Growth in Feminist Organizations', *Feminist Studies 20*, No.2, Feminist Studies Inc.

Rosener, J. B., 1990, 'Ways Women Lead', *Harvard Business Review*, Vol 68, No.6.

Rothchild, J., 1993, 'The Feminine Model of Organization' in Robbins (ed.), *Organization Behaviour*, 6th Edition, London: Prentice Hall.

Sen, G. & Grown, C., 1998, *Development, Crises and Alternative Visions: Thrid World Women's Perspective*, Earthscan Publication.

Stott, M., 1978, *Organisation Women*, London: Heinemann.

Tuttle, L., 1986, *Encyclopaedia of Feminism*, London: Arrow Books.

Wolf, N. 1993, *Fire with Fire,: The New Female Power and How it will change the 21st Century*, London Chatto and Windus.

Producing Feminist History in Electronic Form

by Gail Chester

Preface

In about 1982 I first met with some other Women's Liberationists to start collecting our history while it was still happening and still fresh in our minds. Even then, the difficulties of trying to produce a faithful history, representing many different viewpoints, was obvious. And indeed, the project never progressed beyond the initial discussions because we could not resolve the differences, even among the women in that room. Since then, while being pre-occupied with other projects, I have retained my earlier concerns. Thus, despite being a computer illiterate, I was intrigued by Ruth Wallsgrove's[1] passing remark a couple of years ago, about the potential of computers for gathering a range of women's recollections into a history of the Women's Liberation Movement (WLM).

My opportunity to think about whether Ruth's idea could work came when I was studying the electronic book as part of my MA in the History of the Book. By total coincidence (except perhaps in our shared sense of increasing urgency), just as my course was starting, in October 1995, I was invited to a gathering of women who had been involved in the Essex Road Women's Centre (ERWC), to reminisce and discuss the possibility of collecting its history. Although the possibility of collecting and storing material electronically was raised (by other women as well as me), this was not a major focus of the meeting, and the proposals I put forward in the following article have not been widely discussed by women from ERWC. Owing to work and other pressures, progress on the project in general has been slow, and not a great deal has happened since the original meeting.

Meanwhile, other women have been thinking along very similar lines. At the Women's Studies Network Association conference in July 1996, I found out that the Feminist Archive, Bradford was about to produce its first draft of a WLM chronology covering 1969 to 1979 (Arledge Ross and Bearse, 1996). This draft was essentially a paper version of Ruth Wallsgrove's idea of a computer time-line which got me going in the first place. And at the conference I also heard about the South Wales Feminist History and Archive Project, being co-ordinated at the University of Glamorgan[2] by Avril Rolph, who said, '. . . it occured to me from the outset that using a multi-media format could help to document the Women's Liberation Movement in a much more diverse and interesting way than just textual descriptions.' (pers. comm.)

Although I did the research for this paper as part of an academic course, my main concern throughout has remained the political and practical implications of producing authentic feminist history. As a long-time feminist activist, I wish to see our history preserved and another wave of the WLM encouraged. It seems to me that we can employ useful bits of the new technology for our own benefit, and that now is therefore a good time to introduce the suggestions presented here. If the paper dwells more on the technicalities than the politics, it is because I feel that readers will be less familiar with the former.

Because of the possible unfamiliarity of the material, a few points need highlighting at the outset. I am not suggesting that recording our history electronically is the only way to do it – far from it. I wish to acknowledge that these are useful tools which it would be unwise to ignore, but they are no more than tools, and are only useful in the proper political context. Secondly, I am dealing with information and technology which dates extremely quickly. This paper was mainly written and researched in June 1996, with a few amendments made in December 1996, so by the time you read it, new technologies and applications will almost certainly have appeared. Internet connections may no longer be valid. Thus some of the details may be wrong, though I believe the general principles will not be.

Finally, it may not be clear that, although I refer to *an* electronic history, there are actually several forms of electronic publication, any or all of which could be useful for this project, and which involve different levels of privacy. The main technologies I am concerned with are CD-Roms, E-mail discussion groups, and Web pages. CD-Roms are disks wich are most analogous to a printed book, in that they are inserted into individual computers, and 'read' there.[3] E-mail allows computer communication analogous to writing a letter, which may be sent to another individual person, and in the case of e-mail discussion groups (also known as bulletin boards, conferences, newsgroups, and so on), a specified closed group of people, or an open and unknown group of people. Web pages are placed on the Worldwide Web (part of the Internet), and are analogous to advertisements, being available to be read by anyone with access to the Web who is interested in finding them. Pages cannot generally be altered, except by the person who compiled them, and they may consist entirely of text, or incorporate images and even, occasionally, sounds. As with print publishing, electronic publishing requires that the appropriate medium is used for a particular message, and I have tried to indicate in the paper the relevant uses and limitations of each.

Implicit in my thinking, but not expressed in the body of the paper, is my awareness that many of the original publications and methods of organising of the WLM have been women-only. This presents a dilemma for any attempt to make the material more widely available, which becomes more acute the further one ventures into cyberspace. This is a problem that is also being addressed by other projects, and cannot be ignored. As Jalna Hanmer (1996) says, referring to the Feminist Archive, Bradford:

> Working to retain the past is also a radical feminist activity – in an activist and intellectual sense – in the here and now. WLM publications and activities were usually women-only in Britain. To respect the women-only distribution policy of these publications makes it even more difficult to obtain funding, and therefore secure the future of these sources, but remaining loyal to the intentions and thereby the politics of its authors and editors, is a way to maintain an herstorical organisational

tradition. Seeking to secure women-only anything is as subversive now as it was in the 1970s . . . (Hanmer, 1996:549)

The message is clear. We must not abandon the latest set of toys to the boys, but should adopt those parts that are useful for our own purposes.

Introduction
There are two distinct sets of problems to be considered in undertaking an electronic history of the WLM, and the issues need looking at separately. Firstly there are the problems associated with attempting to produce a history of the movement (or even an important representative part of it); and secondly there are the problems which arise from attempting to gather any collection of very diverse materials into an electronic format and make it accessible to its intended audience or audiences.

I shall start by dealing briefly with the issues which arise when thinking about any history of the WLM, as inevitably this will affect decisions about formats, what material to include, and so on. It is generally agreed by contemporary feminists that recording the history of the WLM would be a good idea for various reasons. Information will probably be more reliably collected while the main actors still retain clear memories and have not thrown away all their ephemera, and it is important to provide information and inspiration for succeeding generations, as well as raw material for further study and analysis.

Women teaching in the area of contemporary history have become acutely aware of the gaps, and some members of the Women's History Network and the Women's Studies Network Association have been discussing how to pool resources to improve the situation. They have established the need for primary and secondary source databases, and are attempting to assemble a bibliography of useful texts. Progress on the project has been slow because of the paucity of material and the other commitments of the women involved.[4] Talking to some of them reinforced my belief in the importance of attempting to record women's history, even while highlighting some of the difficulties.

These discussions echo a more general concern with gathering information by and about women, which was reflected by a conference on 'Women, Information and the Future' at Radcliffe College's Arthur and Elizabeth Schlesinger Library on the History of Women in America, held in July 1994. Several papers at the conference were devoted to discussions about the collection of women's history material in various countries, including Britain (the Fawcett Library and the Feminist Library). In her preface to the conference proceedings (Moseley, 1995), Joan R. Challinor, Chair, Schlesinger Library Advisory Committee, notes:

Three fundamental convictions, long promulgated by the Schlesinger Library, inspired the organizers of the conference:

• Women need full and unrestricted access to information if they are to take their rightful place in world affairs.

- Women should be involved in every stage of gathering and disseminating information and should determine what information is to be collected, how, in what form, and how it is to be shared.
- All information gathered by the United Nations and its 185-member countries should include complete data on women; this information should be disseminated in a form accessible to women in every geographic and demographic setting.

The conference organizers agreed that women's information networks should be encouraged, to foster reciprocity and cooperation and to ease communications across national boundaries and geographic divides. Such information networks promote the ability to think creatively and to work collaboratively and will be essential if women are to take their rightful place in the world of tomorrow. (Challinor in Moseley, 1995:xiv)

Nevertheless, all past serious attempts to produce histories of the British WLM have failed before they have even started, for a variety of interlocking reasons. As Debbie Cameron explains:

Writing the WLM's history is difficult and gives unusual scope for interpretation. Unlike most political movements, the WLM was always a relatively loose and decentred configuration of diverse groups rather than a hierarchical organisation with official policy documents and authoritative central records. And though there are plenty of individuals who can bear witness to the events that interest a historian, relying on their testimony brings its own problems. In a leaderless and decentralised movement where women do not speak as official representatives, who you talk to makes a difference to the picture you get. And testimony is bound to be affected by hindsight - a problem for all oral history, but especially for oral political history. Women may well discuss their actions and beliefs twenty years ago in ways designed to enhance their political credentials in the very different climate of the present. (Cameron, 1993:11)

Furthermore, despite its apparent homogeneity to the outside world, there are significant political differences between feminists, which can lead to women not trusting others to represent them fairly and/or collect the 'right' material. Such suspicions can magnify the difficulties of anyone trying to present a wide spectrum of activity and opinion. Cameron's own article is an example of this - she complains about radical feminism having been written out of the few books of feminist history which have been published.

Another political antagonism which is significant for a project of this nature is the one between activists and academics within the WLM. This conflict is more or less evident, depending on the particular project, and in their hearts, women know that the interests of each group are not so different, and that many women are both. A good example of productive collaboration is the Feminist Archive, Bradford, 'A Collection of Grassroots Material from the Women's Liberation Movement', which has been able to utilise resources from the university to pay a part-time worker to complement its long-time volunteers.[5] An extremely honest assessment of the difficulties of trying to combine the roles of feminist academic and activist is provided by Laurie Mercier and Mary Murphy (1991), who were involved in assembling a history of club women in Montana. They write about the many feminist scholars they know who could not persuade non-academics of the importance of history and go on to say:

> As feminist historians, we recognise the importance of women's history in our own lives, in shaping our sense of worth and ability . . . we learned that people gain inspiration from a variety of sources . . . We could work collaboratively, but it was presumptuous to think that all women would or should become historians. (Mercier and Murphy, 1991:182)

However, the difference between their project and a WLM history is that they saw themselves mainly as feminist women doing something *for* "non-feminist" women (however that is defined), whereas I am concerned with feminists doing it for ourselves. Viewing the task from this perspective might hopefully solve some of the problems of the professional historians, though our potential internal political conflicts might give rise to a whole set of fresh ones.

All attempts so far to produce a history of participation in the WLM have been in conventional book form, and have mostly relied on individuals' written testimonies or on interviews.[6] Such records have much potential historical value, but they carry within them the difficulties which face all oral histories. Gluck and Patai (1993) have devoted a whole book to the feminist practice of oral history, but all their contributors are academics confronting 'the intricacies of interviewing across cultural boundaries'. (Gluck and Patai, 1993:3) This is not generally the problem of the ERWC project, although issues of power and control and interpretation of the material are still of great concern. As Gluck and Patai point out:

> Contemporary literary theory – challenging the older historian's tendency to see oral history as a transparent representation of experience – made us aware that the typical product of an interview is a text, not a reproduction of reality, and that models of textual analysis were therefore needed. (Gluck and Patai, 1993:3)

While feminists must remain sensitive to such critiques when analysing material, such considerations must not prevent the material being collected, and various groups, including the Feminist Archive, Bradford, are actively seeking it:

> [We are] currently involved in an oral history project recording the involvement of women in the WLM. The project focuses on women active during the 1970s and before, in Bradford and Leeds, West

Yorkshire. Its aim is to record the history of the movement in the words of the women who know it best and to raise awareness about the Archives and their role in the community. This project is now entering its second year and we hope that publications will be forthcoming. (Appeal letter, November 1995)

What oral histories and written testimonies cannot take into account is the substantial parts of WLM activity which have not been recorded in conventional forms, for example, minutes of meetings, leaflets announcing political actions, even information about people's personal relationships. As the WLM held strongly to the belief that the personal is political, who shared a house or lover with whom at which time, or who was in which friendship networks, could be of political interest for future analysis.[7]

Given the disparate nature of the material, and the great desirability of including a wide variety of political perspectives within any collection of WLM material, it certainly seems that the idea of gathering and storing material electronically holds many attractions, even though it creates its own difficulties. It should already be obvious that it is probably impossible to write *the* history of the WLM, owing to its enormous diffusion, both political and geographical, but the dream remains of trying to piece together a patchwork quilt of overlapping information – temporal, sectoral, political, geographical – so that as full a picture as possible could eventually be achieved. Achieving this dream without using electronic methods, while by no means impossible, would be much more exhausting and would probably not be as comprehensive. The recently published Bradford chronology, covering the period 1969 to 1979 (Arledge Ross and Bearse, 1996), is a good example of what can be achieved using conventional methods. It is a great achievement, which took the compilers two years.[8]

Why Essex Road Women's Centre

When I was starting my research, trying to conceptualise an electronic history of the whole WLM seemed rather too overwhelming an initial task. I decided it would be sensible to start by doing a feasibility study of a small but representative part of the whole movement. It was very fortunate that when I was first mulling over my ideas, Lisa Vine, the woman whose initiative got Essex Road Women's Centre (ERWC) started in 1973, decided that she wanted to collect its history, working with other women who had been involved. She was prompted to do this by the untimely death of Jo Temple, another activist at ERWC, who had left behind some boxes of ephemera, but no recorded personal memories, much to the regret of her friends.

ERWC occupied a shopfront site at 108 Essex Road, Islington, from 1973 to 1976. It was one of about six such Centres in London at that time, with about another 30 around the country. Women's Centres were basically co-ordinating centres and access points for WLM activity, and the degree of involvement with women from the local community who were not feminist activists varied from place to place. ERWC was fairly representative of all the other Centres, whilst of course, having its local specificities. It provides a useful microcosm of the national WLM at that time, as both local and national groups were based there, and its active members seem to have been reasonably representative of the WLM as a whole, in terms of sexuality, class, ethnicity, and so on.

Lisa Vine and a few colleagues called an initial meeting of the ERWC History Project on 9 October 1995, which was attended by more than 40 women. Reflecting later on discussion at the meeting, I concluded that material to be collected comes in the following forms:

- Printed ephemera from the time: mainly leaflets, posters, minutes, notes, song-sheets, magazines, pamphlets.
- Photos taken at the time: for example, of demonstrations, stalls at events, meetings at the ERWC, other WLM events attended by women from ERWC.
- Material audiotaped at the time: mainly songs and performances, some political discussion.
- Archive film material: translated onto video; not translated; tape/slide material.
- Written memories, collected from October 1995 onwards: handwritten, typewritten, word-processed.
- Audiotaped memories from individuals or groups, collected from October 1995 onwards: spoken analysis and anecdote, and songs.
- Videotaped memories, collected from October 1995 onwards: individuals and groups.
- References to ERWC in books of analysis written subsequent to its existence.[9]
- Large physical objects which could only be stored digitally as photos; for example, banners, speculums (for medical self-examination), an Aunt Sally (from an Islington People's Festival).

There seem to be three stages involved in the process of converting this raw data into a history of ERWC: gathering the material; storing it; transmitting it and/or publishing it. All these stages can usefully involve electronic book processes, although, of course, that is not the only way of handling material. It must be decided what is most appropriate in each case, which involves considering all the connected political, philosophical and practical issues.

Gathering the material

Before gathering can start, women need to trust that their material will be in safe hands, so it is important to show evidence of having thought through the issues. At the October 1995 meeting, all the women present were enthusiastic about the original idea of collecting ERWC's history, but were more cautious about the idea of doing it electronically. Two of the issues that were raised were women's anxieties that they would not be able to participate if they could not type, as they did not understand how their contribution could be incorporated; and anxieties about who would have access to the material and at what stage. Such feelings need to be taken seriously as an indication of how alienated many women still feel from new technology. Dealing with difficulties sympathetically would be crucial for encouraging women's participation, and could also provide an opportunity to learn new skills. There is no doubt that a training element would have to be incorporated into the project, if digitising were not going to be left to a very few women, and it may well be better not to digitise at all than have it done incompetently.

Information about women's use of the newest technologies is somewhat anecdotal[10] and is changing all the time, as its use is diffusing and developing so rapidly. But the discernible trends are unsurprising – with women, as with men, younger women and North American women tend to be more comfortable with it, though happily, not all developments are restricted to North America. Sirpa Wrede wrote to the women's-studies discussion list[11] on 7 May 1996, in response to a woman from rural Scotland who was concerned about women's access to the Internet and IT in general:

> In Finland, where I live, in addition to universities and companies, many municipalities are investing in access to the internet. This is mostly still in the introductory stages, but more than 1/3 of Finnish municipalities now use internet. Most of them have installed computers in public libraries and schools, which enables everyone who wants, to access the internet without cost. The idea is often to increase local democracy and to supply a new route to information about local decision-making. However, access as such is not enough. People need skills to make use of the services. Mostly there are very cheap courses available, but many women may still not feel included in these invitations to join the netters.

As Wrede's note suggests, there is little information available about how use is measured – possessing the technology does not necessarily mean it is used. For example, Michele Evard (1996:188) points out that a commercial survey in the US in December 1994 showed that 36% of Internet-accessing accounts were owned by women, but it is estimated that less than 10% of people posting public messages to Usenet newsgroups are women.

The possibility of access to the Internet was not even mentioned at the ERWC meeting, as the women there had more basic concerns about the use of any new technology. Their fundamental concern was that they wanted their history to include the widest possible range of women and opinions, remembering that all women feel marginal sometimes, and they wanted to maintain the element of debate and change within and between different individuals and groups and issues. They particularly wanted to develop the sense of a collective picture and did not want anything introduced that might interfere with this objective. Most women connected with the ERWC project probably still need convincing that electronic methods would increase the possibility of achieving their goals rather than diminishing it.

Storage of material
Although it would be more efficient to resolve the question of electronic storage at the beginning, very little of the gathering of the material can be done electronically, so it is not until this stage that such matters become pressing. For ERWC, as for many archiving projects, storage is an early issue which needs to be resolved, as there is a considerable physical storage

problem. At present, material is stored in many cardboard boxes in many women's homes, while memories await being written up on many further bits of paper. This would take up a lot of space if it were all assembled in one place. It is in response to this difficulty that the electronic storage of archives in general has been suggested. Meanwhile, many questions remain about whether electronic storage is the most appropriate method for such a project.

Andrew Odlyzko (1996) who works for AT&T Research, has been a prominent contributor to the discussion about the electronic publication of scholarly journals (Okerson & O'Donnell, 1995). He claims that concerns about the durability of electronic information (i.e. being unable to retrieve material because the machine has broken down after becoming obsolete) is largely unjustified:

> Magnetic tapes, and even current optical disks, do not last long. However, it is possible to produce extremely durable digital storage media. For example, the HD-ROM recording technology, developed at Los Alamos, can attain storage densities over 100 times those of current CD-ROMs and, by using materials such as stainless steel or iridium, can guarantee stability for tens of thousands of years, and provide resistance to fire, water damage, rats, and other disasters that can destroy paper data. Since storage densities are increasing rapidly, however, there is no point in using such long-lasting storage methods. If 10 years from now we will be able to store 100 times as much data at the same cost, why pay extra for any medium that provides stability beyond 10 years?

While this may well be true, it ignores the fact that people cannot afford to continually upgrade their equipment, and also that not all material presently in print is equally suitable for electronic storage. In the case of ERWC, it seems unlikely that the women involved would be prepared to destroy the physical artefacts, even if their content could be stored digitally. This cannot be dismissed as soppy sentimentality, as an electronic representation of a hastily produced polemical pamphlet leaves out a great deal of information about the context of its production – the misplaced ink splodge, the quality of the paper and the style of the print are as important for the full appreciation of that document as they are for a medieval manuscript. It should also be emphasised that even if material is stored digitally, there is no need to destroy the original. Each version could (and almost certainly should) happily co-exist, fulfilling different roles in the understanding of history.

Lisa Vine has had some discussion with the Islington archivist, herself a feminist, who has expressed a general interest in taking material. However, at this point, a distinction should be made betweeen the categories of material mentioned earlier. Whilst it would be an attractive idea for perhaps most items to be stored in a public archive and made freely available more or less immediately as physical artefacts, it might well be that recently collected written, audio and video-taped memories, should not be made publicly available for now, until decisions have been made about how the information in them should be utilised, whether in print, electronically, or in other form.

Issues of electronic storage

Given that it is technically possible to store electronically almost all the items likely to be gathered by the ERWC group, a number of important issues must be considered before starting to do this:

- *What should be digitised?* As mentioned above, just because something can be done, it does not mean it should be done. I would not initially digitise any editorial material from magazines, pamphlets, or other published work. It would be useful to have an electronic listing of contents, for easy reference, but even this would not be a priority if resources were limited, which they almost certainly would be. It could be done relatively painlessly by a woman who was, for example, reading through old material anyway, to jog her memory. Whether to prioritise digitising material such as minutes of meetings, which were printed but not published in the normal sense, would depend on how much new material this provided. Interestingly, at the ERWC meeting, some women could not see the point of keeping old agendas and minutes, and did not recognise their value as a relatively objective record of what actually happened, and as memory-joggers. Because of the much larger amount of disk space required to store digital images, it would also not be an early priority to transfer photos, drawings, etc, to electronic storage (although a list of available images would be useful). For the same reason, it would be preferable to directly digitise text by keying it in, rather than scanning it, as a ratio of 1 to 500 in disk space is required. But any feeling of the original appearance of a document is then lost, and it is more work. After taking all these factors into account, it seems that it would be most helpful initially to store all newly-collected memories electronically, so that they could be referred to by other members of the project, and provide a working database. Therefore, in addressing the issues that follow, I shall focus discussion on the electronic storage of newly-gathered memories. While the following issues can, of course, be extrapolated to all the material, it is in the area of personal memories and current beliefs that women are likely to feel most vulnerable, and therefore where these issues are most likely to be contentious.

- *Access.* Who may use the material while it is in electronic storage, and how can a system be developed for granting access, once agreement is reached on who can have it? While a project is restricted to something the size of ERWC, with relatively finite boundaries, it is fairly clear who is a member of the project. They would therefore presumably have unrestricted access to other project members' material, in order to help them compose their own. However, if the project were successful, and/or became part of a larger WLM history project, outside researchers would soon want access to the material, and feminist activists from further afield would also want to consult the material and hopefully contribute their own experiences.

- *Copyright.* This is again easier to control while the project remains within well-defined boundaries – either the woman herself keeps her own copyright, or she agrees to grant it to the ERWC project. In the world of electronic publishing in general, there is much debate and anxiety about copyright protection, primarily for commercial, but also for moral, reasons. According to Richard Wake (1995):

> The biggest obstacle [to electronic solutions to pressure on academic libraries] may prove to be the issue which as yet seems to show the fewest signs of progress. How should the copyright laws be applied to electronic publications? Existing legislation seems to offer few certainties where electronic publishing is concerned. Academic authors and publishers have views which, on the whole, do not coincide. Though librarians have less of a stake in the solution, all parties should be anxious for an early solution that is clear and will encourage, not hinder, the development of electronically-based publications.

And naturally, copyright concerns are also present in the substantial debate about electronic scholarly publishing that is being conducted on the Internet and elsewhere (Okerson & Mogge, 1994; Okerson & O'Donnell, 1995; Odlyzko, 1996; many contributors to ebook-list, h-mmedia and other academic discussion lists). Various writers' organisations, whose brief is mainly to protect commercial authors' interests, have come together to produce a paper addressing their concerns about electronic rights in current contracts (Association of Authors' Agents et al, 1996), as they want to protect both existing material when it is used electronically and any new work done directly for electronic publication.

- *Confidentiality and slander.* This is closely related to issues of access - how far something is considered insulting is often a function of how it is likely to be used and how public it will be. If these are serious concerns, then thought needs to be given to who will be empowered to exercise editorial judgements about any of the material. There can also be advantages in having information and opinion accessible, as this makes it possible to correct errors and facilitate debate, rather than maintaining the uncomfortable impression that myths are being perpetuated, but being unable to do anything about it. Again, the context of the access is of prime importance.
- *Cost of storage and transfer.* There may be various elements of cost, depending on the availability of suitable equipment and the existing computer skills among members of the project. If a lot of material is not initially produced in digital form, it will need transferring, and if appropriate methods of indexing have been agreed (see below), they would need incorporating. Women's tendency to have less access to technology was reflected at the ERWC meeting in the small number of women who felt confident to discuss the idea of doing the project electronically; those who did were all involved in information professions - a librarian, a literary agent, myself. Would someone have to be trained and paid to digitise, and whose equipment would be used?
- *Location of storage.* This is not necessarily a problem in the initial stages, when each woman or several women could keep part of the

material on their own disks, but before long, various parts of the material would need to be brought together. In some respects, the advantage of doing the project electronically is that the people involved do not need to be in the same physical place – even with as well-defined a focus as ERWC, the women involved have dispersed widely since the 1970s.[12] Geographical dispersal may be a good reason for gathering material electronically, but the project still needs some central co-ordination and storage of material to develop any coherence. This is no different from material gathered and stored traditionally – decisions must still be made about how the material is going to be used, which parts of it may be published, and in what form. At this stage, I am assuming that there are not going to be significant numbers of women with access to networked computers. I will discuss later some of the options which could open up if this were the case, at which point, decisions would definitely need to be made about having access to a server, with all the issues of finance and control that that implies.

• *Indexing.* Each item will be made into a file which should be able to be accessed in various ways. It would be highly desirable to incorporate the indexing from the start, which involves deciding on the group's categories and classification system at the outset. There is now widespread recognition of the shortcomings of the established systems, such as Dewey and Library of Congress, thanks to the efforts of Sanford Berman (1971, reissued 1993) and other progressive and feminist librarians, yet there is still no straightforward way of classifying information that derives from a perspective counter to the mainstream.

In addition to the ideological difficulties of devising an indexing system for the ERWC history, there are also technological and practical issues to be considered, as good navigational tools are of paramount importance when compiling electronic documents. This is a global problem, in recognition of which OCLC and NCSA ran a three-day workshop (Caplan, 1995) to start defining a simple, usable standard for describing network-accessible information resources.[13] There are at least three major factors to consider if the ERWC index is to be satisfactorily user-friendly: choosing a method which many different women can operate to input accurately; enabling diverse types of material to be fully indexed – photos[14], audio-tapes, etc, as well as text; attempting the very difficult task of trying to work out in advance the different approaches users may wish to take to the material. Dealing with this last point requires decisions about how each file should be indexed. It should probably be done in at least the following ways: chronologically; geographically; according to the political position/ ideas/terms/concepts involved; the issue/campaign concerned; the author; other women involved; date of composition.

Transmitting and/or publishing the material
Collecting the ERWC's history is envisaged as an ongoing project, depending mainly on the time and energy of the women involved, so material could be issued at various stages, drawing on the electronically

stored material (and, of course, non-electronically stored material). There are a number of relatively straightforward forms in which material could be provided relatively cheaply, none of which are mutually exclusive, and could be produced at different times:

- A series of self-published pamphlets covering women's recollections and analysis of what happened in various groups, subject areas, or time periods.
- Commercially produced books, covering similar areas to the above, but longer, more professionally produced.
- Audiovisual presentations. There are lots of different possible approaches here – suggestions have included a museum installation.
- Text-only CD-Rom, presenting documents, not necessarily with connecting commentary, but simply as an archive. Depending on the quantity of material, it may be possible to produce this on a floppy disk.
- Interactive, multimedia CD-Rom. Similar to the above, but with digitised images and possibly sound. Again, choices would have to be made about whether to present a simple archive of source material, or whether a firmer editorial shape would be imposed. Fisher (1994) presents a straightforward account of the process, which seems to take most of the pain out of constructing a CD-Rom, once some basic skills have been acquired.

At the initial ERWC meeting, extreme doubts were expressed about the feasibility of producing CD-Roms at an affordable price, yet a school teacher in Hackney recently produced 50 disks of her students' work for £570.00 (personal communication) – less than the cost of most academic paperbacks, if one has access to the machinery to read it. The price of commercial CD-Roms are also starting to fall. Derek Meakin (1996) writes optimistically of the retail price of a CD-Rom falling to £5.95, while Zigzag Multimedia has recently started marketing CD-Roms for children at £9.99. Much of the mainstream publishing industry remains gloomy about the difficulties of selling sufficient CD-Roms to recoup its huge financial investment, but they have a conception of market size which in no way corresponds to the niche market that a WLM CD-Rom would be aiming at, and would find relatively easy to reach. An ERWC CD-Rom would have none of the high overheads or need to make profits for investors that commercial CD-Rom publication involves, and it may even be possible to find a feminist or progressive publisher who would publish the disk as good publicity for themselves.

Now that *CD-Roms in Print* is a regular publication, there is no reason for not marketing CD-Roms like books, yet both buyers and sellers remain very cautious in their attitude to the new technologies. For example, one often only finds out about printed books or journal articles when they are drawn to one's attention, and this is accepted as a fact of life which is not generally unendurably frustrating (unless you are the author!). Yet people tend to get immensely irritated by the apparently random or accidental nature of finding out about new CD-Roms or the existence of material on the Internet. This may be because electronic publishing is so recently established, or because the Internet is not something that can be physically held, or because it can take a long time to browse. Publicising print books is regarded as more systematic because it has existed for much longer, but in reality is often as haphazard.

Meanwhile, the Internet is getting more organised. For example, in the academic area, government funding has been given to IHR-Info to provide a gateway to the Internet for historians, and to SOSIG to do the same for social scientists, while in the booktrade, publishers and booksellers are learning to exploit the Internet – though it remains unclear whether it is envisaged primarily as a system for delivery or promotion of material (Weedon, 1996).

There could be benefits to ERWC in becoming involved with the Internet from both these points of view. A web site could be developed now to provide an announcement of their existence, with some sample material, which might well encourage other women to contribute to and extend the project. Such developments could then lead, at a later stage, to some of the more elaborate conferencing possibilities discussed below, as well as possibly leading to the development of a more sophisticated hybrid CD-Rom, which allows material on the CD-Rom to be updated via the Internet (Murdoch, 1996; Weedon, 1996). As with every other aspect of this project, everything depends on the time and energy of the women involved, and whether any way can be found of financing it.

Constructing a web page is becoming simpler all the time, with various types of guide to the subject. For instance, there is a page entitled 'Tools to Weave Your Own Web' in Charles (1995: 61-62), which guides readers via interactive floppy disk to Internet sites where they can track down software and get other help; Goldsmiths College is running a course on Creating Web Pages using HTML (details on http://www.gold.ac.uk/guides/c606.htm); and the home page of Sun Microsystems has a user-friendly 'Guide to Web Style', which aims to help people create better web pages. There are even several experienced real-time women who will gladly offer advice. For those with Microsoft Word 6 or 7, Internet Assistant is a no-charge add-on to enable one to ceate web documents as part of the word processing package, and Microsoft also produces FrontPage for creating and managing web sites. Even if using these packages is not quite as simple as Microsoft claims, the fact that the user does not need to know HTML to create web pages, and that a web site can be posted to other web servers and Internet service providers once created, suggests that quite soon, relatively little technical expertise or finance will be required to develop and maintain a web site proficiently.

A note of caution was sounded by Marion Brady,[15] who maintains the web site at Imperial College, London. She pointed out that maintaining a web page can be a lot of work. For example, they receive 200-300 email messages on their Webmaster each day, and even though most of them simply require forwarding to appropriate departments within the college, someone has to do it. These messages come in through people clicking on the email hotspot at the end of their web page. It is not necessary to have such a connection, but it certainly discourages easy feedback if there isn't one. ICL presumably gets such a weight of messages because it is a world-renowned centre of excellence in computing and, Marion's presence notwithstanding, male-dominated. It should definitely be possible to invite responses to a web page in such a way that any messages that were not germane could be ignored.[16]

Moving beyond ERWC

At an early stage of my research it seemed to me that a small-scale project like the ERWC history could link in with or expand into a wider WLM history by establishing a moderated, closed email discussion group, which would be a good way for women round the country to be in dialogue with each other. It seems to have a number of advantages over the Worldwide Web, being simpler, cheaper and quicker to access, as well as allowing multilateral communication. As my reading progressed, I was introduced to more sophisticated methods of electronic communication, and I could see their benefits, especially if the project were to expand to become a national WLM history. However, the obvious and serious drawback of all of these schemes is that for most of them, everybody concerned has to have access to the right equipment, and this takes lots of money, while using it requires high motivation.

There is mounting evidence of the Internet being used for various innovative academic projects (see, for example, Popham and Hughes (1996); Deegan, Lee and Timbrell (1996)). At its simplest, individual academics, such as Ebben and Kramarae (n d 1996?) and Odlyzko (1996), are posting essays to be freely available for discussion. While the Internet offers no guarantee of permanence, what it does offer is speedy and potentially wide transmission for an article whose readership might otherwise be very restricted; and once it is printed out for reading, its durability is at least equivalent to that of a photocopy. Matthew Kirschenbaum has just developed a new web site for online references and resources relevant to electronic theses and dissertations in the humanities, courtesy of the University of Virginia Library's On-Line Scholarship Initiative, whilst closer to home, the Institute of Historical Research of London University is inaugurating a computer-based seminar system, Electronic Seminars in History. The seminars will transmit academically reputable papers and discussion on them to the email accounts of participants, before storing the material in a browsable archive.

Developments such as these represent innovative use of basic existing Internet technology, but meanwhile the technology continues to advance fast, and technologies that have been available in the United States for a couple of years are now being introduced here. For example, Tari Lin Fanderclai (1996) discusses her use of MUDs (multi-user synchronous Internet communications) with a group of students in English. MUDs have mainly been used for game-playing upto now, and users require some training to feel comfortable with them. But from this description of them by Fanderclai, their potential for serious study and debate should be obvious:

MUD stands for "Multi-User Domain." MediaMOO is a MOO, which is a kind of MUD; MOO stands for "MUD, Object-Oriented." Other kinds of MUDs include MUSH, MUCK and MUSE. Although there are differences among the various kinds of MUDs, the basic idea is the same: Users connect to the MUD using telnet or any of various MUD clients. Each user connects to his or her own character (some MUDs provide guest characters for users who have not yet obtained characters of their own). Using those characters, users can move around the various rooms on a MUD, talk to other users, and interact with the various objects on the MUD. Everything a user sees on a MUD is presented in text; for example, when the user moves his or her character into a room on a MUD, he or she is presented with a text description of the room. On many MUDs, users are able to add their own rooms and objects to the MUD. (Fanderclai, 1996:241).

Another recent development is the intranet – like the Internet, but with access restricted inside one company or organisation. The BBC is currently developing one, called Gateway (*Ariel*, 1996). According to Mel Lowe, of Corporate Internal Communication:

> . . . as with the Internet, it offers huge possibilities. It is now possible to publish many of our manuals, directories, research, archives and databases in this way. If you think how quickly that can be done, and if you no longer have to print these things, you can save a great deal of money. Nor do we have to create lots of different IT processes to distribute this material across the BBC. But the really exciting thing is that the intranet is more than just a one-way flow of information. The technology gives us a platform from which we can access data prepared by many different applications, and through which we can feed back response. (*Ariel*, 1996:8)

Like other companies, such as Federal Express and British Telecom, which already have operational intranets, the BBC has a widely dispersed, computer-literate workforce. However, as Andy Lewis, who is responsible for implementing the BBC's intranet points out:

> . . . it is vital that there is a solid infrastructure upon which the intranet can run before it is introduced to all 12,000 users – from servers on the network to browsers on PC. Three key things will determine its success: reliable content, reliable access, and reliable infrastructure. (*Ariel*, 1996:9)

What Lewis does not add is 'which will depend on reliable amounts of money'. It is also interesting that he assumes that the intranet will be set up using PCs. The *Financial Times IT Review* (June 1996) recently devoted four pages to network-centric computing, which relies on network computers (NCs), also known as 'thin clients', because all the software will no longer have to be on each PC, but will be available on the network as required, so that each machine will be much cheaper (current estimates are around £350), which might appear to be a return to the mainframe, but this time the source of software could be the Internet. And obviously, users outside a network will still need to use a PC.

With these dazzling yet inaccessible options whizzing round my brain, I returned to earth via Mark Bryson of Lancaster University[17], who maintains a web site on asynchronous computer conference systems, listing 15 different systems which could be useful. I began my discussion with him feeling that Lotus Notes would be a good way for women to communicate, because it organises incoming material easily. However, it requires considerable training to use, and, most significantly for a dispersed project such as a WLM history, each person in communication has to have the same software. After discussing the benefits of Lotus Notes and various other conference systems, Mark Bryson said, unprompted by me, that he thought the best bet for the WLM history project would be a private email discussion group!

There seem to be two possible routes for establishing an email discussion group. Within the academic environment, one could approach the postmaster at a convenient institution and ask if they have an email discussion list service. Alternatively, GreenNet would be happy to accommodate such a list, as long as the list moderator (i.e. co-ordinator) was a GreenNet subscriber. GreenNet is an Internet access provider, similar to commercial organisations, such as Compuserve and Demon, but serving the progressive community. It is the British member of APC (the Association for Progressive Communications), the global computer communications network for environmental, peace, human rights and development issues. Friedland (1996) discusses the equivalent organisation to GreenNet in the USA, the Institute for Global Communications (IGC).

According to Marion Brady, there are groups in the US offering free web space for feminist organisations, which may be attractive, but GreenNet also provides Web access at a reasonable price, and will assist users to get their web sites listed on search engines, such as Yahoo and Alta Vista, which is crucial for advertising your existence.

Conclusion
Having investigated the various aspects of the project, I believe it is perfectly feasible for a group of women with limited resources to produce a history of ERWC electronically. How much of it is published electronically depends on the enthusiasm of the women involved, and their ability to call in some extra expertise as necessary. On this basis it should be possible to produce a CD-Rom, establish a web page and an email discussion group, if required. It would also be possible to extend this into a national project, although it would almost certainly not be possible to do so without paid workers - so maybe the best way to proceed would be on the basis that the WLM always organised, with autonomous groups, overlapping and liaising as appropriate, building a network from the grassroots outwards. In this way, it may be possible to retain some of the excitement of the original movement, conveying a sense of how it was at the time. Whether it will be

possible to achieve another of the major goals of the women at the original ERWC meeting – to keep control of their own history, and not have it made bland by outside experts - is more doubtful. Once any material is published, it is impossible to keep control of it, and especially if it is decided to produce a collection of documents, whose very purpose is to invite further investigation, then distanced analysis will start. But these are not problems unique to electronic publication, and if the women of ERWC do not do it for themselves, it will not be done at all.

Acknowledgements

A number of people have made the production of this paper possible: Ruth Wallsgrove, whose remark first got me thinking, and who has encouraged me as the work has progressed; Diana Patterson, who clearly and patiently revealed the mysteries of computers to me, and had faith in me; David King, who provided the domestic and other support without which I could never have started. To them all, I am eternally grateful. I would also like to thank Dena Attar, Penny Cloutte, Jalna Hanmer and Diana Shelley for their comments on the draft of this paper.

Notes

[1]   Another WLM activist with a longstanding interest in feminist history, who now works in the computer industry. My thanks to her for her continuing interest in this project.

[2]   Their introductory handout (n.d.) says:
. . . We will begin by investigating personal histories and source materials from the 1970s and 1980s, and will produce an archive of taped interviews, and a database of documents and materials held by institutions and individuals.
We believe that it is essential to undertake the project from a feminist perspective, in which the experiences of women, and the materials produced by the movement, are central. . . .
As well as material in existing collections . . . much relevant material is still in private hands, such as your attic or filing cabinet! We hope that women will allow us access to this material so that we can catalogue it for inclusion in the Guide to Sources. . . . We will produce the guide in a printed form and on disc in searchable database form. We are also investigating production on a multi-media CD-Rom.

[3]   Recent innovations allow material to be downloaded from the Internet onto CD-Rom, which has important implications for keeping material updated. However, such complications do not affect the basic descriptions I am giving here.

[4]   Information gathered from a handout distributed at the Women's Studies Network conference 1995, an advert in the Women's History Network Newsletter, August 1996, and a conversation with Gerry Holloway,

convenor of Women's Studies at the University of Sussex, and one of the project co-ordinators.

5   Feminist Archive, Bradford, appeal letter, November 1995; newsletters, issues 1 (December 1995), 2 (March 1996), 3 (June 1996).

6   For example, *Once a Feminist*, (ed.) Michelene Wandor, London: Virago, 1990; *68, 78, 88*, (ed.) Amanda Sebestyen, Bridport: Prism Press, 1988.

7   This is borne out by my conversation with Elizabeth Crawford, author of the forthcoming *Biographical Dictionary of Women's Suffrage, 1870-1928* (Taylor & Francis, 1997). As part of her research, she has compiled information about the substantial family relationships and interconnections between many major suffragists and their publishers.

8   Now that the first draft is published in print, the compilers are inviting feedback:

> This chronology is intended as a reference for researchers and others interested in the herstory of women's activism. It is hoped that [its] publication will stimulate debate and encourage women to fill in the gaps from their own experiences. By definition this chronology is incomplete. It is very difficult to chart every single WLM related activity and group . . . [T]he researchers request that any woman who notes a missing entry that is appropriate to this chronology let us know, so that we may add it. (p.2)

If they have to rely only on responses from women who come across the print version only via the Archive, they may not get much feedback. Using electronic communication, they could not only advertise the chronology's existence more widely, at least among academic women, but if they stored responses electronically, they could handle a range of responses within one document which would probably be too confusing if they tried to do the same in print.

9   A couple of examples were given at the meeting, one being a discussion of ERWC by Lynne Segal in her contribution to *Beyond the Fragments: Feminism and the Making of Socialism* (Segal, 1979). Lynne is now a professor at Middlesex University and she was very involved in ERWC. She mentioned this article herself, and some women disagreed strongly with the analysis she put forward at the meeting. To me, this incident highlighted the problems to be faced when trying to assemble a history of events, the analysis of which is clearly still contentious many years later. Re-reading Lynne's article to write this paper, it was obvious how an electronic version of it could help to overcome some women's feelings that Lynne had been 'allowed' to make the definitive statement about ERWC. Using hypertext links to the original text, as many women as wanted could add their comments on Lynne's piece, and on each other's. The end-product would be a multi-layered electronic document representing a variety of opinions that could be cross-referred with each other. Such an exercise would be very confusing if it were attempted in print, and would give rise to substantial questions of editorial control. (Landow (1992) discusses these issues.)

10 See, for example, the articles in Cherney and Weise (1996). Also, the

impression that women's use of the Internet is more restricted than men's seems to be confirmed by the fact that on three occasions when I was cruising women's cyberspace (WWWomen!; Women in the Age of Computers; Charles (1995); Helen Fallon's site; Joan Korenman's list) in mid-afternoon GMT, when the lines are usually clogged because the Americans are awake and connecting, I got through to my chosen sites almost immediately.

[11] My bibliography contains a list of all the electronic sources I consulted.

[12] It was interesting what a high proportion of women on the contact list still live in Islington or Hackney – this may, of course, be partly a function of who has stayed in contact with the organisers, who themselves still live locally.

[13] The full report of this workshop is available at http://www.oclc.org:5046/oclc/research/conferences/metadata/dublin-core-report.html

[14] The Hulton Deutsch picture library is now available on-line over ISDN, and has devised a simple but effective indexing system for searching its more than 200,000 images. (Web site – http://www.u-net.com/hulton)

[15] My thanks to Marion Brady for spending time in discussion with me.

[16] Although the issue of sexual harrassment on the Internet has been the subject of considerable media hype, especially in the US, Stephanie Brail (1996) makes it clear that anxiety about attacks from men is far from being unnecessary feminist paranoia.

[17] My thanks to Mark Bryson for spending time in discussion with me.

References

Printed works consulted

Arledge Ross, Elizabeth and Bearse, Miriam L., compilers, *A Chronology of the WLM in Britain: Organisations, Conferences, Journals, and Events, with a Focus on Leeds and Bradford, 1969-1979*. First Draft. Research Paper no. 1. Bradford: The Feminist Archive, Bradford, 1996.

Association of Authors' Agents et al, *Electronic and Multimedia Publishing – Guidelines for Authors*. Draft version. London, n.d.[1996?].

Bailey, Charles, 'Network-Based Electronic Publishing of Scholarly Works: A Selective Bibliography', *The Public-Access Computer Systems Review* 6, no.1 (1995). Version 21, May 1996. Downloaded from <http://info.lib.uh.edu/pr/v6/n1/bail6n1.html>.

Berman, Sanford, *Prejudices and Antipathies: A Tract on the LC Subject Heads Concerning People*, 1993 edition, with a foreword by Eric Moon. Jefferson, NC: McFarland, 1993. (First published in 1971 by Scarecrow Press, Metuchen, NJ.)

Brail, Stephanie, 'The Price of Admission: Harrassment and Free Speech in the Wild, Wild West' in Lynn Cherney and Elizabeth Reba Weise, (eds.) *Wired Women: Gender and New Realities in Cyberspace*. Seattle: Seal Press, 1996.

Cameron, Debbie, 'Telling it Like it Wasn't: How Radical Feminism Became History', *Trouble and Strife*, no. 27, Winter 1993, pp.11-15.

Camp, L. Jean, 'We Are Geeks, and We Are Not Guys: The Systers Mailing List' in Lynn Cherney and Elizabeth Reba Weise, (eds.) *Wired Women: Gender and New Realities in Cyberspace*. Seattle: Seal Press, 1996.

Caplan, Priscilla, 'You call it corn, we call it syntax-independent metadata for document-like objects', *The Public-Access Computer Systems Review* 6, no.4 (1995), pp. 19-23.

Charles, Julie, *Women on the Wire: A Modem is a Girl's Best Friend*. Accompanied by a 3.5" disk. Highwire, Point and Click Internet Series. Toronto: Reed Books Canada, 1995.

Cherney, Lynn, and Weise, Elizabeth Reba, (eds.) *Wired Women: Gender and New Realities in Cyberspace*, Seattle: Seal Press, 1996.

Deegan, Marilyn, Lee, Stuart, and Timbrell, Nicola, (eds.) *An Introduction to Multimedia for Academic Use*, Oxford and Hull: Universities of Oxford and Hull, 1996.

Ebben, Maureen and Kramarae, Cheris, 'Women and Information Technologies: Creating a Cyberspace of Our Own'. Published on the Internet at <http://gertrude.art.uiuc.edu/wits/introduction.html> and downloaded.

Evard, Michele, 'So Please Stop, Thank You: Girls Online' in Lynn Cherney and Elizabeth Reba Weise, (eds.) *Wired Women: Gender and New Realities in Cyberspace*. Seattle: Seal Press, 1996.

Fanderclai, Tari Lin, 'Like Magic, Only Real' in Lynn Cherney and Elizabeth Reba Weise, (eds.) *Wired Women: Gender and New Realities in Cyberspace*. Seattle: Seal Press, 1996.

Financial Times IT Review, Special Feature on Network Centric Computing. 5 June 1996, pp.7-10.

Fisher, Scott, *Multimedia Authoring: Building and Developing Documents*. London and Cambridge, MA: Academic Press, 1994.

Friedland, Lewis A, 'Electronic democracy and the new citizenship', *Media, Culture and Society*, vol. 18, no. 2, April 1996, pp. 185-212.

Gluck, Sherna Berger, and Patai, Daphne, (eds.) *Women's Words: The Feminist Practice of Oral History*, New York and London: Routledge, 1991.

Hanmer, Jalna, 'Taking Ourselves Seriously' in Renate Duelli-Klein and Diane Bell, eds. *Radically Speaking: Feminism Reclaimed*, London: Zed Books, 1996.

Hildenbrand, Suzanne, 'Electronic Graffiti or Scholar's Tool?: a Critical Evaluation of Selected Women's Lists on the Internet' in Eva Steiner Moseley, (ed.) *Women, Information and the Future: Collecting and Sharing Resources Worldwide*, Fort Atkinson, Wisconsin: Highsmith Press, 1995.

Introduction to multimedia for booksellers, 4pp A4 free leaflet. London: Booksellers Association of Great Britain and Ireland, March 1996.

Landow, George P., *Hypertext: the convergence of contemporary critical theory and technology*. Series - Parallax: Re-visions of Culture and Society, Baltimore and London. Johns Hopkins University Press. 1992.

Meakin, Derek, 'There's still a multimedia future', *The Bookseller*, 20/27 December 1996, p. 17.

Mercier, Laurie, and Murphy, Mary, 'Confronting the Demons of Feminist Public History: Scholarly Collaboration and Community Outreach' in Sherna Berger Gluck and Daphne Patai, (eds.) *Women's Words: The Feminist Practice of Oral History*, New York and London: Routledge, 1991.

Moseley, Eva Steiner, (ed.) *Women, Information and the Future: Collecting and Sharing Resources Worldwide*, Fort Atkinson, Wisconsin: Highsmith Press, 1995.

Murdoch, Simon, 'Hybrids: will they overtake the old varieties?', *Multimedia Bookseller*, May 1996, pp. 16-17.

Odlyzko, Andrew, On the road to electronic publishing',. Preliminary version, April 15 1996. Forwarded via the Red Rock Eater News Service <rre@weber.ucsd.edu> to H-Mmedia, and downloaded from there.

Okerson, Ann and Mogge, Dru, (eds.) *Gateways, Gatekeepers, and Roles in the Information Omniverse: Proceedings of the Third Symposium.* Washington: Association of Research Libraries, 1994.

Okerson, Ann Shumelda, and O'Donnell, James J., *Scholarly Journals at the Crossroads: A Subversive Proposal for Electronic Publishing - An Internet Discussion about Scientific and Scholarly Journals and Their Future,* Washington: Association of Research Libraries, 1995.

Popham, Michael and Hughes, Lorna, (eds.) *Computers and Teaching in the Humanities*, Oxford: CTI Centre for Textual Studies, 1996.

Pritchard, Sarah M., 'Women's Studies Scholarship: its impact on the information world' in Eva Steiner Moseley, (ed.) *Women, Information and the Future: Collecting and Sharing Resources Worldwide*, Fort Atkinson, Wisconsin: Highsmith Press, 1995.

Roper, Jonathan, 'The Heart of Multimedia: Interactivity or Experience?', *Convergence: the journal of research into new media technologies*, vol. 1, no. 2, Autumn 1995, pp. 23-25.

Segal, Lynne, 'A Local Experience' in Sheila Rowbotham, Lynne Segal and Hilary Wainwright, (eds.) *Beyond the Fragments: Feminism and the Making of Socialism*, Second edition. London: Merlin Press, 1979.

'Trawling for net gains', *Ariel*, April 30 1996, pp. 8-9.

Wack, Mary, 'Chaucer in 2001' in Ann Okerson and Dru Mogge, (eds.) *Gateways, Gatekeepers, and Roles in the Information Omniverse: Proceedings of the Third Symposium.* Washington: Association of Research Libraries, 1994.

Wake, Richard, 'Academic bypass on demand', *The Bookseller*, June 30 1995, p. 36.

Weedon, Alexis, 'The Book Trade and Internet Publishing', *Convergence: the journal of research into new media technologies*, vol. 2, no. 1, Spring 1996, pp. 76-102.

Williams, Granville, *Britain's Media - How They Are Related.* Second edition. London: Campaign for Press and Broadcasting Freedom, 1996.

Internet resources consulted
Email discussion groups
<ebook-list@aros.net> on electronic publishing

<h-mmedia@msu.edu> on computers in humanities teaching
<sharp-l@iubvm.ucs.indiana.edu> on the history of the book
<womens-studies@mailbase.ac.uk> on women's studies, mainly British

Other information sources
<http://ihr.sas.ac.uk> IHR-Info (The Institute for Historical Research)
<http://www.wwwomen.com/> 'WWWomen! The Premier Search Directory for Women Online!'
<http://www.wwwomen.com/category/comput1.html> WWWomen! on Women in the Age of Computers
<http://www.december.com/cmc/mag/1996/mar/toc.html> *CMC Magazine*, special issue on Women and Gender Online, vol. 3, no. 3, March 1996.
<http://gertrude.art.uiuc.edu/wits> Bibliography of women and IT
<http://lucien.sims.berkeley.edu/women_in_it.html> Web-ster's Network - Women in Information Technologies
<http://www.primenet.com/~shauna/women.html> International Directory of Women Web Designers
<http://osi.lib.virginia.edu/ediss.html> Electronic thesis/dissertation site
<http://www.aura.com/library/omnimedia> Omnimedia Electronic Books
<http://www.lancs.ac.uk/usese/ktru/mbryson.htm> Mark Bryson's web page about computer conference systems (asynchronous, not video-conferencing)
<http://www.dcu.ie/staff/hfallon/thesis.htm> Directory of Gender Related Internet Resources for Academic Research, compiled by Helen Fallon, Dublin
<http://www-unix.umbc.edu/~Korenman/wmst/forums.html> Joan Korenman's gender related electronic forums list - regularly amended and updated, very useful
<http://www.bubl.bath.ac.uk/BUBL/Women.html> BUBL Worldwide Web Subject Tree, information on women's studies
<http://www.sun.com/styleguide/> User-friendly advice on creating web pages from some workers at Sun Microsystems
<gopher://silo.adp.wisc.edu:70/00/.uwlibs/.womenstudies/.infotech/.infoful> Bibliography on information technology and women's lives, concentrating on publications with a feminist approach. It is also available in print (it contains more than 750 citations) from the Women's Studies Librarian for the University of Wisconsin System, 430 Memorial Library, 728 State St, Madison, Wisconsin, USA
<support@gn.apc.org> Email address of GreenNet, British progressive Internet access provider. Phone: 0171 713 1941

Publishers' printed catalogues consulted
Dorling Kindersley Multimedia, Spring 1996.
Hulton Deutsch On-line, Spring 1996.
Oxford University Press Electronic Publishing, Spring 1996.
Zigzag Multimedia, Winter 1996/7.

Looking for T46: Lesbians in Beijing

Frances Connelly and Monika Reinfelder

Looking for T46 in the mud at the NGO (Non-Governmental Organisations) Forum site in Huairou, China, was no feast. T46 – the lesbian tent – was located at the far site of the Forum amongst other 'diversity' tents. For some of us it was not too difficult, friends from all over the world acted as signposts. The many cuddles, kisses and hellos just delayed us getting to our destination for hours. For those who had never been to such a mega event everything seemed disorientating, in spite of signs and a clearly defined map. Sadly, one woman only found out about the existence of the tent when back in London!

Our intention is not just to provide an account of the activities of the tent, nor to give an exposition of the precise workings of United Nation (UN) conferences in general or the Fourth United Nations World Conference on Women (FWCW) in particular; rather the argument is for the internationalisation of lesbian politics. While this can well happen, and indeed it does, without such conferences, Beijing did provide a useful tool in bringing together lesbians from all over the world for networking, consolidating campaigns, and for broadening each others' horizons, all of which are prerequisites for, and part of, lesbian politics.

In the West the UN and its organisations are viewed with suspicion or lack of interest by many lesbians (Khambatta, 1996; 9 & 14). And yet, on an international level lesbians have actively participated in, and influenced such events for many years. Lesbians have made contribution to 'other issues' (eg women's human rights, health, education, development), but have been denied space as out lesbians. In Beijing lesbians made history by securing their own space for the first time in the history of the United Nations. At the first UN women's conference in Mexico in 1975 few courageous lesbians spoke out, and there was still discussion about the legitimacy of lesbian participation at the third conference in Nairobi in 1985. Lesbian presence and visibility in Beijing/Huairou was very much the result of the emerging international lesbian movement.

If searching for the lesbian tent proved a bit of a chore, the preparation for it certainly required some international effort. Although it was the International Gay and Lesbian Human Rights Commission (IGLHRC) that took on the negotiations with the UN Facilitating Committee of the conference, the idea originally came from the Thai lesbian group Anjaree. Anjaree is very active in the Asian Lesbian Network that, together with the Latin American and Caribbean Network, and some lesbians from the West, was instrumental in getting sexual orientation included in the draft of the *Platform for Action*. This document was prepared by the UN Commission on the Status of Women at the last preparatory conference in New York and was finally agreed at the FWCW in Beijing in 1995. It was at the New York conference that sexual orientation was included, albeit in brackets which signified that it required further discussion. Its inclusion was the result of the work of the Lesbian Caucus that included lesbians from all over the world. Patria Jimenez, from the Mexican group El Closet de Sor Juana addressed the Commission on the Status for Women in a formal speech urging them to include sexual orientation in the document (Reinfelder, 1996; 21-23). Latin American lesbians had been well organised. Prior to the Latin American and Caribbean regional preparatory conference in Buenos Aires lesbian groups from ten Latin American countries met in Lima to formulate their demands. The Asian Lesbian Network too was actively involved in all of the Asia/Pacific preparatory conferences trying to ensure that lesbian issues would not be neglected.

Each of the five UN defined regions (Latin America/Caribbean, Africa, Asia/Pacific, Europe/North America, Arab) was invited to draw up its own regional Platform for Action. The European/North American regional preparatory conference was the only one that successfully ensured the inclusion of sexual orientation. The UK government agreed to the document and should therefore be committed (at least in theory!) to

> reflect the full diversity of women, recognising that many women face additional barriers because of such factors as their race, language, ethnicity, culture, religion, sexual orientation, disability, socio-economic class or status as indigenous people, . . .

The final *Platform for Action* produced in Beijing includes a series of recommendations which, unfortunately, place no legal obligation on individual governments. It can, however, be used for campaigning and lobbying purposes. The focus of the *Platform* are twelve 'critical areas of concern' that governments have pledged to pay attention to in their attempts to reduce discrimination against women: poverty, economic inequality, education, health, violence against women, effects of conflict on women, power-sharing, mechanisms to promote the advancement of women, mass media, environment, the girl child, and human rights.

The Lesbian Tent

At the Forum delegates from NGOs campaigned around issues related to these twelve areas. Activists specifically focusing on lesbian issues made lesbian human rights (or rather lack thereof) their main concern. The tent was run by a committee of women from the five regions. A daily open meeting facilitated information sharing and planning. Volunteers translated where possible and each day the meeting was moderated by a woman from a different region. No one had anticipated the volume of visitors, both lesbian and non lesbian, to the tent. They included governmental delegates from the official conference, scores of journalists and even a famous Chinese opera singer. Visitors were of all nationalities, and many heterosexual Chinese women came in a spirit of solidarity. One said:

> I think that people have their own choices about who they love or what kind of people they want to be so I don't think that government or any kind of organisation should put on any kind of restriction or force them

to change what they feel or what kind of people they should be. I don't think that's fair. I think that people really should have their own choices. I hope really that one day we could look on them [lesbians] without discrimination or feel any resentment towards them or feel that they are abnormal . . .

Many closeted women from countries where lesbianism is underground and/or illegal came for information and support. For example, some Asian women wanted to talk about how to avoid arranged marriages, African women wanted to know where to find lesbians in their countries, others sought advice on how to visit Western countries. As one of the organisers explained:

We have also been able to address many questions from a lot of African women and other women from the world who come in and say, well, what are lesbians, well, questions like do you have children, what do your family think? Questions about monogamy and HIV, so I think that the atmosphere of openness and accessibility and discussion of a lot of taboos just around sexuality has occurred here. That is a climate that we create, have all created together. So that has been extremely empowering for me . . . the visibility of African women here, myself and the two South Africans, gives African women a point of entry, . . . they can't just say "it's a Western thing, . . . we don't have that in our country," and I can say, I'm a Kenyan lesbian, do you want to talk about it? And we have had two hour sessions with some women some days.

The International Lesbian Information Service (ILIS) and IGLHRC had produced global human rights report on lesbians (Anderson, 1995; Rosenbloom, 1995) and they also distributed information about lesbianism in Chinese, which was confiscated by the Chinese authorities, but further copies generated much interest and support from Chinese women. The authorities also ignored our request for media discretion and their harassment only stopped after intervention from the UN Facilitating Committee of the Forum; unlike their harassment of Tibetan women in exile which continued until the end of the conference. The fact that the main targets were the lesbian tent and Tibetan women in exile resulted in consolidating the solidarity between the two groups.

Workshops on lesbian issues took place every day both in the tent and elsewhere in the Forum. Topics included lesbian health, lesbian mothers, art and sexuality, lesbian human rights, a 'lesbian speakout' in the youth tent, fundraising for lesbian organisations, email, etc. There were regional workshops, as well as an international panel, which helped to encourage or consolidate regional organising. Europeans recognised that Latin American and Asian lesbians were far better organised on a regional basis and therefore explored possibilities of improving communication and exchange between East and West Europe. Western European women working in the former Yugoslavia noted that many of the women aid workers and visitors were in fact lesbians who thought that they should hide their lesbianism there, whereas in fact it would be more helpful to the local women to be open, to provide information and act as alternative role models. Following much interest from heterosexual Asian and African women two very popular workshops were held on respectively Asian and African 'lesbianism for the curious', which also helped in dispelling the 'lesbianism is a white disease' myth. A Filipino participant explained:

Before Beijing I was asked: "Anna, are you going to the UN conference as a lesbian or as a media person? I suggest you go as a media person otherwise you lose your credibility." Although many people say they support lesbian issues, there are a good number of women from the Filipino delegation who do support lesbian issues, they feel, that if they push for it they might become marginalised. You see the Philippines is the spokesperson for the Group of 77. Quite a powerful position, I mean to say a lot of people will be lobbying them for various things, . . . the Churches and the rightist groups, and they have to deal with those groups. To get things about sexual orientation being part of the agenda provided an opportunity for discussion. Women who wouldn't normally discuss lesbian issues even in a supposedly very liberal feminist movement, like the one we have in the Philippines, were still afraid to get labelled as lesbian supporters. But because now it's gone to the level of the UN they have to discuss it, and they have to ask us, they have to consult with lesbians and they have talked among themselves about lesbian issues. And they will not dare, those who are political, they will not dare say the wrong thing . . .

One of the most important events to take place in the Forum was the Global Tribunal on Accountability for Women's Human Rights, organised by the Center for Women's Global Leadership. Twenty two women from around the world gave powerful personal testimonies on the way in which their lives had been damaged by gross violations of basic human rights. One of the speakers, Daphne Scholinski, testified on her experience of being incarcerated in psychiatric hospitals for four years as a teenager, diagnosed as suffering from a 'gender identity disorder'. While there she was sexually abused by both staff and 'patients' and was in the end only released when her father's health insurance ran out.

I am 29 years old and currently live as an artist/writer, San Francisco, California. I am here today as a surviving living testimony, and to give voice to the experience of many lesbian, gay, bisexual youth and young people who do not conform to traditional gender roles. Thousands of us continue to be stripped of dignity and brutalised by psychiatric abuse in institutions or are struggling to survive after psychiatric incarceration. I must stress LIVING because many never make it this far, due to the high suicide rates resulting from this abuse or the internalized fear and shame of their experience . . . We need to create a safe space for us to continue breaking the silence that has allowed this issue to be ignored for far too long . . . and that clearly identifies homophobic psychiatric abuse as a violation of the most basic human rights.

Daphne's speech received a standing ovation and a very emotional response from the lesbian tent participants who had attended the Tribunal in her support. Amnesty International pledged to fight for the release of lesbians who are known to continue to be incarcerated in psychiatric institutions today.

The most visible event outside the tent was the lesbian parade (demonstrations were forbidden) which lasted for about two hours and which was supported by about 500 women. It was the largest 'parade' to take place, and was well publicised in advance by leaflets and a press release which promised that there '. . . will also be a "coming out" event where women from numerous countries will identify themselves as women loving women in different languages to show the world that "we are everywhere"'. Lesbians demanded concrete action and called on the FWCW to recognise the freedom of women to determine their sexuality, to integrate the concerns of women regardless of sexual orientation throughout the *Platform for Action*, and to direct governmental, non-governmental and inter-governmental organisations to include these concerns in policy formulation and implementation.

The media showed much interest in all events organised and the press conferences in the tent were well attended, journalists asked reasonably well informed questions and were concerned to dispel some rumours. As for example the claim that lesbians would visit tourist sites in China, take off all their clothes and have sex. Officials had been trained especially to throw sheets over such unsightly happenings! The director of IGLHRC explained that such rumours were invented to discredit our serious work which was to campaign against human rights abuses of lesbians. Women from Barbados, Thailand, South Africa, and North America answered questions relating specifically to their countries.

However, the tent, like the Forum and conference as a whole, had its down side. The conspicuous absence of lesbians with disabilities caused much consternation. At the main conference women with disabilities demanded reimbursement for their expenses as much of the Forum as well as the official conference had been inaccessible. Their tent at the Forum was placed amongst the 'diversity' tents which would have meant a long climb over many steps and stones with wheelchairs getting stuck in the mud. Only a day's direct action ensured a different venue. Even then many workshops were inaccessible with women in wheelchairs having to be carried up staircases. Hotels were often inappropriate and expensive, in particular as women had to bring their own helpers which doubled hotel bills. During the three weeks we were there we saw one signer: the brilliant permanent performer of Sweet Honey in the Rock. When Gertrude Mongella, Secretary-General of the Conference, was challenged, she claimed the issue to be 'new' (sic).

The Lesbian Caucus
The official conference presented a very different picture from the Forum: no mud, lots of luxury, and miles away from the Forum. This was deliberate to prevent interaction of NGOs with the official delegates. However, it did not prevent the Lesbian Caucus from making itself very visible at this

conference, its members wearing large blue 'Lesbian Rights are Human Rights' badges. The Caucus had previously constituted itself in the lesbian tent. For us being members of the Caucus proved the most amazing experience of lesbian skill sharing. The daily meetings were extremely labour intensive, but always humorous, inspiring and exhilarating. There were roughly 30 caucuses consisting of members of NGOs, all putting pressure on the official delegates through lobbying. Apart from five regional caucuses they focused on specific issues like refugees, migrant workers, north/south, health, and women's human rights. It was the latter that overlapped and worked most with the Lesbian Caucus.

Meanwhile the official delegation worked on the draft of the *Platform for Action*, often well into the night. Sexual orientation proved one of the most contentious issues: it was finally removed from the document at 4.30am of the final day. However, the Lesbian Caucus claimed victory: 'The closet doors have swung open wide at the FWCW'. Never had lesbians been so visible at a UN conference, nor had sexual orientation been debated with such intensity and seriousness, and at such length. A lesbian demonstration had been staged at one of the plenary sessions with a banner that claimed human rights for lesbians. The international press had shown much (sympathetic) interest. Especially when for the first time a lesbian, Beverley Ditsie from South Africa (the only country in the world in which discrimination against lesbians is unconstitutional), addressed a major UN conference, requesting the inclusion of sexual orientation in the final document. Although it was finally deleted this was a trade off which had left another important paragraph (96) in the text:

> The human rights of women include their right to have control over and decide freely and responsibly on matters relating to their sexuality, including sexual and reproductive health, free of coercion, discrimination and violence. (United Nations, p 59)

This is the most progressive statement on sexuality ever to be included in a UN document. In addition, 40 countries committed themselves to interpret discrimination based on 'any other status' as including sexual orientation.

Not all was well, one lesbian accidentally found herself in a meeting of fundamentalists, led by North Americans, pouring out venom. Lesbians were compared to paedophiles, sodomists (!?), to those practising bestiality or ' doing it with the devil', and seen as aids carriers, as evil, and more. Visibly shaken by this, and in spite of all the support that surrounded us, it was difficult to recover from such an onslaught. Rebecca Sevilla from Peru had already taken issue with this when she courageously spoke at the Forum's plenary on the rise of conservatism. She identified this form of attack as a fear stemming from the correct recognition that lesbians are a threat because of the freedom, independence and autonomy we represent.

What now?
Notwithstanding the many difficulties that we did indeed encounter, the

support, the solidarity, the proof of outstanding lesbian abilities and courage left us all inspired and determined to continue the international struggle. The IGLHRC organised a tribunal on human rights abuses in New York attended by lesbians from other regions. A symposium was arranged in Holland that allocated funds to lesbian groups in the South. Lesbians of the Latin American and Caribbean Network met again at the 7th Latin American and Caribbean Feminist *Encuentro* in Chile at the end of 1996. Patria Jimenez from the group El Closet de Sor Juana became the first out lesbian MP in Mexico in 1997. The fourth conference of the Asian Lesbian Network took place in Manila in December 1998. The African Network was much consolidated, and East-West European links were formed.

Individual countries, too, have seen many new initiatives. In South Africa, Beverley Ditsie formed a new group, Nkateko, women only and more concerned with grass-roots lesbians than GLOW (Gays and Lesbians of Witwatersrand) which she formerly belonged to. Namibia, for the first time, saw a media debate on homosexuality, catalysed by the conference which was attended by lesbians from that country. The group CLIC (Can't Live in the Closet) in the Philippines received a grant for a research project on lesbians. In the UK lesbians lobbied both before and after the conference and ensured the inclusion of two concrete demands in the report of the consultation between the government and NGOs: the repeal of Section 28 and the amendment of the Sex Discrimination Act to include sexual orientation (Department of Education and Employment, 1996; 34). All of the above are but examples of activities inspired by the events in Beijing. As such the extension of 'Women's Rights are Human Rights' (formally acknowledged for the first time at the 1993 United Nations World Conference on Human Rights in Vienna) to include lesbian human rights is a step forward. For lesbians in numerous countries such campaigns as well as international support may at present be the only hope of escape from the most sinister aspects of the institution of heterosexuality.

Working internationally as a lesbian differs very much from working at a national level. Differences are assumed, not ignored or denied, but the focus is on commonalities. We write as White/Western women and acknowledge the importance of addressing issues of caste, class, race, ethnicity and disability; the need to deconstruct middle classness, 'whiteness', Englishness, ablebodiedness; and the necessity to continuously challenge North/South inequalities. However, internationally our differences are more apparent, which provides the opportunity to focus on commonalities. Some of the squabbles in the lesbian communities in the UK seem extremely childish when compared with a concern to abolish the death penalty for lesbians in Iran! For many lesbians in the world to squabble with each other, to discuss differences, is a luxury, if not a dream. We believe in contributing to this dream becoming a reality.

References

Anderson, S. (ed.) 1995, *Lesbian Rights are Human Rights!* Amsterdam: International Lesbian Information Service (Nieuwezijds Voorburgwal 68-70, 1012 SE Amsterdam, The Netherlands).

Department for Education and Employment, 1996, *Global Platform for Action: Consultation Exercise*, London: Department of Education and Employment.

Khambatta, A., 1995 'Beijing: Bollocks!', *Bad Attitude*, 8.

'Lesbians take on the UN', 1996, *Trouble & Strife*, 33.

Reinfelder, M. (ed.) 1996, *Amazon to Zami: Towards a Global Lesbian Feminism*, London: Cassell.

Rosenbloom, R. (ed.) 1995, *Unspoken Rules: Sexual Orientation and Women's Human Rights*, San Francisco: International Gay and Lesbian Human Rights Commission.

United Nations, 1996, *Platform for Action and the Beijing Declaration*, New York: United Nations.

Marginalised Discourses: Making Black Lesbian Mothers Visible in Feminist Theory

Akuba Quansah

In the so-called 'postmodern nineties' in which models of space/location and voice claim to celebrate a non-oppressive heterogeneity in its various manifestations, (for example, that of gender, class, sexuality, disability, and so on), black[1] lesbian mothers[2] find themselves continually marginalised in such theoretical discourses. Within feminist academia, issues of representation and voice have never been so fiercely debated than in contemporary times. Not only do we not have the authority to speak and represent other subjects but we must interrogate our own subjectivities – so much so, that we (or some of us at least) have no sense of 'self' but 'selves'. Certainly, if one adopts a resolutely postmodernist stance, it no longer seems unproblematic to posit a fixed, salient, transhistorical lesbian identity. 'Lesbian', as with other social identities, is now conceived of as a shifting metaphor.

Postmodernism, drawing on Jordan and Weedon's (1992) explanation, advocates that there is no unitary, authentic knowledge in our social world. Rather, knowledge works in various competing forms which represent conflicting groups and interests (op.cit: 203). According to Jordan and Weedon, feminists using this approach challenge all essentialist explanations of femininity and masculinity, and stress instead the ways in which subjectivity is fragmented, ambiguous and constructed within social processes and actions. In other words, there is no homogenous reality to which women can claim in order to ensure feminist activism. In rejecting essentialism, feminists adopting a postmodernist stance, claim to create space for the articulation of non-hegemonic voices. As black feminist cultural theorist, bell hooks, has postulated, this approach can be liberating and empowering as it encourages marginalised voices – such as those of black subjects – to redefine antiquated ideas of identity (hooks, 1991: 28). Yet, inspite of the emancipatory potential, it seems that postmodern feminism is still unable or unwilling to incorporate adequately wider categories of 'black lesbian' and 'black lesbian mother' to the definitions of what it means to be a woman. This paper arises out of the growing disillusionment and frustration I am experiencing as a black lesbian mother, lecturing and studying in British academia since 1988. When reading various social science and humanities literature, and especially when attending feminist-oriented gatherings, I am continually reminded of the conspicuous lack of black lesbian participation *per se* in theory formulation and research. In the main, White and Black mainstream feminists are continuing to ignore the subject of black lesbian motherhood in theory in much the same way as Queen Victoria's refusal (as legend has it) to

71

acknowledge the existence of lesbian-ness[3] when legislating against gay (male) sexuality.

Take, for instance, Romans' research study of lesbian motherhood, 'Daring to Pretend?'. Although she raises some important issues regarding the life-styles and family structures of lesbian mothers in the United Kingdom of the late 1980s, her sample, as she herself admits, consisted predominantly of white, middle-class lesbian mothers. Black, disabled and working class lesbian mothers were all excluded, yet she states that:

> the research does claim to have achieved a reasonable age range (Romans, 1992: 100).

Romans was right to include age as a focal point, given that it is also a much neglected area of analysis in social (including feminist) research. However, she should have also considered cultural specificity since age impacts on different people and social groups in different ways. In neglecting issues of race, class and ability, her research falls short of its intended objective, which is to show how different lesbian mothers manage their life-styles in terms of specific coping strategies. Far from demonstrating diversity amongst lesbian mothers, Romans simply reproduces that same old problem of exclusionary intellectualism which bell hooks challenged in her book, 'Yearning'. She writes that postmodernism is:

> dominated primarily by the voices of white male intellectuals and/or academic elites who speak to and about one another with coded familiarity (hooks, 1991).

In highlighting the specificity of the black lesbian mother, the intention is not to privilege her over and above other politicised and textualised women (including white lesbian) subjects, with whom she may share some common experiences. Yet, I do still feel an overwhelming urge to articulate the contradictory dynamics that motherhood presents the black lesbian mother with. I am engaged, of course, in an exploratory exercise, one which offers no definitive answers but rather aims to galvanise more provoking questions and interest about black female alternative sexualities, not least from black lesbian mothers themselves.

Perhaps the most appropriate starting point then is to first question the relevancy of the term 'lesbian' to black women in same sex relationships, with or without children. Whilst I am aware that the term 'lesbian' has been used so far in a relatively unproblematic sense, many black lesbians in Britain and elsewhere in the world either reject it outright or use it selectively on the basis of its historical and cultural specificity to Western Europe. There are, of course, white women in women-identified relationships who too problematise 'lesbian' and/or reject it as an ontological category because of its emphasis on gender and erotic binarism. Queer theorists[4], for example, advocate the use of the term 'queer' instead of 'gay' and 'lesbian' as it is deemed to be genderless in the sense that it deconstructs the conceptual/contextual connnections between biological, social and erotic sex.

In feminist discourse defining 'lesbian' proves to be an ever challenging task. For example, Rich (1980) proposes a general 'lesbian continuum', ranging from those who may be in relationships with men but have links with other women to those with a full emotional, sexual and political commitment to women, Stimpson (1982: 244), on the other hand, rather graphically describes lesbianism as a 'commitment to skin, blood, breast and bone'. Yet, the various different definitions of the term 'lesbian' in feminist discourse have done nothing to stem the flow of criticisms which, in recent years, have been levelled against it by many black women with alternative sexualities. Inspired by Lorde's use of the term 'zami', in her novel which also carries the same title, London-based black poet Dorethea Smart justifies her own preferred usage of this term, instead of 'lesbian', on the basis of its specificity to 'African/Caribbean culture' (Smart, 1993: 38). As Lorde writes,

"Zami", A Carriacou name for women who work together as friends and lovers. (Lorde, 1982: 155).

Later that decade, 'Zami' was also used for the title of two consecutive black lesbian UK conferences. Yet the term is not without its own definitional problems either. In being Caribbean-derived, questions can be raised about its relevancy to women who are directly descended from Africa. As Femi Otitoju[5] states,

"zami" Is about an experience in the Caribbean. The words 'lesbian' and "zami" do not have to be transferred geographically; each definition describes a particular experience.

Similarily, in several dialects spoken amongst the matrilineal Akan of Ghana the word, 'supi' is used colloquially to refer to women who have sexual relationships with other women. Although heterosexual marriage and motherhood are reported to be the norm for women in rural and urban Ghana (Ama Ata Aidoo, 1984), a 'supi' is usually found in a women/girls-only community, such as a boarding school. As Bleek (1976) notes,

homosexual activities are practised by girls who want to release sexual tensions but are afraid to become pregnant when they go with men.

As a woman of Ghanaian descent, the terms 'supi' and 'maame' (the latter meaning 'mother') are, of course, personally relevant to me, not least because the amalgam of these terms, 'supimaame' translates as 'lesbian mother'. In my terms, it means a woman of African descent who is both a mother and a lover of women in one or several contexts; spiritual, emotional, physical, sexual and political. 'Supimaame', like 'zami', adds breadth to the definition of what it means to be a woman from an Africentric viewpoint. Rather than attempt to essentialise black lesbian mothers' experiences into the idiom of the Akan, it is hoped that the concept of 'supimaame' will merely serve as a resource of self-empowerment for those who wish to adopt it. Apart from being African-derived, 'supimaame' does not seem to break down readily into a binary oppositional category, like lesbian/mother which, according to Pat Romans, presents a contradictory relationship in that biologically-determined factors and social constructs intermingle confusedly. A lesbian is stereotypically conceived as an abnormal and/or unfeminine woman who, according to Martin and Lyon (1972), lures innocent girls or women into an unknown fate, whilst a mother conjures up the conception of a 'normal' woman who is fulfilling, as MacIntyre (1976) asserts, a 'natural maternal desire'.

To begin to understand something of the position of the black lesbian mother or 'supimaame' in British society today it is useful to draw on African/American lesbian feminist, Smith's concept of 'simultaneity of oppression'. In 'Home Girls' (1986) she argues for a multi-issued approach to politics when considering the position of black women in Africa and the African diaspora. The one factor that unites black women, as with other marginalised groups, cross-culturally is that we[6] experience multiple oppressions non-hierarchically. As Smith (op.cit: xxxii) puts it,

> everything out there was kicking our behinds - race, class, sex and homophobia.

This concept of the simultaneity of oppression has had a major impact on the formulation of black feminist thought by emphasising the multiplicity of contexts in which competing oppressions manifest themselves. It is also a useful precursor for conceptualising the specific situation of the black lesbian mother in Britain in terms of the concept of ubiquity of resistance. It seems to me that a black lesbian mother has to resist multiple oppressions from one central site, namely, her home place. From her temporary or fixed abode she not only has to feed, clothe and shelter herself and her child(ren) daily, but she must fight many conflicting social battles around issues of identity within her immediate communities and the society at large. 'Home' becomes a symbolic site through which motherhood (including co-motherhood), lesbian-ness and resistance are experienced and articulated ubiquitously. She resists, for example, institutional and personal racism from both white heterosexual men and women and white gay men and lesbians; she resists white and black homophobia, and white and black sexism; she resists anti-children attitudes within the black and white gay and lesbian communities; she resists poverty and the institutional violence of the Child Support Agency (CSA)[7]; she resists negative paternity intervention such as legal disputes over custody and access, and she resists family exclusion. Moreover, on an intellectual level she resists white Eurocentric ideologies, feminists or otherwise, on lesbian motherhood.

Romans (1992) points out that it is the lesbian mother, of all the members of the gay community, who feels the need to maintain links with both the heterosexual and lesbian and gay communities. I would add that black lesbian mothers, on the whole, tend to maintain stronger links with their black communities, albeit some of them arbitrary than their white lesbian counterparts. Their relative physical 'blackness' make them far more visible to racist individuals so resisting racism, even if it means forming allegiances with some black heterosexual men and women, as well as their black gay brothers may be prioritised at particular times in their everyday realities. After all, being 'out' or remaining in the closet about an alternative sexuality involves a relative degree of choice. Blackness, on the other hand, is not a choice that can be so easily compromised without risking physical self-harm.

Some feminist perspectives tend to attribute the commitment and desires of a lesbian to have children to patriarchical ideology and institutions. For example, separatist lesbians often view lesbians who maintain links with men of all sexual orientations, and particularly lesbians who have conceived children by heterosexual sex and/or have male children (by whatever method) as upholding male supremacy. As Solanas (1988) writes,

Women raising male children hope that because of their influence, the child will not grow up to be a pig . . . but it is impossible . . . societal conditioning and socialisation are vastly powerful.

All too often motherhood (and fatherhood) is equated with heterosexuality, as if to suggest that only heterosexuals are entitled to procreate and rear children. However, there are indeed many heterosexuals who, individually or in partnerships, consciously choose not to have children, and to argue the contrary is to ignore the diverse realities of life that men and women experience.

Being a lesbian mother of African descent is not necessarily antithetical to her kinship systems. Though based in Britain, those lesbians who have been reared by African/Caribbean parents or guardians have been socialised into the expectation that children are an essential signifier of fully-fledged adulthood. Marriage, partnership, sexuality and motherhood are not necessarily interconnected. For example, in African matrilineal (such as the Akan of Ghana) or patrilineal societies children are important for the institution and transmission of property rights (Carmel Dinan: 1983). Black lesbians descending from such cultural backgrounds, in having children, could merely be reinforcing a 'rites of passage'. Children often become the medium through which their sexualities are expressed, celebrated and hidden at once. For example, the biological black lesbian mother, like her white counterpart, would have had a direct or indirect association with the father of her child or children in order to ensure procreation; that is, self or medical insemination, or heterosexual sex. Fostering and adoption and artificial insemination, however empowering these methods might be – since they enable lesbians to conceive without heterosexual sex – are not made easily accessible to many black (and white) lesbians due to legal and financial constraints.

In the UK, Section 28 parliamentary debates presupposed that gay male and lesbian parents were 'pseudo-parents' who had pretend families. It was also proposed to prohibit teaching the 'acceptability of homosexuality as a pretended family relationship' in an attempt to counter the displacing of the conventional nuclear family by gay and lesbian parents. In terms of fostering, Paragraph 16 of the Children's Act guided Social Services to exclude gay people as potential parents, and it was only after intense lobbying that this clause was abolished. Lesbian parenting was attacked again in the Human Fertilisation and Embryology Act 1990, which stipulates that a woman will not be provided with artificial insemination unless consideration is given to the welfare of the child, including the need of that child for a father. Consequently, doctors and counsellors at medical centres must now decide whether or not prospective mothers who do not have partners would be capable of catering completely for the child's ne(eds.) The repercussions of these legal constraints have been widely felt by many black lesbians seeking to have children. Some end up conceiving their children through heterosexual sex, sometimes casually. Others would have had their children within the context of a previous heterosexual partnership. It is this latter group of black lesbian mothers (though not exclusively) who experience extreme disapproval and disdain from some lesbians, feminist or non-feminist, but predominantly white. Conceiving children heterosexually, for some childless lesbians, appears to bring with it accusations about closet heterosexuality. The mere fact that a lesbian has or chooses to have children, as Romans (1992: 104) asserts, can so often label her as a "pretend" lesbian.

The black lesbian mother, like her white lesbian counterpart, is so often torn between concealing her sexuality from her child(ren); from the genetic father of her children if conceived non-anonymously; from family members, those at work and school, whilst trying simultaneously, in some lesbian and gay circles, to prove that her lesbian sexuality is still intact. Playing down her sexuality in her everyday interactions with the family, school, and heterosexual friends enables her to maintain support systems which would otherwise be denied. In this respect, she tends to pose a greater threat to her kinship structures if motherhood is resisted as an 'option'. Yet, she also presents a threat to black (and white) heterosexual men since some will happily use the man's sperm to procreate but distance themselves sooner or later from heterosexual relations, if sexual intimacy, and sometimes emotional intimacy become part of the expected package.

Issues of maintenance and financial support are also relevant. As with other single parents, many black lesbian mothers are forced onto benefits which are below subsistance levels. The policies of the Child Support Agency (CSA) plunge them further into a trap of material disadvantage and disenfranchisement. If a black lesbian mother does not disclose the appropriate information regarding the father of her child(ren), her welfare benefit risks being affected. She is forced into either colluding with the biological father of her child(ren) in order to retain some of the maintenance which the State is so desperate to recoup; or into co-operating with the Department of Social Security and may, consequently, risk physical and verbal abuse. Not co-operating with either causes particular dilemmas. She cannot risk court, for this could mean lesbian exposure, a reduction of her support systems and a possible custody battle. Yet, she also does not wish the father, who happens to be biologically related to her child(ren), to use the issue of maintenance to survey her private life and invade her personal space, or to use his social contact time with the child(ren) to mask a hidden agenda such as the desire to rekindle intimate relations with her.

As I bring this paper to an end, I ask, where does all this leave the black lesbian mother in relation to feminist discourses? According to Romans (1992) lesbian mothers currently combating dominant ideologies on gender, motherhood and the family tend to be white, articulate and middle-class, and that the situation for black lesbian mothers is unclear. This kind of observation can only serve to obscure and mystify the experiences of black lesbian mothers. In fact, the position of black lesbian mothers could never be clearer. We exist, we are many, and we are diverse in our daily struggles against grassroots and academic oppression. When Wilton (1995) says that in order to survive and resist, any marginalised/stigmatised group is obliged to establish a rudimentary sense of group identity, I am in agreement with her. We can not dismiss our identities as black lesbian mothers, as they are essential to resisting widespread oppressions.

Whilst deconstructing lesbian-ness has offered a new insight into some experiences made marginal in feminist theory, it does not change the materiality of one's circumstances. I appear to speak from a position of relative 'privilege', and with this, I realise that the manner in which my ideas have been presented may be exclusionary too. Yet, as with many other marginalised women, I am not yet liberated from the oppressive forces of racism, homophobia, classism, sexism, and 'maternal burn out'. Moreover, outside academia, with other black lesbian mothers, and other marginalised 'sisters' we engage in feminist debates regularly, where some empathetic awareness of our relative struggles is possible. Postmodern feminism may indeed liberate at the point at which one is talking postmodernism from the position of the silenced. Nevertheless, to rephrase Wilton's statement, (1995), it has yet to protect us adequately from the oppressions of White heteropatriachical materiality.

Notes

1   Unless otherwise specified, the term 'black' will refer to an African ancestry although I realise that in Britain it **can** and **is** being contextually broadened (in a political sense) to include women and men who descend through one or both parents from Asia and Latin America as well as the politics of identifying communities, see Mason-John (1995) and Mama (1984).

2   By using the term 'black lesbian mothers' I do not wish to essentialise and totalise all black women with children in same-sex relationships into an undifferentiated category of experiences because, clearly, like any other group, they constitute heterogenous realities. It is beyond the scope of this paper, however, to discuss this point in further detail, but it is one in which, I feel, warrants further research generally.

3   Throughout this paper I prefer to use the term 'lesbian-ness' rather than 'lesbianism'. I agree with Wilton (1995) that 'lesbianism' is too rigid a

term and suggests a pathological state whereas the former indicates a more fluid set of meanings.

[4] A detailed account of 'Queer theory' is beyond the scope of this paper. For further reading see Wilton (1995).

[5] Otitoju in Mason-John (1995).

[6] At times, the term 'we' is used subjectively to indicate that the issue(s) raised also impact on my own life.

[7] The Child Support Agency is a Government funded agency which was set up in 1993, under the Child Support Act, and is responsible to the Department of Social Security. It is responsible for collecting information about and tracing absent parents, and assessing, collecting and enforcing child maintenance. Although the duty to maintain children applies to all cases where child maintenance is an issue, the Child Support Act imposes specific obligations on parents with care and control of children Government benefits, such as Income Support and Family Credit. Such parents are required, first, to authorise the CSA to take action to recover maintenance, and secondly, to co-operate with the agency by providing the necessary information to help trace any absent parent and to assess and collect any monies owed. According to the Act, any parent who has convinced a Child Support Officer that she or he has 'good cause' (such as, the risk of harm from the absent parent) for withholding permission, will not be required to give any information. For non-exempt parents who fail to comply with either requirement or where 'good cause' has not been accepted, a benefit penalty (a reduction in benefit), can be imposed. By 'institutional violence' I am referring metaphorically to the forceful and confrontational manner in which the CSA, acting on behalf of the Secretary of State, recovers or attempts to recover maintenance. The rigid requirements of the CSA put the lesbian mother on benefit, whatever her ethnic origin, under considerable risk of abuse or aggravation from the absent parent if she decides to co-operate, or at the risk of intensified economic scarcity if she does not comply to the requirements of the agency.

References

Aidoo, A.A., 1984, 'To be a woman', in Morgan, R. (ed.) *Sisterhood is Global*, 2nd edn. pp.261-268, Penguin Books.

Bleek, W., 1976a, *Sexual Relationships and Birth Control in Ghana: A Case Study of a Rural Town*, Amsterdam, Anthropological-Sociological Centre.

Dinan, C., 1983, 'Sugar daddies and gold-diggers: the white collar workers in Accra', in Oppong, C. (ed.), *Female and Male in West Africa*, London: Allen and Unwin.

hooks, b., 1991, *Yearning; Race, Gender and Cultural Politics*, London: Turnaround.

Jordan, G., and Weedon, C., 1992, *Cultural Politics: Class, Gender, Race and the Postmodern World*, Oxford: Blackwell.

Lorde, A., 1982, *Zami: A New Spelling of My Name*, Watertown, M.A.:

Persephone. (Repr. Trumanburg, NY: Crossing Press, 1983).

MacIntyre, S., 1976, 'Who wants babies? The social construction of instincts', in Barker D., and Allen, S. (eds.) *Sexual Diversions in Society*, pp.150-73, Britain: Tavistock.

Mama, A., 1984, 'Black women, the economic crisis and the British state', *Feminist Review*, 17, 21-35.

Martin, D., and Lyon, P., 1972, *Lesbian Women*, New York: Bantam.

Mason-John., V., 1995, *Talking Back: Lesbians of African and Asian Descent Speak-Out,* Cassell.

Rich, A., 1981a, 'Compulsory heterosexuality and lesbian existence', *Signs*, 5, 4, 631-60.

Romans, P., 1992, 'Daring to Pretend?' In Plummer, K. (ed.) *Modern Homosexualities: Fragments of Lesbian and Gay History*, pp.98-107, London: Routledge.

Smart, D., 1993, 'If the label fits, wear it', in Mason-John, V., and Khambatta, A., (eds.) *Lesbian Talk; Making Black Waves*, Scarlet Press.

Smith, B., 1986, *Home Girls: A Black Feminist Anthology* (ed.), Kitchen Table, Women of Colour Press.

Solanas, V., 1988, 'Beginnings of our consciousness: defining lesbian separatism', in Lucia-Hoagland, S., and Penelope, J. (eds.) *For Lesbians Only: A Separatist Anthology* pp.31-37, Only Women Press Ltd.

Stimpson, C.R., 1988, 'Adrienne Rich and feminist-lesbian poetry', in Stimpson (ed.) *Where the Meanings Are: Feminism and Cultural Spaces*, pp.140-54, London and New York: Routledge.

Wilton, T., 1995, *Lesbian Studies. Setting an Agenda,* London: Routledge

'A real giving up of self': Children's Needs and Maternal Subjectivities in Narratives of Middle-class Motherhood

Steph Lawler

The child-centricity of most feminist and nonfeminist accounts of mothering deflects feminist attention from central questions: What are the effects of current conditions of mothering on *mothers*? And how might *mothers* benefit from a revisioning of motherhood? (Daly and Reddy, 1991:3. Emphasis in original).

Introduction

For all the millions of words which feminists have devoted to analyses of mothering, one issue remains relatively neglected: the questions of how knowledges about, and constructions of, childhood work to define motherhood, and of how these knowledges and constructions inflect mothers' sense of self[1]. In this article, I want to take up Daly and Reddy's questions, above, to focus on one important 'condition' of contemporary Euroamerican motherhood: the question of how motherhood itself is defined and constituted, and the effects of this constitution on mothers themselves. In particular, I am concerned to explore some of the costs of the meanings attached to motherhood on women whose mothering is marked as 'normal' and 'natural'.

What I am particularly concerned with here is the ways in which motherhood is constituted in relation to knowledges about childhood, and especially in relation to apparently liberated and liberating 'child-centred' knowledges. My argument here is that the social category 'mother' is discursively constituted in relation to, and indeed in response to, a prior social category - that of 'child'. Hence, what counts as (good) mothering is extrapolated from what children are considered to need. As Woollett and Phoenix argue:

> conceptualizations of motherhood and of good mothering merely reflect ideas about children. What children are thought to need for development is generalized to define good mothering (Woollett and Phoenix, 1991: 40).

In this sense, then, the category 'mother' is formulated on the basis of the category 'child', and children's needs become the imperative grounding of 'good (enough) mothering'[2]. While some feminist analyses have problematized this linkage to the extent that they have proposed equal parenting between women and men (Chodorow, 1978; Benjamin, 1988), 'mothering' as a category largely remains intact. As Walkerdine and Lucey argue, although the activity of 'mothering' is often detached from the person of the biological mother, 'implicitly the arguments remains: children have needs and mothering is necessary as a *function* to meet them' (Walkerdine and Lucey, 1989: 19. Emphasis in original). In other words, 'anyone can mother', but *someone* has to do it.

As Walkerdine and Lucey suggest, what makes 'mothering' as a function so apparently immune to problematization is that the category 'child' is rarely problematized in analyses of mothering. As a result, and despite the insights offered by writers who have subjected the category 'child' to critical scrutiny[3], conventional and normalized conceptualizations of 'the child' of 'childhood' and of children's 'needs' are usually incorporated into analyses of mothering, making it difficult to radically critique conventional notions of motherhood[4]. In the next section, I will consider some contemporary Euroamerican conceptualizations of 'the child', and look at some of the implications, for mothers, and for children themselves, of these conceptualizations.

good enough children?

Need is also a political instrument, meticulously prepared, calculated and used (Foucault, 1979: 26).

As Stainton Rogers and Stainton Rogers argue, childhood is 'knowledged into being' (1992: 15). In other words, the category 'child' is produced through knowledges about the child, rather than through innate and inherent characteristics of the people known as 'children'. Overwhelmingly, the knowledges which surround childhood in contemporary Euroamerican societies are generated by what have come to be called the 'psy professions' - the disciplines of psychiatry, psychology, psychotherapy, pedagogy, and so on. Although the knowledges produced by these disciplines have the status of universal 'truths', several commentators have pointed to the cultural and historical specificity which engender such 'truths', and to the political preoccupations which surround them. (Walkerdine and Lucey, 1989; Rose, 1991; Woollett and Phoenix, 1991)

Psy has generated numerous knowledges about childhood, not all of them homogeneous or coherent: however, I want to concentrate here on one particular aspect of psy's conceptualization of childhood, which recurs again and again in both feminist and nonfeminist work (Kellmer Pringle, 1980; Eichenbaum and Orbach, 1982, 1992; NSPCC, 1989; Ruddick, 1990). This is the conceptualization of 'need' as being the foundational basis of childhood[5]. The needs of children are constituted (through psy) as timeless and universal, stemming from inherent properties of the child her/himself. Mothering becomes constituted in terms of a *response* to these 'innate' needs[6]. Yet, children's 'needs', like childhood itself, are socially constituted on the basis of specific historical and political preoccupations (Walkerdine, 1984; Walkerdine and Lucey, 1989; Woodhead, 1990) and on the basis of how the 'normal (adult) person' is defined in any particular cultural / historical setting (Stainton Rogers and Stainton Rogers, 1992). Contemporary Euroamerican societies tend to valorize autonomy as a property of the person (Haraway, 1987; Rose, 1991; Fraser and Gordon,

1994), and hence one of children's primary needs is usually held to be the need to develop autonomy (Winnicott, 1964, 1965; Kellmer Pringle, 1980; Adcock and White, 1990). Hence, the development of the child is considered to inhere in the unfolding of a self which is innately autonomous - free from the impositions of others, self-governing[7]. A narrative is established in which the child's voyage to adulthood becomes centred around the emergence (or non-emergence) of the autonomous 'true self'. Certainly, this concept is sometimes reworked so that autonomy comprises forms of relationality (Eichenbaum and Orbach, 1982, 1992; Everingham, 1994) but it is the development of autonomy which nevertheless remains the ultimate goal[8]. And because it is 'autonomous', this 'normal, natural' self will be able to 'achieve' in the social world (Walkerdine and Lucey, 1989).

However, and for all its 'normality' and 'natural-ness', the autonomous self is not seen as unfolding all by itself: it must be *nurtured* by the mother's sensitive care (Winnicott, 1964; Kellmer Pringle, 1980; NSPCC, 1989) - by, for example, her use of forms of regulation in which the regulation itself is hidden, rather than overt; by her 'responsiveness' to the child, and her use of reason as a regulatory principle. It is 'sensitive mothers', then, who successfully establish their children as autonomous. 'Sensitive mothers' are constituted as meeting the child's need for autonomy, and hence making them into fully human subjects. The mother's place in the narrative of the 'true self' becomes one of enabling (or not enabling) this self to emerge. She can only do this by meeting the child's needs. The child-centricity of this approach is usually assumed to be 'empowering' and transformative. But, as I will go on to argue, this discourse is tyrannical in its establishment of the need for relentless self-monitoring and self-scrutiny, and deeply conservative in its individualizing of social hierarchies and oppressions.

As I see it, there are three principal problems with these conceptualiz-ations of selfhood and its roots in childhood. Firstly, the narrative of the emergent, autonomous self, so promising of freedom, relies on a project of self-monitoring and self-surveillance. As Rose argues in his critique of psy:

[T]he norm of autonomy secretes, as its inevitable accompaniment, a constant and intense self-scrutiny, a constant evaluation of our personal experiences, emotions and feelings in relation to images of satisfaction, the necessity to narrativize our lives in a vocabulary of interiority. The self that is liberated is obliged to live its life tied to a project of its own identity (Rose, 1991: 254)

Psy discourses have become increasingly important in regulating lives. They have 'escaped' from specialist enclaves (Fraser, 1989) to find expression in media discussion, in social welfare services, and in the general parlance of everyday life. Their frequent repetition across a range of sites makes them particularly intractable: they become, not just theories, but *truths* about human nature, the 'inner' self, relations between persons, and so on. In this respect, psy has become an authority, 'albeit one who has replaced the claims of god and religion with those of nature and the psyche' (Rose, 1992: 364).

The authority of psy is hidden, however, because it works, less through demands for obedience than through techniques of normalization; less through the threat of penalties than through the promise of rewards. Psy works, at least in part, through harnessing our desires. The most apparently personal and intimate parts of our lives, our desires and pleasures, have come to be both produced and regulated within its systems of normalization. If contemporary Euroamericans seem to be free from sovereign power, this may be because we are increasingly adept at regulating ourselves.

The knowledges of psy (including its promised self-knowledge), far from being an escape from power, involve the workings and indeed the extension of power. Through the kinds of 'technique of the self' which Rose identifies, social actors become subjectified in the two senses identified by Foucault (1982): firstly, they are *subjected* to discourses; and secondly, they are *made into* subjects through discourse. In this way, power works productively within the human subject - stimulating particular meanings, particular desires, specific forms of pleasure, and, indeed, constituting specific forms of human subject.

In this sense, then, the maternal subject is created and re-created through knowledges about childhood, and mothers are subjectified by these knowledges (Ambert, 1994). Knowledges about children and their needs become 'technologies of the [maternal] self' (Foucault, 1988) through which mothers must act upon themselves, producing good (enough) mothering within themselves, and constructing themselves as good (enough) mothers.

A second problem with these configurations of childhood, and of selfhood, lies in their fundamental voluntarism: in the slippage between *feeling* autonomous and *being* autonomous. With a construction of autonomy as a property of the person comes an occlusion of the social barriers which militate against most persons' achievement of autonomy. In other words, no amount of feeling autonomous is going to do away with social hierarchies of gender, class, 'race', and so on. But the twist here is that failure to achieve can now be located within the person - it is not social mechanisms which are held to 'hold us back' but an individual psychopathology, an unhealthy lack of autonomy (Walkerdine and Lucey, 1989; Fraser and Gordon, 1994). And there is a further twist: since mothers are already positioned as those persons responsible for the development of autonomy, it is mothers who can be blamed when autonomy fails to evince itself (Caplan and Hall-McCorquodale, 1985; Bradley, 1989).

This leaves all mothers in a vulnerable position: they become the guarantors of a specific type of self within the child, and, since social order is held to result from this 'well-adjusted' self, they become, ultimately, the guarantors of social harmony (Walkerdine and Lucey, 1989). However, some mothers are in a more vulnerable position than others. Mothers of daughters have the responsibility for ensuring that their daughters overcome structural relations of gender inequality. But, cross-cutting this, mothers who are Black and/or working-class have an added responsibility, in that their children's 'success', of which they are the guarantors, can only be achieved by those children 'escaping' from structurally disadvantaged positions of class and 'race'. Indeed, it is important to note that it is the mothering practices of White, middle-class women which are constituted as the norm within discourses of the mother and child: mothers who are Black and/or working-class become the 'others' against whom normality is defined. Their mothering practices are constituted as 'wrong', as 'inadequate'[9]. Their children's failure to 'achieve' is located within their mothering. Further, these knowledges are not free-floating: they are incorporated into the practices of those whose task it is to monitor mothers and their children, and who must regulate those mothers who cannot be relied upon to regulate themselves. Questions are asked about why these mothers are getting it wrong, and the task then becomes one of 'enabling' them to get it 'right'. In press and other media reports, in academic case studies, in the notes of medical and other professionals, these women's mothering is exposed to scrutiny. Only rarely do those discourses which themselves position these women as 'getting it wrong' come under any kind of scrutiny or critique[10].

My third critique of the narrative of the autonomous self centres on its child-centricity: this narrative is that of the daughter/son, not that of the mother. Indeed, the mother is the *object* of the narrative - the dual facilitator of, and threat to, the child's emergent autonomous self. In nurturing the child's self, the mother's own self-narrative is eclipsed, and indeed, her own subjectivity can threaten to disappear. While a capacity to care for others and put their interests before one's own might be a wholly desirable quality, this eclipsing of the mother's self in favour of that of the child has a number of less desirable implications. For example, much child care advice works on the principle that the mother's needs are *identical* to those of the child. The British child-care writer Penelope Leach, for example, is typical in her claim that:

> [T]aking the baby's point of view does not mean neglecting your, her parents' viewpoint. Your interests and hers are identical. You are all on the same side, the side that wants to be happy, to have fun.(Leach, 1988: 8)[11].

But as both Urwin (1985) and Marshall (1991) note, these two (potentially conflicting) sets of needs are harmonized through the mother's needs claims being *eclipsed by* those of the child - through the mother's (separate) personhood being discounted. The overwhelming emphasis within child-centred discourses on meeting the child's needs positions the mother as little more than both embodiment and the fulfilment of her children's 'needs'.

Further, the very conceptualization of children's needs can work as a stick with which to beat mothers who are culturally marked as 'out of line'. In recent British press coverage, for example, the notion of 'children's needs' has been used to castigate lesbian mothers, single mothers and working-class mothers. Similarly, in the U.S. 'underclass' debates, much of the subtext has revolved around the representation of poor mothers, single mothers, Black mothers, as 'bad mothers', expressing their moral turpitude

in putting their own (short-term) wants before the chil   ociety's)
'needs'[12]. Tremendous prominence is given to the notion   iildren of
these women will suffer: that their 'needs' could n   by such
unsuitable mothers. This notion is backed up by quotat   'experts'
in the psy professions. Again and again within thes   ntations,
children's 'needs' are set against maternal 'wants', prese   rticularly
intractable argument. Who can argue against childre   ? 'Need'
implies both a more objective reality and a greater legi   an 'want'
(Woodhead, 1990).

It seems then, that the 'good mothers' present in child-care advice have no desires other than the desire to be a good mother. The 'bad mothers' of recent British press reports and of the 'underclass' debates in Britain and the U.S., however, have plenty of desires: what they do not have are legitimate needs. These kinds of formulation contribute to a normalizing project by which mothers are governed. They contribute, too, to schemata of understanding through which the self may act on itself. Who would want to be a bad mother? When maternal selves and maternal demands are set against children's 'needs', any discursive space in which mothers could assert their own demands, their own subjectivities, is virtually closed off. In the next section, I will explore this issue through an examination of maternal narratives.

Good enough mothers?

These maternal narratives are taken from empirical research on the mother-daughter relationship, in which I carried out repeated, semi-structured interviews with fourteen White women living in the north-west of England. All of these women were mothers of daughters: three were working-class, from working-class birth families; seven were middle-class, from working-class birth families; and four were middle-class, from middle-class birth families[13].

All of the women in this study defined mothering in terms of children's 'needs' (and especially their emotional needs). Children's needs were the *point* of mothering. All of the women also defined their position as mothers as ones in which their children's needs 'came first'. But what did they come before? The women tended to cast this situation in terms of their children's needs coming before their own desires. In other words, within these women's accounts, what mothers *want* should be subordinated to what children *need*. In some ways, this looks like the kind of constitution of good motherhood I outlined above, in which maternal desires and subjectivities are effaced in favour of childhood needs. However, there are important differences. While this construction simply obliterates desires in good/normal mothers, these women (who did see themselves as good mothers) also saw themselves as having desires independent of those of their children, and considered that their desires might clash with the needs of the child. However, only one desire - the desire to be the good mother - could claim any legitimacy when faced with children's needs, or even children's demands.

However, and perhaps not surprisingly, it was the women who made the heaviest investments in 'child-centred' discourses who most repeatedly invoked the wants/needs binarism in speaking of their relationships with their daughters and sons, and these women, too, who expressed most anxieties around the issue of their daughters and sons 'being themselves'. These women - nine in all - were all middle-class (though some had been born into working-class families); all had been trained in the 'caring professions' (teaching, social work, nursing, counselling), and a majority had had extensive contact with psychotherapy, either as clients or as practitioners (or both)[14]. Hence, these women 'knew' the discourses of the self and of childhood generated from psy knowledges, and, indeed, these discourses explicitly informed their accounts. Not only did they use the formulation wants/needs to speak about their relationships with their children, but they also saw the nurturing of autonomy within their daughters (and sons) as one of the most important tasks of motherhood (for some, it was the most important task of motherhood).

In the rest of the article, I want to concentrate on the accounts of these nine women for two reasons. Firstly, I want to disrupt the constitution of middle-class motherhood as normal, and in no need of investigation or problematization; secondly, I want to examine what happens to maternal subjectivities when mothers do make heavy investments which position them as little more than the embodiment and the fulfilment of children's ne(eds.)

With their knowledge of the 'right' way to mother, and with their commitment to child-centricity, these women's mothering would be 'read' by psy discourse as exemplary. Their class position is unmarked, silently occupying the ground marked as 'normal' against which other groups of mothers become defined as pathological, and, indeed, some of these women are employed to regulate the mothers whose mothering is deemed to be pathological. Their knowledge is assumed to derive from an intrinsic understanding of the mother-child relationship, rather than something they have learned.

This position of 'normality' is undoubtedly a position of privilege. Yet there is a tremendous cost here. I have written elsewhere of the ways in which psy knowledges pathologize working-class women (Lawler, 1995, 1999), and I want to stress that I am not claiming that middle-class women are somehow *more* oppressed in this respect than working-class women. However, I do want to argue that, even when mothers apparently 'get it right', they can only do so at the cost of at least the partial effacement of their subjectivity. As I will argue later, the women do resist, but there is limited space within which to do so. Like the middle-class women in Walkerdine and Lucey's study, these women are 'manacled to sensitivity' (1989: 83), engaged in a project of self-monitoring and self-evaluation which centres around the daughter's achievement of autonomy.

Autonomy was, indeed, a recurring motif in these women's accounts. When they spoke as daughters, they spoke frequently of their need to achieve autonomy and independence from others, and especially, from their mothers. But when they spoke as mothers, the focus shifted to the daughter's achievement of autonomy. All of the women in the study defined 'good mothering' in terms of meeting children's needs, but, for the women under discussion here, a primary need was the daughter's need to 'be herself' - to be self-directed, free from the impositions of (m)others. So, for these women, an important task of motherhood - for some, the most important task of motherhood - was the nurturing of the daughter's (and the son's) autonomy - and, because autonomy was seen to be the foundation of 'normal' selfhood, the nurturing of the daughter's (and the son's) 'true self'.

In other words, then, when speaking as daughters, these women expressed a tremendous investment in the achievement of autonomy in themselves: but when they spoke as mothers, this autonomous self apparently becomes relational, existing in terms of meeting children's needs, primary among which is the need to achieve autonomy. But of course, these women are both mothers and daughters: so what happens to the autonomous self when the subject-position 'mother' is taken up? Indeed, when contemporary Euroamerican personhood is taken to be innately autonomous, how can we situate a maternal subjectivity when maternity is tied to relationality, rather than to autonomy? It is to these questions that I now turn.

Losing the self

Nobody within a discourse of meeting needs talks about the mother, what effect being "constantly available" might have on her. No one talks about how she must constantly struggle to maintain the rich environment of which she is guardian or how much hidden effort is made; while the child is enjoying 'liberation' and autonomy, this to some extent depends on the mother's oppression (Walkerdine and Lucey, 1989: 106. Emphasis in original).

As I have already indicated, all of the women in this study equated 'good mothering' with the subordination of the mother's desires to the child's needs.) For the women I am discussing here, however, the subordination of their desires to their children's needs was often linked with some expression of a 'loss' of the self, especially, though not exclusively, during the early years of their children's dependency. For example:

SL: What are the sacrifices to being a mother?
Hazel: I think when they're young, it's a real giving up of self. ... I think the sacrifice is giving up like your own ambitions, your own self, and putting those on the shelf, putting those aside for a while, and concentrating on the child-rearing [15].

Elizabeth: I think even then [when her children were younger] I was aware that there was a lack of identity. I wasn't fully my own person.

SL: What are the sacrifices?
Rachel: Well not living your own life entirely, I think, when you have the children. Because they're always there and, to me, anyway, they come first. ... I think balancing doing your own thing and being a mother

must be quite difficult. I think I've not really tried to balance it very much. I think I've, er - I feel I know what I should be doing as a mother, so I do that, but I maybe don't do a lot of what I want to do.

The phrases 'not living your own life' and 'not being your own person' may sound commonplace to contemporary Euroamericans: they are bound up with the cultural belief that we have an authentic, intrinsic self, and that it is possible to either live out or not live out this authenticity, to 'be' or to 'not be' this self. But I want to ask what these phrases *mean* in this context. How is it possible to 'give up' the self, to be other than the self?

If motherhood is tied to a form of femininity based on relationality, rather than autonomy, then autonomy is impossible from within this position. And because autonomy is held to be a normal and substantive state of personhood, then the take-up of the subject-position 'mother' - a position tied to relationality - evokes the sacrifice of personhood. If persons are centrally and fundamentally autonomous, mothers, existing only in relation to and in response to children's 'needs', are going to have difficulty counting as persons.

Motherhood, in this context, seems to represent a rupture in these women's selfhood, a breach of the autonomy which is held to be constitutive of the person. It marks a breach in the self-narrative through which lives are understood and constituted as coherent (Ricoeur, 1991; Ewick and Silbey, 1994; Somers and Gibson, 1994). Paul Ricoeur's (1991) analysis of identity may cast some light on this rupture. Ricoeur distinguishes between two principal uses of the concept of identity: identity as selfhood *(ipse)*, and identity as sameness *(idem)*. Ricoeur argues that identity as sameness implies continuity: identity as selfhood is also understood on the basis of this feature of continuity; hence, he argues, persons are understood as being continuous, in terms of being the same entity, from foetus to old age. Here, both understandings of identity - as selfhood, and as sameness (continuity) coincide.

However, Ricoeur argues, identity as sameness also implies permanence, and it is here that identity as selfhood may not coincide with identity as sameness. If the self changes over time, then it is not an identity based on permanence. When this permanence is lost, as in a breach of the 'self' which went before, the subject may experience the self as 'nothing' - as lost: 'Who is 'I' when the subject says that (s)he/it is nothing? Precisely a self deprived of assistance from sameness - *(idem)* identity' (Ricoeur, 1991:198).

Hence, although there is still a speaking subject, still an 'I' to say, 'I am nothing', the loss of sameness-identity may precipitate a 'dark night of personal identity' (Ricoeur, 1991:199), in which the self *feels* as though '(s)he/ it is nothing'.

If women experience motherhood as a loss of the self, then, this may be because the self of the mother is distinct from the pre-maternal self. While the pre-maternal self, for these women, is constituted on the basis of (a struggle towards) autonomy, the maternal self, constituted on the basis of a response to children's 'needs', evokes the very opposite of autonomy. In contradistinction to the supposed autonomy of 'normal' personhood, maternity is constituted on the basis of relationality. Although autonomy is militated against by the fact of a woman's *being* a woman, it is in motherhood that autonomy seems most difficult to achieve. Hence, women may experience maternity as a rupture in the self, a lack of permanence with what went before. Certainly, and as I discuss below, no mother is *only* a mother. Certainly, too, as children grow older and, to a certain degree, more independent, mothers may find themselves with more time to take up subject-positions other than mother. Nevertheless, mothers *as* mothers are tied to a relational subject-position, in which they are both the embodiment and fulfilment of their children's needs.

However, as Ricoeur argues, there is still an 'I' to say, 'I am nothing'. Hence, it is possible for this self to find ways of reinscribing itself. These women did, indeed, find ways of reinstating their self-narrative: in the next sections, I will focus on the techniques they used to do so.

The discourse of choice

Don't expect gratitude; your child did not ask to be born - the choice was yours (Mia Kellmer Pringle, 'Ten Child Care Commandments').

Motherhood - in the sense of the getting of a child - is now supposed to (ideally) be a choice (Strathern, 1992a)[16]. As Strathern puts it:

However one looks at it, procreation can now be *thought about* as subject to personal preference and choice in a way that has never before been conceivable. The child is literally ... the embodiment of the act of choice (Strathern, 1992a: 34. Emphasis in original).

The story of becoming a mother - at least in its ideal form - is a story in which choice is exercised, and reproduction occurs through the exercise of this choice. But choice has a specific meaning to contemporary Euroamericans, and this meaning not only gives shape to the story of reproduction, but also marks out the personhood of the chooser. According to Strathern (1992a: 36), in the 'enterprise culture', 'choice has become the privileged vantage from which to measure all action'. Strathern also suggests (1992b) that choice has come to be constitutive of personhood: not to choose is to be less of a person, and conversely, personhood is secured through the exercise of choice. So, if mothers' personhood is threatened through their relationship to children's 'needs', the language of choice may be a means of reinstating that personhood:

Rachel: I feel that I chose to have them [children] and, you know, therefore it's a relationship that I chose to have and therefore it's a very necessary one...
SL: When you say that it's a necessary relationship, what does that mean?
Rachel: Well, because I feel they need me.
Elizabeth: I suppose you sacrifice your identity to a large extent. Maybe it's different nowadays because so many more women go out to work

and have a career as well as a family. Whereas I was at home for twenty years. ... I certainly don't regret it. I felt I did the right thing in being there, particularly when the children were young. ... And I don't consider I've sacrificed a career or anything because I made a choice. So I had my - my job there, really. ... Sacrificed is the wrong word, really, because it was a choice[17].

For both Rachel and Elizabeth, it is choice which structures their maternal stories. Yet what both women also express is the very rigidity of the system of choice: their choices, and hence their desires, are literally embodied in their children, whose imperative needs must then structure the mother's life. Having made the choice to have children, having satisfied their desires in this way, there can be no expression of discontent. Choice, in other words, brings with it a responsibility, and mothers must carry in themselves the responsibility for exercising this choice. So, for Elizabeth, choice wipes out any potential for understanding her life in terms of sacrifice. For Rachel, her choice sets up a chain of causation ('and therefore ... and therefore ...') the end result of which is her children's neediness. In a sense, she has exercised choice *on behalf of* her children (since they did not ask to be born). Therefore, her children's choices, or desires, must be reinstated in the form of needs.

If the exercise of choice is linked with consumption (Keat, 1990; Strathern, 1992a) what, if anything, is being consumed? What is being 'consumed', in a sense, is a form of self-enhancement - in this case, not the enhancement of the selves of the women, but the enhancement of the selves of their children, which is mothers' principal task. The responsibility for producing children's properly socialized selves lies with mothers and, conversely, if there are any problems, it is mothers who are likely to be blamed (Caplan and Hall-McCorquodale, 1985; Bradley, 1989). The choice to produce children carries the injunction to produce (psychologically) *perfect* children. Since the only way to do this is to meet children's 'needs', mothers should subordinate themselves to those needs. Their desires are harnessed to this aim; having made the choice, and having had their desires fulfilled, mothers should not expect anything *else*. As in Kellmer Pringle's 'child-care commandment', the language of choice erases the possibility of further desires on the mother's part.

Yet Rachel narrates her younger self as full of desires, representing herself as a girl who constantly demanded (and got) her own way, to such an extent that her mother's nickname for her was 'Rachel-Wanting'. But now, Rachel hardly seems to express any wants at all (other than the desire to be a good mother), and, when she does, she is clear that those wants should be subordinated to those of her children. Rachel presents herself as a mother whose life is totally organized around the desires of her children. Her maternal narrative is marked by a subjugation of her own wants to those of her children. Of all the woman I spoke to, Rachel was most explicitly critical of the nuclear family, yet she remains within it because she believes it is the best way available to her in which to bring up children, and her children have, in any case, expressed their demand that she should live within it. When she quarrels with her husband, she says that she feels guilty because she fears that it will make her children insecure. And she does not engage in pursuits she enjoys if her children veto them.

How did this wanting and demanding girl become the woman who seems to give her own wants hardly any legitimacy at all? Where did Rachel-Wanting go? The language of choice hardly seems sufficient to contain all this desire. As I discuss below, Rachel uses humour to express a sense of herself outside of the position 'mother' (and, apparently, to antagonise her children!). But she also defers her longings on to a time in the future when, as she sees it, she will not have to meet her children's needs: indeed, she says that she will refuse to do so. She will not, for example, have to live in a marriage - an institution she sees as only viable 'in terms of bringing up kids':

> I think the nicest old age I can imagine for myself would be living in somewhere like Knightsbridge, with a cat or two, and just tottering around ... tottering off to Harrods for your half pound of mince [laughs]. But not with a man about. I mean what use are they by then?

Rachel's projection of the fulfilment of her desires into the future renders her narrative of herself as one in which her desires are not so much lost as deferred: perhaps Rachel-Wanting is only temporarily absent. In the interim, however, her use of the language of choice, like Elizabeth's, inscribes her as a person, since only persons can 'choose'. 'Choice' is a problematic discourse, implying, in this context, the responsibility for tremendous self-management on the mother's part, but it does at least open up some space within which mothers can inscribe themselves as persons.

Redefining 'need'
Another way in which women asserted a sense of themselves was through a process of defining their children's needs, such that they (at least at times) coincided with their own. But rather than the women's needs-claims being subsumed under those of their children, as is the case with many cultural representations of mothering, in the women's formulations, children had to recognize the *separate* needs-claims of the mother: indeed, they *needed* to do so.

> **Kate:** I think [to be a good mother] you've got to have endless supplies of love and concern about the needs of the other person, but at the same time you've got to be able to set boundaries so that you're not totally washed out by it all. You've got to be able to provide yourself with time and some kind of nurturing from someone else, or perhaps from the child, even, erm, so that you can get refreshed. I think you can be a very bad mother if you put so much into it that you're left drained yourself and left with nothing. It's a matter of, erm, setting limits, I suppose, both in time and space.

Kate uses the imperative constitution of children's needs to make claims about maternal needs. In other words, maternal needs-claims (which might otherwise be de-legitimated as 'desires') are legitimated on the basis that they meet children's needs. In a reversal of more customary discourses, Kate, and other women who redefined 'need' in this way, is able to inhabit the category 'good mother' at the same time as asserting her own separate existence.

Several women presented their own and their children's needs as congruent in this way, most often in accounts of divorce and separation. All of the women who had been divorced expressed feelings of guilt in relation to their children. For a woman to end a relationship with her children's father may, after all, be an undeniable manifestation of her own wants. Seeing the situation in terms of benefits to the child is a means of minimizing the tensions which must inevitably occur as a result of this exercise of wants. But not all women were able to see their divorces in this light. The extract below is taken from a group discussion; the women present had been talking about the difficulties of being a single parent, of having to provide everything for the child[ren]. While Lynne presents her own needs and those of her children as congruent, Dawn is clearly not convinced:

> **Lynne:** When I don't come up with the ironed shirt, or the cake, or whatever it is I'm supposed to come up with as this perfect mother, I just say, 'Well, failed again!' Because I just will not try and be this perfect person, for them or for anybody. You know, they have to learn that I have limitations and not expect everybody else to be perfect. ... But I think it makes them into better people. Recognition of the parent's need, I think, makes them into more understanding people, so I don't feel guilty about it.
> **Dawn:** Well, I suppose it was a constructive learning for them, but I can't say it's one I would have chosen.

Even women who do seem convinced by this marrying of needs, however, do not sustain this position throughout their accounts. Most of these women still saw themselves as 'losing the self'. Bringing together children's and mother's needs in this way, then, represents some resolution to this loss, but only a partial and temporary one.

Escaping motherhood

> You might believe that Daisy has no gaiety left in her, but this is not true, since she lives outside her story as well as inside (Carol Shields, *The Stone Diaries*, p.123).

I want to finally consider another technique used by the women to recoup a sense of self which they saw as 'lost' during motherhood. This was the assertion of a self which 'escaped' from the subject-position 'mother'. Their accounts here are a reminder that 'mother' did not constitute the whole of these women's subjectivities or selves: they lived outside of the maternal story, as well as inside it. These women are daughters, lovers, friends, sisters. Some of these positions sit more easily with contemporary Euroamerican conceptualizations of personhood than the position 'mother'[18]. So, some women straightforwardly dissociated themselves from the signifier 'mother' at various points in their accounts. Anna, for example, sees 'all mothers' as having to mediate between family members. Yet she does not see herself as having to do this. In our first interview, she said:

> **Anna:** Mothers are always in that awkward position in the middle, aren't they? Having to balance all kinds of loyalties.

In the second interview, we returned to the subject, and I asked her:

> **SL:** Have you ever been in that position?
> **Anna:** Erm, no ...... I honestly don't think I have.

Is Anna not a 'mother' then? Her account strongly suggests that her self-identity is bound up, not only with the category 'mother', but with the category 'good mother'. She is confident about her motherhood and clearly considers she has done it reasonably well. At the same time, Anna wants to dissociate herself from what she sees as conventional motherhood, which she associates with her own mother. Anna, then, both is and is not a mother: she refuses to align herself with what she sees as a 'stereotypical' type of motherhood; but, like the other women here, she considers that maternal wants should be subordinated to childhood needs, and that to do so is the mark of a 'good mother'. What is important, though, is that Anna represents her maternity as not encapsulating her self. Lynne goes further, in representing her mothering as almost antithetical to her self:

> **Lynne:** The time that those responsibilities [of child-care] take up is time that's taken away from me to be myself.

Like Anna, Lynne considers herself to be a good (if imperfect) mother. And, like Anna, she represents her self as 'escaping' the category mother. There is an excess to the self in these women's accounts, something which cannot be contained within the position 'mother'.

For other women, it was the intervention of an alternative category - that of 'child' - which assisted their dissociation from motherhood. The category 'child' is characterized by both its neediness and its personhood, so the taking up of childish/like behaviour can be a way of reasserting selfhood. For example, Rachel, who, as I noted earlier, presented herself as without desire in her relationship with her children, found ways of breaking out of this maternity, by behaving in ways which her children (and especially her daughter) found out of place with Rachel's position as 'mother'. Rachel draws attention to herself, asserting a presence within a category which is otherwise marked only by its responsiveness. And, in doing so, she seems to relish her daughter's discomfort:

> **Rachel:** I embarrass her a lot, she says [laughs]. I think she probably thinks I'm a bit, erm - a bit immature for my age. She says I don't act like other mothers.
> **SL:** What d' you do that's so embarrassing?

Rachel: Well, I go round town singing and that's no good. I laugh too much and that's no good. Erm, I take my clothes off too happily. ... So that kind of thing is totally embarrassing. ... She's often said, 'Why don't you act like other mothers?' ... That's the thing - 'So-and-so's mother would never do that'. That kind of thing. ... And perhaps I do it all the more then.

If the subject-position 'mother' is one in which selfhood is eclipsed, and experienced as 'lost', then by placing themselves outside of this category, however temporarily, women may be able to regain the lost (pre-maternal) self. But it is important to reiterate that there is no doubt that any of these women consider themselves to be 'good mothers'. Within their accounts of dissociation, then, they engage in a process of *redefining* 'good motherhood'. Despite their heavy investments in a discourse which is problematic - the discourse of childhood and its imperative 'need' for autonomy - these women are in no way 'cultural dupes'. While their maternal narratives indicate a loss of the self, the self is inscribed through other narratives within their accounts - narratives which inscribe them as persons. In this way, the assigned category 'mother' can be taken up and used as a source of individuality, and these women can become mothers who are not 'really' mothers, but who, nevertheless, are 'good mothers'.

Concluding remarks

The type of mothering represented in these middle-class women's accounts is so normalized, so taken for granted as being 'right', that it has generally escaped problematization. Against this standard, other understandings of motherhood and childhood can so easily be pathologized.

This in itself is a question which needs serious consideration: otherwise, conventional and normalized accounts of motherhood will continue to pathologize those women already marked as 'Other'. My aim in this paper, however, has been to expose some of the dangers of techniques of normalization for those mothers who are apparently 'getting it right'.

There is no asocial space to which any of us could retreat - no space 'above' or 'beyond' power. Even the resistances in which we engage are not outside of the workings of power: as Michel Foucault argues, 'everything is dangerous' (Foucault, 1983: 343). However, as Daly and Reddy (1991: 3) suggest, we can engage in a 'revisioning' of motherhood. My contention in this article has been that a radical revisioning of motherhood requires a revisioning of childhood and of personhood, and an examination of the political interests and political preoccupations which currently underwrite all of these categories.

Notes

1 Important exceptions to this neglect include Urwin 1985; Walkerdine and Lucey, 1989; Woollett and Phoenix, 1991.

2 I take this phrase from Winnicott, 1964, although several later authors have also made use of it (see, e.g. Bettelheim, 1987; Adcock and White, 1990. See also Ruddick, 1990 and Phillips, 1996 on the good-enough feminist mother). Although the phrase 'good-enough mother' does suggest that perfection is neither necessary or desirable, a close look at work which uses the term indicates that to be 'good enough' is a considerable achievement, and, for Winnicott at least, involves the almost total subjugation of the maternal self to that of the child.

3 See, for example, Walkerdine and Lucey, 1989; Walkerdine, 1990, 1997; Jenks, 1996; James et al, 1998.

4 See, for example, Chodorow 1978; Ruddick 1990; Phillips 1996. For an excellent critique of the failure to problematize children's needs, see Doane and Hodges, 1992.

5 As Nancy Fraser (1989) points out, 'needs talk' tends to centre around the *satisfaction,* rather than the *definition* of need: hence questions such as how needs get to be established as 'real', in what circumstances, and by whom, become occluded.

6 This is the line explicitly taken by writers like Winnicott, who argues that 'The needs of infants and small children are not variable: they are inherent and unalterable' (Winnicott 1964, 179). More recently, and from a feminist perspective, Sara Ruddick (1990) suggests that a basic, universal category of maternal work exists in relation to a fixed and universal set of children's 'needs'. For a critique of the universalizing of children's needs, see Woodhead, 1990.

7 'Autonomy' as an ideal type of the self has already been the focus of much feminist criticism. It has been argued, for example, that the social valorization of autonomy sets up a norm against which women's 'relational selves' come to be seen as lacking (Gilligan, 1982; Gilligan and Rogers, 1993; Jordan, 1993). However, my critique is on somewhat different grounds to this, as I will go on to argue. I see the postulating of *both* autonomy *and* relationality as properties of the self as setting up specific norms against which persons can be measured and found wanting. Further, mapping out these properties onto gendered selves 'fixes' and unifies those selves: for example, it obscures the ways in which women may take up 'autonomous' positions, and men, 'relational' ones (see Sayers, 1986).

8 In Eichenbaum and Orbach's work, for example, autonomy arises out of the fulfilment of 'dependency needs' (Eichenbaum and Orbach, 1982; 1992). This is a theme which has remained remarkably constant since Winnicott in the 1950s.

9 See, for example, Kellmer Pringle's (recently republished) work, The *Needs of Children*, in which she equates 'democratic' with middle-class and 'authoritarian' with working-class parents.

10 Important exceptions here include Walkerdine and Lucey 1989; Walkerdine 1990, 1997; Woollett and Phoenix 1991; Singer 1992.

[11] The term 'parents' is now commonly used in child-care advice and other sites in preference to 'mothers'. However, there is evidence that this is little more than a linguistic device: it is clear that 'motherhood' and 'fatherhood' are not positioned equivalently, and also that, within this kind of representation, 'parents' often means 'mothers'. See Marshall, 1991.

[12] For analyses of the place of mothers in the 'underclass' debates in Britain and North America, see Collins, 1991; Morris, 1994; Slipman, 1994; de Acosta, 1997; Skeggs, 1997.

[13] I asked the women to self-define both class and 'race'. Defining class at all can be a minefield, especially since women are often defined by the class position of their male partners: but I wanted to know about the women's perceptions of their own class position. In fact, their self-definitions accorded with the 'official' definitions of class used in Britain, measured by the Standard Occupational Classification. All of these women were in, or had last been in, heterosexual relationships. With a small-scale study like this, I am not, of course, claiming that the findings could be generalized or that they are representative. I am more interested in getting at the complexity of the women's accounts. For a full account of the methodology, see Lawler, 1999.

[14] Hence, these women occupied a specific kind of middle-class position, marked in terms of education and knowledge, rather than primarily in terms of economic wealth.

[15] All names are pseudonyms. Throughout this article, the following are used to mark extracts from interview transcripts: three dots (...) indicate that material has been edited; six dots (......) indicate a pause; square brackets indicate non-verbal communication, e.g. [laughs].

[16] This is especially so in the wake of the new reproductive technologies. See Strathern, 1992a for a fuller analysis.

[17] This is not the place to discuss Elizabeth's alignment of self-actualization, or 'having an identity' with careers, but it is worth noting that this was an alignment made by most of the middle-class women, unlike working-class women who saw the home as offering greater potential for self-actualization. Clearly, these differential alignments are connected with classed divisions in the paid labour market, and with different meanings and conditions attached to different forms of work.

[18] However, as I have already indicated, their autonomy - and hence their personhood - is militated against by the fact of their femaleness.

References

Adcock, M. and White, R. 1990, (eds.), *Good Enough Parenting: A Framework for Assessment*, London: British Agencies for Adoption and Fostering.

Ambert, A-M., 1994, 'An international perspective on parenting', *Journal of Marriage and the Family*, no. 56: 529-543.

Benjamin, J., 1988, *The Bonds of Love: Psychoanalysis, Feminism and the Problem of Domination*, New York: Pantheon.

Bettelheim, B., 1987, *A Good Enough Parent: The Guide to Bringing Up Your Child*. London: Thames and Hudson.

Bradley, B., 1989, *Visions of Infancy: A Critical Introduction to Child Psychology,* Oxford: Blackwell.

Caplan, P. and Hall-McCorquodale, I., 1985, 'Mother-blaming in major clinical journals', *American Journal of Orthopsychiatry* 55: 345-353.

Chodorow, N., 1978, *The Reproduction of Mothering: Psychoanalysis and the Sociology of Gender,* London: University of California Press.

Collins, P. H., 1991 *Black Feminist Thought: Knowledge, Consciousness and the Politics of Empowerment.* New York: Routledge.

Daly, B. O. and Reddy, M. T., 1991, 'Narrating mothers', in B.O. Daly and M.T. Reddy, 1991, (eds.), *Narrating Mothers: Theorizing Maternal Subjectivities.* Knoxville: University of Tennessee Press.

de Acosta, M., 1997, 'Single mothers in the USA: unsupported workers and mothers', in S. Duncan and R. Edwards, (eds.), *Single Mothers in an International Context,* London: UCL Press.

Doane, J. and Hodges, D., 1992, *From Klein to Kristeva: Psychoanalytic Feminism and the Search for the 'Good Enough' Mother,* Ann Arbor: University of Michigan Press.

Eichenbaum, L. and Orbach, S., 1982 *Outside In ... Inside Out: Women's Psychology: A Feminist Approach,* Harmondsworth: Penguin.

Eichenbaum, L. and Orbach, S., 1992, *Understanding Women,* London: Penguin.

Everingham, C., 1994, *Motherhood and Modernity: an Investigation Into the Rational Dimension of Mothering,* Buckingham, Open University Press.

Ewick, P. and Silbey, S., 1994, 'Subversive stories and hegemonic tales: toward a sociology of narrative', *Law and Society Review* 29, 2: 197-226.

Foucault, M., 1979, (trans. A. M. Sheridan) *Discipline and Punish: the Birth of the Prison,* Harmondsworth: Penguin.

Foucault, M., 1982, 'The subject and power', in H. Dreyfus and P. Rabinow, *Michel Foucault: Beyond Structuralism and Hermeneutics,* Chicago: University of Chicago Press.

Foucault, M., 1983, 'On the genealogy of ethics: an overview of work in progress', in P. Rabinow, 1984, (ed.), *The Foucault Reader: an Introduction to Foucault's Thought,* Harmondsworth: Penguin.

Foucault, M., 1988, 'Technologies of the self', in L.H. Martin, H. Gutman and P.H. Hutton, (Eds.), *Technologies of the Self,* London: Tavistock.

Fraser, N., 1989, *Unruly Practices: Discourse and Gender in Contemporary Social Theory,* Cambridge: Polity.

Fraser, N. and Gordon, L., 1994, 'A Genealogy of Dependency: tracing a keyword of the U.S. welfare system', *Signs* 19 (2): 309-336.

Gilligan, C., 1982, *In a Different Voice: Psychological Theory and Women's Development,* Cambridge, MA: Harvard University Press.

Gilligan, C. and Rogers, A., 1993, 'Reframing daughtering and mothering: a paradigm shift in psychology', in J. van Mens-Verhulst *et al*, (eds.).

Haraway, D., 1987 '"Gender" for a Marxist Dictionary: the sexual politics of a word', in *Simians, Cyborgs and Women: The Reinvention of Nature,* London: Free Association Books.

James, A., Jenks, C. and Prout, A., 1998, *Theorizing Childhood,* Cambridge: Polity.

Jenks, C., 1996, *Childhood,* London, Routledge

Jordan, J., 1993 'The relational self: a model of women's development', in J. van Mens-Verhulst *et al,* (eds.).

Keat, R., 1990, 'Starship Britain or universal enterprise', in R. Keat and N. Abercrombie, (eds.), *Enterprise Culture,* London: Routledge.

Kellmer Pringle, M. K., 1974, 'Ten child care commandments', in I. Vallender and K. Fogelman, ((eds.)), *Putting Children First: A Volume in Honour of Mia Kellmer Pringle,* Lewes: The Falmer Press.

Kellmer Pringle, M. K., 1980 *The Needs of Children,* London: Hutchinson.

Lawler, S., 1995, 'I never felt as though I fitted': family romances in the mother-daughter relationship', in L. Pearce and J. Stacey, (eds.), *Romance Revisited,* London: Lawrence and Wishart.

Lawler, S., 1999, *Mothering the Self: Mothers, Daughters, Subjectivities,* London: Routledge.

Leach. P., 1988, *Baby and Child: from Birth to Age Five,* Harmondsworth: Penguin.Marshall, H., 1991, 'The social construction of motherhood: an analysis of childcare and parenting manuals', in A. Phoenix *et al,* (eds.).

Morris, L., 1994 Dangerous Classes: the Underclass and Social Citizenship, London: Routledge.

NSPCC, 1989, *Putting Children First: an NSPCC Guide,* London: NSPCC.

Phillips, S., 1996, *Beyond the Myths: Mother-Daughter Relationships in Psychology, History, Literature and Everyday Life,* London: Penguin.

Phoenix, A., Woollett, A. and Lloyd, E. 1991, (eds.), *Motherhood: Meanings, Practices and Ideologies,* London: Sage.

Ricoeur, P., 1991, (trans. D. Wood) Narrative identity, in D. Wood, (ed.), *On Paul Ricoeur: Narrative and Interpretation,* London: Routledge.

Rose, N., 1991, *Governing the Soul: The Shaping of the Private Self,* London: Routledge.

Rose, N., 1992, 'Engineering the human soul: analyzing psychological expertise', *Science in Context* 5, 2: 351-369.

Ruddick, S., 1990, *Maternal Thinking: Towards a Politics of Peace,* London: The Women's Press.

Sayers, J., 1986, *Sexual Contradictions: Psychology, Psychoanalysis and Feminism,* London: Tavistock.

Shields, C., 1994, *The Stone Diaries,* London: Fourth Estate.

Skeggs, B., 1997, *Formations of Class and Gender,* London: Sage.

Slipman, S., 1994, 'Would you take one home with you?', in C. Murray, *Underclass: the Crisis Deepens,* London: IEA Health and Welfare Unit.

Somers, M. R. and Gibson, G. D., 1994, 'Reclaiming the epistemological 'Other': narrative and the social constitution of identity', in C. Calhoun, (ed.), *Social Theory and the Politics of Identity,* Oxford: Blackwell.

Stainton Rogers, R. and Stainton Rogers, W., 1992, *Stories of Childhood: Shifting Agendas of Child Concern,* Hemel Hempstead: Harvester Wheatsheaf.

Strathern, M., 1992a, *After Nature: English Kinship in the Late Twentieth Century,* Cambridge: Cambridge University Press.

Strathern, M., 1992b, *Reproducing the Future: Anthropology, Kinship and the New Reproductive Technologies,* Manchester: Manchester University Press.

Urwin, C., 1985, 'Constructing motherhood: the persuasion of normal development', in C. Steedman, C. Urwin and V. Walkerdine, (eds.), *Language, Gender and Childhood,* London: Routledge and Kegan Paul.

van Mens-Verhulst, J., Schreurs, K. and Woertman, L., 1993, (eds.), *Daughtering and Mothering: Female Subjectivity Reanalysed,* London: Routledge.

Walkerdine, V., 1984, 'Developmental psychology and the child-centred pedagogy: the insertion of Piaget into early education', in J. Henriques, W. Hollway, C. Urwin, C. Venn and V. Walkerdine, 1984, *Changing the Subject: Psychology, Social Regulation and Subjectivity,* London: Methuen.

Walkerdine, V., 1990, *Schoolgirl Fictions,* London: Verso.

Walkerdine, V., 1997, *Daddy's Girl: Young Girls and Popular Culture,* London: MacMillan.

Walkerdine, V. and Lucey, H., 1989, *Democracy in the Kitchen: Regulating Mothers and Socialising Daughters,* London: Virago.

Winnicott, D. W., 1964, *The Child, the Family and the Outside World,* Harmondsworth: Penguin.

Winnicott, D. W., 1965, *The Family and Individual Development,* London: Tavistock.

Woodhead, M., 1990, 'Psychology and the cultural construction of children's need', in A. James and A. Prout, (eds.), *Constructing and Reconstructing Childhood,* London: Falmer Press.

Woollett, A. and Phoenix, A., 1991, 'Psychological views of mothering', in A. Phoenix *et al*, (eds.), *Motherhood: Meanings, Practices and Ideologies,* London: Sage.

National Identity and the Female Body

Sophie Nield

Nationalism, as the story is generally told, begins as Sleeping Beauty and ends as Frankenstein's monster. The nation . . . was awakened to her destiny, not by one handsome prince, but by a variety of distinguished servitors . . . And why had Sleeping Beauty been sleeping? She had been put to sleep, these servitors explained, by wicked kings and self-seeking aristocrats . . . Would Sleeping Beauty live happily ever after? Yes, indeed, but only after these wicked influences had been destroyed in the struggle now approaching. Yet in the course of that struggle, Sleeping Beauty began to develop some unlovely characteristics. On closer inspection, it transpired that she was in fact partly composed of lumps of flesh torn from other bodies politic. And further, the world was filling up with such creatures, all noisily awake, and all demanding attention and sympathy. Hordes of such fierce maidens filled the world, quarreling over the lands they wished to absorb.[1]

This is the opening paragraph of K.R. Minogue's (1967) monograph *Nationalism*. Minogue extricates himself from this analogy by asking rhetorically whether it is frivolous to compare 'the foremost ideology of the modern world with a fairy tale?' and arguing that no, this is acceptable, because nations themselves construct such fairy-tales around their origin and inevitability. What he does not question is his own gendering of the nation as female, as a 'beauty' waiting to be awoken, that, once wakened, reveals 'herself' as a grotesque and monstrous female body. Within this paragraph we have the two central and determining concerns of this essay. Firstly, the construction of narratives of continuity around nations, which are often relatively recent political constructions, causes them to be 'naturalized' as political entities consisting of human communities so 'natural' as to require no other definition than self-assertion. Secondly, my concern is with the emblematisation of nations as the female body. This, I will argue, is also rooted in an artificial 'naturalization': the use of the female body as emblem of an abstract idea begins in the alignment of women within society with 'nature' and not 'culture'. One naturalization authenticates the other in a discourse which becomes closed and circular. This is precisely the circularity of thought activated and demonstrated by Minogue above.

The allegorical female form is not a rarity. Most towns in Britain will have a version of Justice – a classical figure of a woman, blindfold, carrying scales and a sword, who stands atop the law courts. Anonymised female figures are often present in public statuary as Virtues. Victory as a woman is also familiar – monuments in Berlin, London, Paris, Rome, Vienna and New York all represent this incarnation of the apotheosis of the martial maid, Nike/Athena. Retrieved from her earlier pagan incarnation, she provides the mould for the chaste language of virtue, and becomes the model for Justice,

Prudence, Temperance and Fortitude. Athena herself was adopted as an emblem for Victorian Britain.

Marina Warner tells us that the allegorical female figure either wears armour, in order to demonstrate by deep association its law-abiding chastity, emblematic of its wholeness and impregnability, or it proclaims its virtue by abandoning protective covering. 'The breast of a woman, as distinct from the generic human bosom, acts as sign of nature . . . the exposed breast can signify a matron and nurturer, and a type of the protective state . . . Liberty's exposed breast signifies freedom from eroticism. . . . It extends and denies an erotic invitation. It is also a source of power, the original source of sustenance.'[2] The representation of a land as female taps into these connections, and will be the subject of analysis here. The placidity of the maternal figure, or even the martial maid whose victory 'redounds all the more blazingly to her causes because she is weak'[3] insert themselves into a wider set of discourses surrounding the mother, the virgin and the land: discourses rooted in a naturalization (and equation with 'nature') of motherhood and feminine virtues.

The recent revival of interest in the analysis of nations, nationalisms and the construction of national identities, informed by Benedict Anderson's (1983/1991) *Imagined Communities*, has emphasized the ways in which the nation-state must be imagined and symbolized before it can be seen to exist. Anderson's point of departure is the 'formal universality of the socio-cultural concept (of nationality)[4], when 'nations' themselves are often modern, artificial or constructed. Ernest Renan, writing in 1882 at the point of emergence of many nations in Europe, attempts to track their specificity. Unable to find a satisfactory and universally applicable set of criteria for the self-evidence of the existence of nations, he proposes a potential reason for the loyalty of the individual to their place of origin.

> A nation is a soul, a spiritual principle. Two things, which strictly speaking are just one, constitute this soul. One is in the past, the other is in the present. One is the common possession of a rich legacy of memories; the other is actual consent, the desire to live together, the will to continue to value the rich heritage that has been received in common. It presupposes a past; however, it is epitomized in the present by a tangible fact: consent.'[5]

Writing a hundred years later, Anderson, too, recognizes that 'nation-ness' is a 'cultural artifact of a particular kind'[6], in other words, one which seems to have no material existence or definable origin, and appears to exist through and in the mutual consent of the people to recognize that existence. He defines the nation as 'an imagined political community – imagined as both inherently limited and sovereign'[7].

The female figure as emblem is part of the rendering visible of this entity which only has existence as an imaginary. As Michael Walzer wrote 'The state is invisible; it must be personified before it can be seen, symbolized before it can be loved, imagined before it can be conceived.'[8] The symbolic representation of a nation is the site at which the imaginary

102

takes form in matter and is given definition and presence. It is where the ephemeral, tricky concept of nation is pinned down and made manifest; the coherent representation of Anderson's 'cultural artifact'. Attesting to the difficulty of imagining the state without symbols is the frequent personification of the state – Louis XIV's 'L'etat, c'est moi'. Likewise, the destruction or overthrow of a particular national regime or state often involves 'symbolcide' – the toppling of statues, the burning of flags, the desecration of monuments, all of which 'are' the previous regime.

Nations are not, of course, only emblematised as female, but the associations of nations with male figures often incorporate real male rulers – Lenin, Stalin, Hitler (apotheosized by the cry 'Germany is Hitler and Hitler is Germany' by Goebbels at the 1934 Party Rally) or at least, figures with agency. As Marina Warner reminds us, when John Bull or Uncle Sam express their anger, it is their own anger they express. Liberty does not express her own freedom (Warner 1996: 12). The nations which have a dominant male emblem often have parallel cults of motherhood, or rigid systems of 'honour' which reside in the chastity of women: one thinks here of 'Mother Russia' for example. The use of the female body in allegorizing virtues such as liberty, justice and so forth cannot therefore be read as empowerment of actual women. Rather, these representations serve to reinforce and reiterate already existing tropes of male agency and female passivity, which are naturalized within wider discourses connecting that which is rational and of 'culture' with the masculine, and that which is irrational and closer to 'nature' with the feminine. These elisions must also be seen as a socially constructed and maintained circle of discourses which act upon and through each other to perpetuate the status quo.

The implication of the elision of the 'female' with the 'natural' has several implications for the analysis of the image of the female body in the imaginings of states and nations. The evolution of societal forms has privileged the 'cultural' over the 'natural': the role of 'culture' is to transcend, or regulate 'nature', by turning natural conditions to its purposes. 'Culture' is therefore seen as both superior to 'nature', as it controls it, and as an exemplification of the dominance of humankind over the wild, the irrational and the uncontrolled.[9] In the context of this binary discourse, women, allied with 'nature' and therefore the 'uncontrolled', must be subject to regulation by the regulated and regulatory world of the 'cultural'. They are thus positioned as 'inferior'. Yet they also occupy a crucial position at the boundary of the nature – culture dichotomy: through their maternal and domestic positioning, it is women who undertake the initial culturing of the child. Initiation ceremonies, rites, or simply moments of cultural behaviour act to separate children (boys in particular) from the world of the mother and introduce them to the world of culture, and the father.

This has three key implications: firstly, the recognition that the realm of women (although societally imposed, and perhaps discursively maintained by women's assumed connection to the world of children) is something that the child must move above and away from in order to function properly within the cultural. This is also present in classic Freudian analysis, which recognizes the acquisition of language, the abjectification of the bodily (Kristeva 1982), and the suppression of 'primal' instincts as part of the child's entry into the realm of the law of the Father, or the oedipal patriarchy. The second point of relevance here lies in the positioning of the female and the family as needing protection from the invader or outsider. The integrity of the family, in other words, must be maintained in order to ensure the continuing passage of children into regulated society. Thirdly, and perhaps more crucially in this context, there are interconnecting positions ascribed to the mother. She is, in part, threatening and potentially dangerous, as she is connected with the realm of the natural and the irrational: her desires must be contained. Identification with the mother is powerful and yet continually repressed in culture: it must be diverted, and rendered acceptable. This occurs in part in the prefiguring, in her early symbolic separation from her children, of the ideal of maternal self-sacrifice, and the dual role ascribed to her in the abstract representations under discussion here, as well as wartime propaganda, as the sender of sons to war. The ideal of maternal self-sacrifice takes precedence over, and to some extent renders safe, the primal fear of the devouring mother: in post-Freudian terms the archaic pre-phallic mother whose world must be transcended in order for one to remain in the regulated world of rationality.

In her 'Thinking of . . . Her . . . as Ireland', Elisabeth Butler Cullingford writes that 'the allegorical identification of Ireland with a woman, variously personified as the Shan Van Vocht, Kathleen Ni Houlihan or Mother Eire, is so common as to be rhetorically invisible'. Of course, she continues, this identification is neither natural nor archetypal, rather, it is constructed through various complex and less complex cultural and iconographic representations. Cullingford's focus is specifically the constructions of a female Ireland in the work of the poets W.B Yeats, Padraic Pearse and Seamus Heaney. Yet she too positions the debate within the terms of the nature/culture schism:

> The representation of the land as female is a function of the patriarchal opposition between male Culture and female Nature, which defines women as the passive and silent embodiments of matter. Politically, the land is seen as an object to be possessed, or repossessed: to gender it as female, therefore, is to confirm and reproduce the social arrangements which construct women as material possessions, not as speaking subjects.[10]

The equating of women with the natural, and the resulting status of women within societal formations, does more than permit the naturalization of the metaphor of land as woman. It also, paradoxically, permits the use of the female body as emblem of the higher aspects of human culture. Firstly, actual women were historically neither expected nor permitted to have dealings in the worlds which these emblems signified: the law, medicine, government, war. Thus the presence of the female body as abstraction is simultaneously indifferent and peaceably maternal: it gives sanction to the formations and activities which it embodies and suffers to be undertaken in its name. Secondly, although subject to its control, the natural is the source of the cultural, and under its protection. Thus the highest aspects of culture must be seen to be in the interests of that source. They must be seen to be connected to that source, to originate from it, and to be legitimized by it. The cultural would seem to need the validation of the natural.

Of course, the emblematisations are subject to alteration. Cullingford tracks, through representations in Irish literature that figure Ireland as a woman, the shift from the land as a sexual partner (a mystical and dangerous woman) with whom the prospective King must have sex, to the introduction of the figures of the vulnerable but chaste maiden, and the self-sacrificing mother, who yields her sons up to war. 'The male myth of woman as pure mother demanding sacrifice of her sons has done untold damage to both women and men. It expresses a fear of the all-powerful mother of infancy that survives in adulthood as misogyny.' Cullingford argues that it is the association of female sexuality and death within which this connection is activated, noting that 'Acceptance of the connection between female sexuality and death as 'essential' or archetypal permits considerable ideological manipulation of the sacrificial mother as a mobilizing image in times of political crisis.'[11] I'm not sure I agree with this point in this uncomplex form. My sense is that by the time her image is utilized as war propaganda or statuary, the mother has become culturally *de*-sexualized, and while certainly the threat of uncontrolled female sexuality can be argued to be the cause of this social and ideological regulation, the representations are actually activated at a more sophisticated stage of their absorption into cultural imaginings. It seems on closer analysis of propaganda images that it is more the implied 'feminisation' of men that is at issue. A famous image for recruitment in Ireland shows a woman berating a man, as they look across to the continent in flames, 'Will you go? Or must I?'

In France, the relationship between abstractions of the female body as specifically maternal or virginal, and the changes in national imaginings and actual figurations of state are particularly interesting. Appearing at different moments are Liberty, Reason, La France, the Republic and Marianne, and it seems that there are two iconographic journeys in place: firstly, the transition from the 'mother' of the nation to a lighter, less matriarchal figure, and secondly, the alignment of concepts of liberty and state with different power structures.

Liberty is not specifically a 'national' image, but one so tied up with national identity as to make little difference. Liberty is the assurance of the 'sovereignty' which Benedict Anderson refers to as an integral facet of the imagined nation.

Derek Gregory tells us that the representation of Liberty as a woman derived from classical antiquity and had achieved a certain degree of iconographical status in France in the late 17th century. It is not surprising, therefore, that after the Revolution in 1789, a decree of 1792 adopted her as the seal of the Republic: 'the image of France in the guise of a woman, dressed in the style of antiquity, standing upright, her right hand holding a pike surrounded by a Phrygian cap or cap of liberty'[12]. Mona Ozouf, in her 1988 cultural history of the festivals of the French Revolution has interesting points to make about these figures. She writes that, although continuing a long tradition of the representation of abstract characteristics and 'national' identities as women (a practice which seems to originate in the rendering of conquered nations as female figures on coins by the ancient Romans), the festivals and monuments of the French Revolution were intended to signify beginning *again*:

> Beyond the *ancien regime* and the upheaval that brought it down, the Festival (of Federation, 1790) also seemed to be a restoration: this beginning was felt to be a beginning again. If the solemnity of the occasion was to have any sacral weight, something in it must go back to the mists of time. This would explain why in the speeches there are so many references to things being 'given back' to the French people . . . but the past that was being rejected was not the whole of the past: in destroying history, the men of the Revolution were merely retying a broken thread . . . with Nature herself, in her primal purity.'[13]

It would, on the surface of things, seem to be a contradiction that the Revolution, whose guiding principle was reason (a product of the cultural) should nevertheless emblematise itself as a woman. Ozouf notes that during the festivals, and more widely in the statuary inaugurated by the Revolutionary government, many of the female figures representative of the great revolutionary themes are blurred: it is Liberty who tends to appear variously depicted as Justice, Equality and Reason (Ozouf, 1988: 98-9). Reason is not frequently emblematised in her own right: the deity of the Festival of Reason in 1793 is actually Liberty. If, however, the signification is of a return to a '*natural*' state of reason, the contradiction is somewhat resolved. For Michelet, writing in 1846, France is a woman, loved by rich and poor alike, associated with nature and the eternal. He wrote 'History, which we . . . decline in the feminine . . . is a rude and savage male. Nature is a woman.'[14] Thus, we assume, the Revolution has installed 'natural' time, the time of women.

Significantly, though, despite this implication of a 'time of women', these emblems of women existed alongside a lived experience of actual women that had little relation to the characteristics embodied. Further, the Parisiennes who took so active a part in the overthrow of the monarchy and the storming of the Bastille, and who are deeply vilified for their wild behaviour by Burke (1790: 90), are rendered invisible by both the propaganda of virtue and the blank calm emblems. (Warner 1996: 287).

As Lynn Hunt has noted 'the collective violence of seizing Liberty and overthrowing the monarchy was effaced behind the tranquil visage and statuesque pose of an aloof Goddess.'[15]

Although the Revolution sought to overturn all existing structures of thought, it retained the use of abstractions of the female body as emblems. This, as we have seen, is a representational structure which, by its very mechanism, maintains the cultural positioning of actual women. Joan Landes writes:

... the assault on patriarchalism was limited both by force...and by the redirection of women's public and sentimental existence into a new allegory of republican, virtuous family life. Liberty herself is a profoundly ironic symbol, a public representation of a polity that sanctioned a limited domestic role for women . . . If Liberty represented woman, surely it was as an abstract emblem of male power and authority.[16]

The Revolutionaries are 'les enfants de la Patrie'; a figure of speech which not only signifies birth as a new beginning, but also the nation as mother, and by extension, female body. This emphasis on nature and motherhood was reflected in the *mise-en-scene* for the Feast of the Supreme Being in 1794, which gave particular prominence to pregnant women. It is a short journey from the sanctifying of the fecund body of the mother to the overprotection of the actual female body.

The status of the actual women of a nation is not necessarily altered as the personification or abstraction of the nation alters. Richard Kearney, cited in Cullingford, notes a change in Ireland from the daughter figure to the 'more militant mother-goddess of the 19th century onwards', yet notes that there is no concomitant shift in the 'social stereotypes of the Irish woman as pure virgin or equally pure son-obsessed mother.'[17] Further, Marina Warner notes that while Athena is being celebrated and Britannia is becoming universally recognized in the nineteenth century, this is mirrored by actual women's, lack of rights – over property, disposal of property, even her own sexual and reproductive autonomy (Warner, 1996: 126).

Marianne, the emblem of Republican France, again was an image that had a reasonably lengthy presence before her incorporation as national emblem. She appears in drama as early as 1637, according to Jeffrey, as a patriotic Jewish princess in revolt against Roman invaders, and reappears in various contexts until becoming the name adopted by the Republic in 1848.[18] Isabelle Julia continues the account:

One of the first concerns of the provisional government of 1848, immediately after the February rising, was to find a figurative representation of the idea of the Republic for purposes of self-assertion and propaganda. Memories of the great Revolution were still associated in peoples minds with the idea of bloodshed. It was therefore necessary to find an image that would be explanatory, reassuring, moderate, decorous and conciliatory. It seemed obvious that it would have to be a female figure: the image of the Republic merged with that of the nation *la Patrie*, and with that of the mother as shield and inspiration. The Republic was therefore personified in a young woman, beautiful, strong-willed and noble.[19]

We have here several important ramifications: firstly that the personification of a state or nation as a woman serves historically specific ends, such as the definition of a new kind of nation, or a move away from a previous administration. Secondly, it causes, whether deliberately or unselfconsciously, an uncritical continuance of the subordination of women within a 'rational' society through the mechanism detailed earlier. As long as the rhetorical device of the abstract female emblem endures, the premises within which it functions are not disrupted. These premises are the elision of women with the natural, from which the image draws its rhetorical power, and the circularity of discourses which causes the 'naturalization' of woman/nature to service the 'naturalization' of nation and vice versa. It would thus appear that there is no possibility of progressive change. There is also in this extract a repetition of Minogue's earlier assumption about the 'obviousness' of the selection of a female figure. It seems unfortunately to be as natural to the French artists of 1848 as to contemporary critics. Thirdly, we are able to conclude that the abstractions of Liberty, and even Marianne up to this point, have not been emblems of the nation, but rather emblems of particular political imaginaries which at different times constituted the nation of France. Gregory continues:

> In 1848 (Marianne) appeared on the second seal of the Republic wearing a diadem of corn with seven rays of the sun encircling her head in a spiked halo . . . a sunburst was the Bartholdi family emblem . . . still more significantly, it was intimately associated with the reign of Louis XIV, the Sun King. To adorn Liberty with a sunburst was thus in a sense to "crown" her, and thereby align her with a tradition of stable and conservative government.[20]

Bartholdi, the designer of the American Statue of Liberty, shifted the allusions of Liberty away from unbridled Nature in favour of an imagery of control and light (Warner 1996: 7). Not only is Liberty tamed and rendered more rational, but also, the incorporation of Royal imagery into her styling goes some way to conflating the emblems, and therefore the actualities, of the opposing political ideologies of France. Marina Warner appears to express confusion over the anomalous appearance of La France on the Pont Alexandre III, built in 1900 'because 'La France' traditionally personified royal France, while Marianne bodied forth La Republique, representative of liberty.'[21] It would seem, rather, that the two figures had become increasingly conflated since the aftermath of 1848. The figuration of the nation is not a separate entity from the nation itself. As I noted earlier, it is the site at which the nation as it is imagined becomes the nation as it is perceived. The one cannot change without the other.

A nation is a made thing: made within the precepts of 'culture', a consequence of reason and rationality. The constructed 'naturalness' of the nation has needed the constructed 'naturalness' of the female body as its emblem. Symbolically, the abstracted female body legitimates and naturalizes the structures it represents. Actually, it serves to perpetuate and maintain, not only them, but also more fundamental and structural divisions along gender lines within societies. 'It is because women continue to occupy the space of the Other that they lend themselves to allegorical use so well; if women had had a vote or a voice, Marianne would have been harder to accept as a universal figure of the ideal.'[22] The historical absence of a self-defined female identity permitted within the culture of the public sphere has left the female form subject to abstraction and determination from elsewhere. The Statue of Liberty, in New York, originally a gift from the people of France to the people of America, and built by Bartholdi, is hollow. Like the abstractions discussed in the course of this essay, she functions by permitting imaginings and desires to be projected onto and inside her emptiness.

In conclusion, though, I think there is a point of optimism. It would seem that it has become harder to appropriate the female form in the ways described here. The architects of the Millennium Dome in Britain had plans for a giant female form which would dominate a space dedicated to the highest in 'cultural' achievement. Once again, it seemed as though the 'natural' and maternal body would legitimize and overlook the 'cultural'. They had, however, to make an embarrassing U-turn, when it became clear that the now present and self-defining public voices of women would no longer permit their bodies to be abstracted in this way. The figure will be androgynous.

Notes

[1]   Minogue, K.R. *Nationalism*, London : Methuen 1967 p.7.
[2]   Warner, M. *Monuments and Maidens: the Allegory of the Female Form.* London: Vintage1996 p.281
[3]   ibid p.149
[4]   Anderson, B. *Imagined Communities.* London: Verso 1991 p.5
[5]   Renan, E. 'What is a Nation(1882) in Woolf, S. (ed) *Nationalism in Europe 1815 to the Present: A Reader.* London: Routledge 1996.
[6]   Anderson, op cit p.4
[7]   ibid. p.6
[8]   Waltzer, M. On the role of symbolism in political thought. *Political Science Quarterly* 82 p.194
[9]   Sherry Ortner's Is female to Male as Nature is to Culture? in Zimbalist Rosaldo, M. and L. Lamphere (eds) *Women, Culture and Society* California: Stanford University Press 1974 is particularly useful here.
[10] Cullingford, E.B. 'Thinking of her ... as ... Ireland': Yeats, Pearse and Heaney *Textual Practice* 4/1 Spring 1990 p.1
[11] ibid p.12
[12] Gregory. D. *Geographical Imaginations* London: Blackwell. 1994 p.330
[13] Ozouf, M. *Festivals of the French Revolution* Cambridge, Mass. 1988 p.34
[14] Michelet, J. *Le Peuple.* Preface. Quoted in Roland Barthes, *Michelet* Oxford: Blackwell 1987 p.198.
[15] Hunt, L' Engraving the Republic: prints and Propaganda in the French Revolution *History Today* October 1980 p.14 cited in Warner op. cit p.287
[16] Landes, J. *Women and the Public Sphere in the age of the French Revolution.* Ithaca: Cornell University Press 1988 p.159, cited in Gregory op.cit. p.331

[17]   Kearney, R. 'Myth and Motherland' in *Ireland's Field Day* University of Notre Dame Press 1986 p.76. cited in Cullingford, op. cit. p.7

[18]   Jeffrey, I. Introduction *La France: Images of Woman and Ideas of Nation 1789-1989* South Bank Centre Exhibition Catalogue 1989 p.27

[19]   Julia, I 'Daughters of the Century' ibid p.90

[20]   Gregory op.cit p.331

[21]   Warner op.cit p.27

[22]   ibid p.292.

References

Burke, E., 1912. *Reflections on the Revolution in France.* (1790) London.

Kristeva, J., 1982. *Powers of Horror: An essay on Abjection.* trans Leon S. Roudiez New York: Columbia University Press.

Locating Gender: Space and Place in Heritage Tourism

Cara Aitchison

Previous gender research has identified and analysed the symbiotic relationship between hegemonic masculinism and nationalism (Yuval Davis and Anthias, 1989; Enloe, 1989; and Walby, 1992). Less frequently discussed, however, is the role that nationalism plays within tourism promotion (McCrone, Morris and Kiely, 1995). Discussions of the interconnectedness of gender, nationalism, and tourism therefore require engagement with the multiple discourses reflected by a range of disciplines and subject fields. In addition to the discourses of gender studies and nationalism, this chapter attempts to examine the *means* and *media* through which gendered representations of nationalism are created, and the *sites, spaces* and *places* within which such representations are constructed. Drawing on previous work by Edensor and Kothari (1994), cultural tourism is viewed as a means by which heritage-related media are used to convey one discourse of gendered Scottish identity derived from a geography of heritage tourism in the sites, spaces and places in and around Stirling.

The relationship between geography and leisure and tourism research is well established (Barbier, 1984; Carlson, 1980; Coppock, 1982; Mowl and Turner, 1995). Since the publication of these earlier articles, however, the discipline of geography has experienced radical and transformative developments in the form of 'the cultural turn' exemplified within 'the new cultural geography'. Recent links between geography and tourism or leisure have, arguably, been witnessed most closely in relation to studies of gender relations, gender identities and sexualities. This evolving discourse of geography and gender has been conceptualised in the form of *spatialised feminism* and *gendered space*. This chapter offers an appraisal of these conceptual developments before embracing the discourse of geography's cultural turn to provide a critical reading of Stirling as a heritage tourism destination.

From spatialised feminism to gendered space

There is a well articulated literature within geography examining the gendered nature of space, place and landscape, but only recently has the new cultural geography begun to conceptualise and theorise gendered *leisure and tourism* spaces. The underpinning literature of spatialised feminism and gendered space now spans over two decades and McDowell (1993a) has identified Burnett (1973) as producing the first paper which discussed gender issues in geography. Burnett, together with other authors from this era, were largely concerned with issues related to either gender and urban space, or gender and 'third world' development. Massey (1984), for example, added a feminist perspective to previous work analysing spatial and social divisions of work and labour. Horst (1981) edited the first book by geographers on 'third world' women and built on previous work which had failed to recognise a gender dimension to the spatial relations of global capitalism.

This early body of feminist knowledge within geography has been referred to by McDowell as collectively forming a type of 'spatialised feminism'. To provide a full and comprehensive review of the literature on geography and gender is beyond the scope of this chapter which merely aims to highlight the area of literature in question and to outline key theoretical developments in the discourse of gendered space as it relates to heritage tourism. Moreover, this literature has already been reviewed thoroughly by a number of feminist geographers (Garcia-Ramon *et al.*, 1988; McDowell, 1993a, 1993b; McDowell and Sharp, 1997; Peake, 1989; Women and Geography Study Group, 1997). However, definitions of both spatialised feminism and gendered space are required here.

Spatialised feminism refers to feminist analysis which identifies and explains the spatial dimensions of power relations between the sexes. Spatial dimensions can be viewed as including the differential use, control, power and domination of space, place and landscape for social, economic and environmental purposes. Analyses of *gendered space* refocus attention from the recognition of inequality to the recognition of difference and this theme has been developed by the recent cultural turn in geography. Since the mid 1980s, therefore, feminist geography has shifted its attention from identifying and evaluating gender differences in spatial relations and patterns to identifying and explaining the social and symbolic constructions of gender and spatial relations; in other words, the spatiality of gender (Mowl and Turner, 1995).

It was Soja (1985) who first introduced the concept of 'spatiality' to emphasise the socially produced and interpreted nature of space. Contemporary cultural geography demonstrates that space, place and landscape - including landscapes of leisure and tourism - are not fixed but are in a constant state of transition as a result of continuous struggles of power and resistance among and between the diversity of landscape providers, users and mediators. The new cultural geography therefore provides a meeting ground for the anti-foundationalist movements of postmodernism, post-structuralism and post-colonialism and its analyses attempt to embrace the complexity of spatiality rather than engaging in the spatial determinism of the early twentieth century or the grand narratives of structuralism from a decade or so ago.

To date, the new cultural geography appears to have focused on consumption rather than production in analyses of leisure and tourism identities. This has been evident in research related to the consumption of leisure and tourism phenomena such as food, fashion and holidays (Mort, 1996; Bell and Valentine, 1997; Forrest and Clift, 1998). One area, however, where attention has been paid to both the production and consumption of gendered space and place has been in relation to leisure and tourism landscapes (Daniels and Cosgrove, 1988; Bender, 1993).

Symbolic and 'Other' landscapes

Theories emphasising the social construction of landscape have illustrated that landscapes are produced, not as physical or objective realities but as 'a cultural image, a pictorial way of representing, structuring and symbolising surroundings' (Daniels and Cosgrove, 1988: 1). Landscape is therefore seen to represent a social and cultural 'geography of the imagination' where social relations and frequently reflected in cultural symbols: 'Whether written or painted, grown or built, a landscape's meanings draw on the cultural codes of the society for which it was made (Rose, 1993: 89).

The new cultural geography has, however, guided against the identification of any direct or simplistic relationship between the material and the symbolic. This 'unharnessing of the symbolic and the sociological', identified by Bondi (1992b: 166), has led some commentators to view such poststructuralist analyses of landscape as having unharnessed their evaluations from any theoretical perspective which provides a sufficiently rigorous analysis of social and material power. Shurmer-Smith and Hannam (1994), in *Worlds of Desire, Realms of Power: a cultural geography*, therefore attempt to address such a critique by providing a series of explorations which analyse the power of the spectacle and the monument. Much of the cultural geography literature referred to above has also been instrumental in developing theories of both gendered power and resistance, together with theories revealing the gendered construction of dualisms and binary oppositions.

The conceptual development of gendered power and resistance has been evident in the work of cultural geographers who have examined the contested and negotiated nature of space and place. Of particular note has been recent work which has addressed the inter-relationships between spatiality and sexuality but such analyses have yet to be extended to an evaluation of heritage production and consumption (Bell, 1991; Bell and Valentine, 1995, Duncan; 1996).

Within feminist geography, the gendered construction of dualisms and binary oppositions has been revealed in relation to the dichotomies of nature/culture, urban/rural, masculine/feminine (Bondi, 1992a: Rose, 1993). The post-Enlightenment adoption of such dichotomies within western society is founded on, and subsequently reproduces, construction of 'the Other' in relation to space and place. The following sections attempt to illustrate how the construction of 'the Other' is central to the gendered representation of heritage. Rose (1995: 116) explains the process of constructing 'the Other' or 'Othering' as 'defining where you belong through a contrast with other places, or who you are through a contrast with other people'. Characterised by binary divides, this process inevitably defines norms and deviants, centres and margins, cores and peripheries, the powerful and the powerless. In the case of Stirling, hegemonic masculinity is defined as central to the nationalist struggle and women are either marginalised or invisibilised from the representation of heritage.

The construction of dualisms or binary opposites is inherently related to the construction of 'the Other'. Drawing on the work of de Beauvoir (1949) and Cixous (1983), it is possible to identify three fundamental relationships within this process. First, the construction of 'the Other' is dependent upon a simultaneous construction of 'the Same', or something from which to be 'Other' to. Secondly, this relationship is one of power whereby that which is defined as 'Same' is accorded greater power and status than that which is defined as 'Other'. Thirdly, that which is defined as 'Other' is accorded a gender and this gender is always female. This three-fold relationship of gendered power is evident in the visibility and centrality of hegemonic masculinity within Stirling's heritage tourist attractions. The construction of binaries and the identification of 'Others' is similarly central to the maintenance of heteropatriarchy as represented by Stirling's masculinist iconography:

> This rough sketch of gender gives us a clue to understanding the political reasons for the substantializing view of gender. The institution of a compulsory and naturalised heterosexuality requires and regulates as a binary relation in which the masculine term is differentiated from the feminine term, and this differentiation is accomplished through the practices of heterosexual desire. The act of differentiating the two oppositional moments of the binary results in a consolidation of each term, the respective internal coherence of sex, gender, and desire (Butler, 1990: 23).

In contrast to this 'marking' of women as 'the Other', however, Irigaray suggests that women cannot be marked out as different from men by a culture which only defines that which is male. As Butler (1990: 10) states, 'For Irigaray, the female sex is not a 'lack' or an 'Other' that imminently and negatively defines the subject in its masculinity. On the contrary, the female sex eludes the very requirements of representation.' Irigaray's perspective is that of women as invisibilised by both culture and linguistic representations which have no method of describing that which lies outside phallogocentric language. Indeed, Stirling's heritage tourism attractions are visibly masculinist and women are largely absent from the heritage landscape which has been mapped out in the spaces and places in and around the town.

Stirling: locating gender in a heritage landscape
Stirling has emphasised both the tourist spectacle and the symbolic monument in an attempt to create an identity of place which distinguishes the town and surrounding countryside from competing destinations. Traditionally, this identity has been constructed around the image of Stirling as 'The Gateway to the Highlands' implying a short-stay tourist destination through which visitors pass en-route to the Scottish highlands. To encourage longer stays and greater income generation, both the local tourist board and the local council attempted to market the area as 'Royal Stirling' and 'Historic Stirling' during the late 1980s and early 1990s. Marketing literature developed since that time emphasises both hegemonic masculinity and nationalism by promoting identification and reification of Robert the Bruce, William Wallace and Rob Roy MacGregor, alongside frequent

references to Stirling Castle as a royal residence of the Stuart Kings.

The production of *Braveheart*, the Hollywood blockbuster which sanctified the life of William Wallace, provided a timely brand image for Stirling's heritage tourism industry. The discourse of *Braveheart* conveyed a particular identity for gender and nation in its foregrounding of both hegemonic masculinity and nationalism. With significant increases in both domestic and international tourism, there seems little doubt that *Braveheart* captured the popular imagination and that the cultural industry, reflected by films such as *The Bruce*, and *Rob Roy*, in addition to *Braveheart* itself, has acted as a catalyst for the cultural tourism industry.

In addition to the links between the cultural industry and heritage tourism, Tilley (1993) stresses the importance of the relationship between architecture and landscape. Here the emphasis is on the interaction between the built environment and the natural environment which can create a specific sense of place and power. Bender (1993: 10), introducing Tilley's work, comments that:

> architecture acts as a lens for perceiving the landscape around monuments. Its relationship with the landscape may prove a powerful means for legitimizing power relations and naturalizing social order.

The representations of both William Wallace and Robert the Bruce occupy the landscape in a number of forms: statues at focal points within and around the town; street names; public houses; tourism promotion signs and symbols; corporate logos; and promotional material reflecting civic pride. All can be read critically as conveying a very particular sense of heritage founded on dominant discourses of nationalism and hegemonic masculinity.

Braveheart country: representations of gender and nationalism

Sharp (1996: 97) comments that: 'National identity is a central aspect of contemporary subjectivity and yet, certainly within the discipline of geography, its articulation with gender has largely been ignored'. She goes on to state that, 'The symbols of nationalism are not gender neutral but in enforcing a national norm, they implicitly construct a set of gendered norms' (1996: 98). This section explores these concepts and assertions by examining the representation of gender and nationalism in the sites, spaces and places in and around Stirling.

Representations of nationalism and hegemonic masculinity are foregrounded by the Wallace Monument which was refurbished to incorporate a variety of new visual displays in time to benefit from the additional tourists generated by the film *Braveheart*. The 220 foot high tower overlooks Stirling and the River Forth and was originally completed in 1869 as a monument to William Wallace who had led the defeat of Edward I of England at the Battle of Stirling Bridge in 1297.

Heritage production within the monument relies on written text, visual imagery and music to recreate the past. Pictures, statues, audio-visual displays, technology induced drama, and costume, combine to create engenderd and nationalist representations of heritage. Tourists entering the monument are overlooked by a bronze of Wallace with his sword drawn and the two-handed broadsword is then displayed on the first floor of the monument as part of a display recounting Wallace's life-long 'struggle' against the English. In a dramatised reconstruction, a talking head of the captured William Wallace evokes nationalist and masculinist pride with his impassioned plea: 'Men must have their power. They seek to influence, to strengthen their position, to be seen as something in other men's eyes'. In this scene, Wallace is constructed as the protector and voice of the nation where the nation could be seen as passive and feminine. Rose (1993) emphasises the feminisation of landscape as a means of portraying woman as nature and man as culture, or woman as the passive background upon which man acts out the foreground. Here, there is a sense in which landscape becomes the nation and culture becomes nationalism: nationalism is the masculinised culture acted out upon the feminised backdrop of the nation.

On the second floor of the monument is the 'Hall of Heroes' where a plaque informs visitors that:

> In this vaulted chamber you'll meet other great Scots, sculpted in marble. Writers, explorers, inventors and statesmen are here, including King Robert the Bruce, Sir Walter Scott, David Livingston, Robert Burns and James Watt, among others.

The 'Hall of Heroes' is a celebration of the men and values of the Enlightenment and, as McDowell (1993b: 316) has commented, 'after an Enlightenment to themselves, it is hardly surprising that its creators are reluctant to relinquish the centre stage'.

Heritage trails: representations of myth and masculinity
The Stirling Heritage Trail opened in 1994 and features many of the historic buildings within the town. The trail is packaged and presented, however, without any critique of the gendered nature of the town's heritage or of the representation of that heritage. The heritage trail starts with 'a soldier's view' from the castle esplanade and includes many other buildings with male histories: the Old Military Prison, the Old Grammar School for Boys, the Old High School, the Tolbooth and Prison, the Mercat Cross, and the Boy's Club. The trail gives a sense in which women are invisibilised from local domestic history as well as from national political history and the heritage represented by Stirling's monuments. Further illustrations of Stirling's male dominated and male-defined history are evident in the names of buildings and their previous uses: John Cowane's House, Glenngarry Ludging, Spittal's House, Darnley's House, Norrie's House, Auchenbowie's House, Mar's Wark, the Argyll's Ludging, and the Erskine Church all take their names from local men with commercial, political or religious standing.

Many of the buildings of the old town are now used as tourist attractions or as restaurants and coffee shops, primarily intended for tourists. These include Stirling's Old Military Prison which opened in April 1996 as a combination of tourist attraction and office space for local businesses. The redevelopment, which took over three years and cost £2.6 million of public money, was funded by Forth Valley Enterprise, Stirling District Council, and the European Regional Development Fund. The attraction is, in part, modelled on Inverary Jail whose 1996 promotional literature stated that the attraction had won a number of awards and recommendations for its displays of 'torture, death and damnation: the story of Scottish crime and punishment 1500 - 1700'. The Inverary attraction features 'an introductory exhibition with blood curdling details of mediaeval punishments' and visitors to Stirling's Old Military Prison are introduced to life-like wax models of male prisoners and guards whilst listening to an audio system conveying the sounds of prisoners in agony during and after torture.

Such representations of history result in a heritage which appears to embrace forms of masculinist myth making in an attempt to promote tourism. Thus Rob Roy MacGregor has had a heroic past constructed for him through postcards, statues and a visitor centre where tourists are encouraged to make up their own minds as to whether Rob Roy was a 'Hero or Villain?'. The language used to describe the less than heroic aspects of his life and character provides few challenges to the type of masculinity and nationalism represented and reconstructed through contemporary heritage tourism. Visitors to the Rob Roy and Trossachs visitor centre are invited to contemplate Rob Roy as a 'rogue' and a 'ruffian'; words which fail to convey the full horror of the violence prevalent at the time. Such representations also serve to enhance the links between male violence and nationalism and critical reading reveals what Butler (1990: 24) has identified as the 'regulatory fiction' of the performance of gender.

This combination of nationalism, hegemonic masculinity and myth-making is perhaps most evident in Stirling's Ghost Walks: evening guided tours on foot with a number of additional costumed characters appearing en route. These tours provide an illustration of the way in which tourists are invited to empathise with particular forms of masculinity and nationalism. For example, the major Ghost Walk starts and finishes with a performance by Allan Mair, the last person to be publicly hanged in Stirling. Mair was hanged in 1843 for the murder of his wife and his ghost is said to haunt the Tolbooth, a building now operating as a restaurant. Whilst much of the information presented during the actor's performance is historically accurate, dramatic license has allowed the performers to construct a pantomime-like scene where Allan Mair protests his innocence to the assembled audience, again in a 'roguish' manner. The crowd is encouraged to voice their belief that Mair must be innocent of the crime for which he is about to be hanged and there are clear parallels between this 'act' and the performance of history (heritage) in relation to Rob Roy. Throughout recent years there have also been theatre productions and street-theatre performances which have continued to blur the boundaries between myth and reality. In 1997 there were performances, events and celebrations held throughout the town to mark the 500th anniversary of the Battle of Stirling Bridge in which William Wallace defeated the English. Coinciding with the

Scottish 'Yes' vote for devolution, these events merged fact with fiction, creating heritage out of history.

These performances of gender have been constructed as both objective and disembodied (Rose, 1993: 100). The identification of the 'interconnections between spatiality, corporeality and visuality' (Nast and Kobayashi, 1996: 75) reveal the significance of the 'tourist gaze' (Urry: 1990) in constructing gendered visions of landscape (Rose, 1993). Through the act of 'the gaze', tourists 'differentially engaged and differentially empowered, appropriate and contest their landscapes' in a variety of ways (Bender, 1993: 17). In the case of Stirling, however, there appear to be few opportunities for alternative readings of such hegemonic representations of gender and nationalism.

Conclusion

This chapter has attempted to locate gender at the centre of an analysis of nationalism and heritage tourism. Feminist geography and cultural geography have offered conceptual and theoretical frameworks upon which to build a spatialised and situated analysis of gender and national identity as performed through the medium of heritage. Illustrative material, drawn from a case study of heritage in Stirling, identified hegemonic masculinity as a dominant discourse in the representation of heritage. Examples of the ways in which masculinity is performed through heritage were discussed in relation to the portrayal of the dominant male icons of William Wallace, Robert the Bruce and Rob Roy MacGregor. Whilst the cultural geography literature frequently reveals the contested nature of landscape, the heritage landscape of Stirling appears only to be contested in terms of national identity, with gender identity remaining disembodied and unproblematised.

Acknowledgments

I wish to thank Liz Bondi, Tim Edensor and Andrew Charlesworth for their constructive comments on an earlier draft of this work. I am also grateful to Nikki Macleod and Steve Shaw who have worked with me in developing research in *Leisure Landscapes*; Gill Valentine who has worked with me in developing research in leisure geographies of gender and sexuality; and David Crouch who encouraged me to develop this work further in his edited collection; *Leisure Practices and Geographical Knowledge*. I also wish to thank the anonymous reviewers of my article titled 'New Cultural Geographies: the spatiality of leisure, gender and sexuality' in *Leisure Studies* 18(1), from which I have drawn much of the theoretical framework for this chapter.

References

Aitchison, C. (1999) 'New cultural geographies: the spatiality of leisure, gender and sexuality' *Leisure Studies* 18(1), 19-39.

Aitchison, C. (1999) 'Heritage and nationalism: gender and the performance of power' in D. Crouch (ed.) *Leisure Practices and Geographical*

Knowledge. Routledge: London, 55-73.

Barbier, B. (1984) 'Geography of tourism and leisure' *Geojournal* 9(1) 5-10.

De Beauvoir, Simone (1949) *The Second Sex*. Penguin: Harmondsworth.

Bell, D. (1991) 'Insignificant others: lesbian and gay geographies' *Area* 23, 323-329.

Bell, D. and Valentine, G. (eds.) (1995) *Mapping Desire: geographies of sexualities*. Routledge: London.

Bell, D. and Valentine, G. (1997) *Consuming Geographies: we are where we eat*. Routledge: London.

Bender, B. (1993) *Landscape: politics and perspectives*. Berg: Oxford.

Bondi, L. (1992a) 'Gender and dichotomy' *Progress in Human Geography* 16(1) 98-104.

Bondi, L. (1992b) 'Gender symbols and urban landscapes' *Progress in Human Geography* 16(2) 157-170.

Burnett, P. (1973) Social change, the status of women and models of city form and development *Antipode* 5, 57-61.

Butler, J. (1990) *Gender Trouble: feminism and the subversion of identity*. Routledge: London.

Carlson, A.W. (1980) 'Geographical research on international and domestic tourism' *Journal of Cultural Geography* 1(1) 149-160.

Cixous, H. (1983/92) 'The Laugh of the Medusa', in E. Abel and E.K. Abel (eds.) *The Signs Reader: women, gender and scholarship*. University of Chicago Press: Chicago.

Coppock, J.T. (1982) 'Geographical contributions to the study of leisure' *Leisure Studies* 1(1) 1-27.

Daniels, S. and Cosgrove, D. (eds) (1988) *The Iconography of Landscape: essays on the symbolic representation, design and use of past environments*. Cambridge University Press: Cambridge

Duncan, N. (ed) (1996) *BodySpace: destabilising geographies of gender and sexuality*. Routledge: London.

Edensor, T. and Kothari, U. (1994) 'The masculinisation of Stirling's heritage' in Kinnaird, V. and Hall, D. (eds) *Tourism: a gender analysis*. Wiley: London.

Enloe, C. (1989) *Bananas, Beaches and Bases: making feminist sense of international politics*. Pandora: London.

Forrest, S. and Clift, S. (1998) 'Gay tourist space and sexual risk behaviour' in Aitchison, C. and Jordan, F. ((eds.)) *Gender, Space and Identity: leisure, culture and commerce*. Leisure Studies Association: Eastbourne.

Garcia-Ramon, M.D., Castener, M., and Centelles, N. (1988) Women and Geography in Spanish Universities *Professional Geographer* 40, 307-315.

Horst (1981) *Papers in Latin American Geography in Honor of Lucia C. Harrison*. Conference of Latin American Geographers. Special Publication No. 1: Muncie, Indiana.

Irigary, L. (1981) 'This sex is not one', on E. Marks and I. de Courtivron (eds) *New French Feminisms*. Harvester: London.

Massey, D. (1984) *Spatial Divisions of Labour*. Macmillan: London.

McCrone, D., Morris, A. and Kiely, R. (1995) *Scotland - The Brand: the making of Scottish heritage*. Edinburgh University Press: Edinburgh.

McDowell, L. (1993a) 'Space, place and gender relations: Part I. Feminist empiricism and the geography of social relations' *Progress in Human Geography* 17(2) 157-179.

McDowell, L. (1993b) 'Space, place and gender relations: Part II. Identity, difference, feminist geometries and geographies' *Progress in Human Geography* 17(3) 305-318.

McDowell, L. and Sharp, J. (eds.) (1997) *Space, Gender, Knowledge: feminist readings*, Arnold: London.

Mort, F. (1996) *Cultures of Consumption: masculinities and social space in late twentieth century Britain*, Routledge: London.

Mowl, G. and Turner, J. (1995) 'Women, gender, leisure and place: towards a more 'humanistic' geography of women's leisure' *Leisure Studies* 14 (2) 102-116.

Nast, H. and Kobayashi, A. (1996) 'Re-corporealizing Vision' in Duncan, N. (ed.) *BodySpace: destabilising geographies of gender and sexuality.* Routledge: London.

Peake, L. (ed.) (1989) 'The challenge of feminist geography' *Journal of Geography in Higher Education* 13, 85-121.

Rose, G. (1993) *Feminism and Geography*, Polity Press: Cambridge.

Rose, G. (1995) 'Place and identity: a sense of place', in D. Massey and P. Jess (eds.) *A Place in the World? Places, Cultures and Globalization.* Open University Press: Milton Keynes.

Sharp (1996) 'Gendering Nationhood: a feminist engagement with national identity' in Duncan, N. (ed.) *BodySpace: destabilizing geographies of gender and sexuality.* Routledge: London

Shurmer-Smith, P. and Hannam, K. (1994) *Worlds of Desire, Realms of Power: a cultural geography*, Arnold: London.

Soja, E. (1985) 'The spatiality of social life: towards a transformative retheorisation', in D. Gregory and J. Urry (eds.) *Social Relations and Spatial Structures*, 90-127, Macmillan: Basingstoke.

Tilley, C. (1993) 'Art, architecture, landscape (Neolithic Sweden)' in Bender, B. (ed.) *Landscape: Politics and Perspectives,* Berg: Oxford, 139-168.

Walby, S. (1992) 'Women and nation' *International Journal of Comparative Sociology* 33(1) 81-99.

Women and Geography Study Group (1997) *Feminist Geographies: explorations in diversity and difference*, Addison Wesley Longman: Harlow.

Yuval-Davis, N. and Anthias, F. (1989) *Women Nation-State*, Macmillan: London.

South Asian Women's Writing in Britain: Biculturality, Hybridity or Fusion?

Ranjana Sidhanta Ash

This paper draws upon a report which explored creative writing – fiction, poetry, drama and performance pieces – by women of South Asian origin living in Britain.[1] It is not an exercise in literary criticism, but attempts to find the subjectivity of women who have left their own lands to live in a foreign one, a subjectivity compounded of memory, nostalgia, cultural contradictions and conflict, and the actual business of building a new life and learning a new language. The writers are women who migrated to Britain from the Commonwealth countries of South Asia – India, Pakistan, Bangladesh and Sri Lanka – or were born in Britain to a parent or parents of South Asian origin. The literature is characterised by the dual vision of the immigrant woman who gazes backwards towards the home and homeland she has left behind, while yet examining her present in alien Britain. Looking backwards through nostalgic memory produces its own distortions of reality as does her encounter with the British version of Western life. The two views create tensions as her ethnic culture and what she perceives as British ways are not always compatible and may be antagonistic. Problems have been presented by, for example, the seclusion of women in the home, and by traditions that demand that women should not go out to work, except through economic necessity, and then in rural surroundings very different from conditions in British factories and offices. To break the hold of traditional notions of female modesty has not been easy nor has it been a smooth transition for the younger generation, exposed to British schooling and peer-group pressure, to negotiate adolescence in this 'bi-cultural' space.

The encounter between two cultures and the inevitable changes that ensue through the processes of acculturation, accomodation and alteration are seen through writing by women that chooses to focus on the lives of Asian women. The three positions selected – biculturality, hybridity and fusion – cannot be rigidly separated, and writers described as bicultural, such as Attia Hosain and Kamala Markandaya, or as diasporic hybrids, such as Ravi Randhawa or Meera Syal, may nonetheless depict differences and change in similar ways. Indeed, the line between cultural hybridity, which produces what has been described as the 'hyphenated immigrant', and cultural fusion, which has seemingly ironed out the anomalies of hybridity to create a new synthesis, is frequently blurred. These categories, then, are not discrete and, significantly, they do not refer to a temporal chronology (a 'progression' from biculturality, through hybridity to fusion), but to the writer's creative subjectivity.

Although their boundaries may be blurred, it is nonetheless possible to offer some provisional definitions of the categories themselves. Biculturality, the sharing of two cultures within the course of daily life, may not be unique to immigrants. However, where daily life, work, the patterns of home-making and parenting, the norms of female behaviour and codes of conduct differ as widely as between most South Asian and British cultures and sub-cultures, the shift from the natal to the host culture within the course of each day, or between specified domains of activity such as work and leisure, can be seen as a mark of biculturality. The category presupposes familiarity with both cultures and a desire to maintain both in their authentic forms, or as authenticated by family, tradition and custom in the homeland. Biculturality is akin to bilingualism – a competence in two languages which play their appointed parts depending on the social context and personal inclination, and which are kept separated and distinct. However, as the bilingual speaker may introduce words from the second language into the first and alter the syntactical order of a sentence, so a bicultural writer can weave heterogeneous cultural strands to suit her design. Nonetheless, the cultural spheres tend to remain distinct and recognisable within their specificities. This pattern is perhaps typified by the novels of Kamala Markandaya.

While the dictionary defines hybridity as 'composed of incongruous elements', for cultural theorists such as Homi Bhabha it is the in-between space between the past and the present, a 'passage between fixed identifications' (Bhabha, 1994: 4). In contrast with assimilationism, which is associated with inequality and the diminishing of the immigrant's culture under the dominance of the host culture, hybridity, says Bhabha, 'entertains difference without an assumed or imposed hierarchy' (1994: 4). Many younger women writers who were either born in Britain or brought up here from childhood, present elements in their work that could be described as hybrid. Ravi Randhawa's fiction, for example, tends to focus on the dynamics of Asian family life within a British context.

Beyond hybridity, however, there is 'fusion' – a word that describes what emerges when the disparate elements of separate cultures are brought together to form something new that nonetheless partakes of, and bears the imprint of, its constituent strands. Fusion recognises cultural differences and the tensions and conflicts that are generated by these differences – but it attempts to reconcile them through some form of synthesis, rather than through an assimilationist obliteration of 'otherness'. New modes of being are sought, rather than a conformity to the demands of the host culture, as is seen in the fiction of writers such as Farhana Sheikh and Atima Srivastava.

Whether one should treat women's writing, the product of their imagination, aesthetic skills and judgement, as autobiographical or representative of their ethnic communities is problematic. It is undoubtedly true that the inexperienced writer tends to draw upon her own experiences, and for the immigrant there is the constant factor of novelty – or outrage – to provide her self expression. Also, according to the testimony of Black and Third World women writers in Britain and North America, the very act of writing, of shaping and choosing words with care, stimulates self assertion and a sense of controlling one's feelings and thoughts. When the writing is organised by a women's collective there is moreover a reinforcement of female solidarity. 'Writing in all its forms, can be a weapon in this process of collectivization and harmonization', argue the editors of a British anthology of writings by Black and Third World Women, '[f]or it details the things which make us what we are' (Grewal, 1988:4). The first anthology published by the London based Asian Women Writers' Workshop also emphasised the importance of collective effort by women who were constantly marginalised and whose literary efforts were ignored. Formed in 1984, the workshop gave its members 'visibility, credibility and access to institutions, publishers and other groups in the community' (AWWW, 1988: 1). A group of university students chose to compile an anthology of writings by women of the South Asian diaspora in the USA, because writing was the only tool through which women scattered across the land could communicate their diverse experiences of life in America: 'We saw that the pieces evoking a sense of a woman's history and identity through her own language were far more powerful than any polished translation' (WSADC, 1993: xvii). A woman's own words, in her own language, capturing her confused feelings of getting to know life in some West Yorkshire town, and her settling into her new life, was one of the aims of the Bengali Women's Support Group based in Sheffield. The women write mainly in Bengali and the stories, poems and reflections are translated into English to provide some of the most 'authentic' testimony of the experience of immigrant life for Asian women in Britain (Chatterjee, 1990; Chatterjee, 1993; Ara, 1994). For the neo-literates among the women the acquisition of literacy produced a greater sense of empowerment than recording their stories orally, a conclusion also found in Newcastle-upon-Tyne where literacy classes in Bengali and Urdu for illiterate women from Bangladesh and Pakistan resulted in the production of an anthology of stories and poetry (Raychandhuri, 1990).

Paula Ebron and A. L. Tsing's 1995 study found that novels written by Asian-American and African-American women writers carry more than the individual writer's subjectivity. For them these texts define and affirm community-based aspirations and provide telling descriptions of minority life by 'insider' voices, voices that have the authenticity to elevate the narrative from the particular to the allegorical. But irrespective of the allegorical or symbolic function of many of the works by Asian women in Britain, their typicality as indicators of the diasporic experience cannot be denied. Although South Asia is itself a vast multicultural region, within which different and diverse women are separated by factors of ethnicity, religion and class, the writing that emerges from the diaspora bears several common features. There is the sense of dislocation when one moves from the familiar to the unfamiliar; there is the added burden of isolation where English is not known or is known imperfectly, as is the case for the great majority of Asian men and women who were educated in their homelands or did not get any formal schooling. Only middle class Asians would have learnt English which remains the language of privilege and power even today, fifty years after decolonisation. Additionally, the presence in Britain of racism which operates institutionally through immigration and asylum laws and has been reinforced by unemployment, urban decline and diminishing civic resources, makes for a commonality of immigrant experience. Frightened by actual incidents of racist violence many Asian women in areas such as London's East End do not dare to go out alone, staying cooped up in tiny apartments in run down inner city tower blocks.

There is now a growing sense of unease at the inter-generation gap in cultural preferences and the possibility of losing one's ethnic identity, an identity which is imposed more strenuously upon women by patriarchal attitudes in their families and communities. There are growing rifts in Asian minority communities as women, especially from the second generation, who may have been born here and have certainly been socialised through British education and peer group culture, no longer accept gender codes defined as 'traditional' (although in many cases, these are invented traditions). Even among the older generation of women, their experiences in Britain have forced them to go to work outside the home, often as a result of their husbands having been made redundant. Such changes also contribute to domestic tension.

It remains undecided whether the modifications in marriage arrangements and the growing numbers of women seeking protection from violent husbands or other male relations, are the result of Western femininst ideas, the actions of women's movements in South Asia, or the inevitable result of social change. That femininsm is not an homogeneous body of discourse or a set of universally accepted modes of change for women is now well established. Contradictions within the broad band of feminist ideology which erupted initially in the USA between African-American women and white feminists, have since spread to Canada and Britain where women's groups are often divided along racial and ethnic lines (Humm, 1994: 170-89). Arun Mukherjee, a Canadian academic from India, has made what she terms 'oppositional aesthetics' her credo to challenge feminist writing that fails to attack racism and imperialism. Her criticism of the privileging of writers such as Charlotte Brontë and Charlotte Perkins Gilman who accepted the ethos of white colonialism is described as reflecting a 'discomfort with feminist theory' that fails to notice that the substitution of dead white male authors by dead white female ones is a practice equally blind to racism and imperialism. While Mukherjee admits that she must join forces with white feminists to challenge the hegemony of dead white male voices, she must also criticise them when their examples of women's experiences are drawn only from their own white middle class culture (1994: xi-xiii).

Although the Asian diaspora in Britain has not, as yet, produced feminist ideologues to match Gayatri Chakravorty Spivak, Trinh T. Minh-ha or Chandra Talpade Mohanty, the debate with Anglo-American criticism has been ongoing since the 1980s.[2] The Asian Women Writers' Workshop articulated their differences in their first anthology, *Right of Way*, published in 1988. Within this volume, the question of feminist identity was central – if they were feminists, was it not an Asian feminism that they supported?

> Many women felt that the word feminist had been sullied by the exclusiveness and racism of white middle-class women and, therefore, was no longer a useful term for us. There were such differences in our

understanding of feminism that in any case the term would have been completely meaningless. (AWWW, 1988: 4)

What emerges from the disagreements with Anglo-American feminism among these women is the complexity of identity for so many Asian women in the British diaspora. One strand, that is common to them all, even when the element of biculturality has begun to be modified through the process of hybridisation, is their attachment to their Asian ethnicity. These women writers, like many others in their community, accept and promote an Asianness, defined by their national consciousness, irrespective of the diversity inherent within the plurality of Asian multiculturality. Contrary to those who find nationalism and contemporary western feminism inimical, there is a remarkable attachment to homelands left behind not merely through nostalgic memory, but also through national identity. Writers retain their Indian, Bangladeshi, Sri Lankan component even when, legally, they have renounced their citizenship and become naturalised British. For the second generation, born in Britain, and therefore, no longer immigrant but citizen, there is surprisingly little of the assimilationist drive to proclaim their completely anglicised identity. They prefer the hyphenated duality of the parental and their own nationality as Indo-British, British-Pakistani or British Bangladeshi.[3]

The allegiance to original national identities on the part of the Asian diaspora can be understood in part by the history of decolonisation and the involvement of men and women in fighting for national independence in the Indian Subcontinent. The ambiguities found in western feminist discourse surrounding the issues of nationalism, the representation of sexual differences and women's political movements, and in ideas such as that of a 'common sisterhood', do not have the same resonances for women from the newly independent countries of the Third World. Kumari Jayawardena in her pioneering work on feminism and nationalism discloses the close links between women's emancipation and the fight for national independence from Eygpt to Korea (Jayawardena, 1986). Even when women returned to their former domesticity after the fervour of national liberation the fire was not extinguished and throughout the countries of Asia, Africa and the Americas, women's movements have joined other forces fighting neo-colonialism and the struggle for democratic rights. It is not surprising, therefore, that immigrant women from India, which has been free from British rule for only five decades, and immigrant women from Pakistan, which is one of the new post-war states emerging from the partition of India in 1947, should carry with them some of the earlier excitement of being free, despite the political and economic problems being faced by these countries. Because of the migration from former colonies to the empire's heartland – a post-colonial Britain that retains much of the culture of colonial superiority, especially in its many manifestations of racism and inequality – the nationalism latent in many Asian immigrants tends to be recovered and reinforced. The national identities being rediscovered, especially by the younger generation, many of whom are British by birth and may not have seen their parental homelands, are also the product of ethnic, religious and political strife between and within South Asian lands, conflict that affects the Asian diaspora in the Midlands of Britain with almost the same intensity as it does India and Pakistan. For Bangladeshis, national pride seems especially strong, in part because their national liberation war against Pakistan was as recent as 1971. Bagladeshi women in East London and West Yorkshire, continue to find February 21 (Martyrs' Day in Bangladesh) a significant and moving subject for their verse and reflective pieces. Rehana Chaudury, who has been in Rotherham since 1976, wants to remember Martyrs' Day in her Bengali poem 'Come Daily, O Twenty-first', because she feels that Bengalis are forgetting the sacrifices made for their language and freedom (Chatterjee, 1990: 24-5). Monuara Badsha, who was a girl during Bangladesh's liberation and now lives in Sheffield, reminds Bangladeshis in Britain that 'the blood of our martyrs was not spilt in vain that day . . . With much strife we have regained our country, Bangladesh, and our language, Bengali' (Chatterjee, 1990: 25-7).

The thread of national identity, not necessarily in its political forms, recurs in many of the works studied. Whether the writer separates the Asian from the British through the location, theme and characters of her fiction, like Attia Hosain or brings the Asian and the British together through external factors such as tourism or global economics, as in Kamala Markandaya's novels, the bicultural writer is absorbed with her Asian inheritance. What is perhaps more surprising, however, is the prominence of the Asian-Indian or Pakistani – rather than the British – component, in fiction and plays within the category of cultural hybridity.

What might be the significant dimension in this attachment to land somewhere in South Asia is its frequent association with the mother. Susheila Nasta, in her introduction to *Motherlands*, an anthology of women's writing from Africa, the Caribbean and South Asia, connects the idea of motherlands, mothercultures and mothertongues with motherhood as a dominant trope in women's writing (Nasta, 1991: xix). National identities, as seen in the Asian women's works, are closely entwined with the mother figure, and in particular with the mother-daughter bond.[4] The anthologies published by the Sheffield-based Bengali Women's Support Group contain many pieces – poems, letters, diary entries – that highlight the women's sense of being Bengali, of belonging to Bangladesh or West Bengal through the personification of the land as mother. In Hasnara Hussain's poem entitled 'Bangladesh, While Living in London', she expresses the nostalgia of the immigrant who looks in vain for the flowering trees and lily covered ponds of her native land and concludes with memories of bidding farewell to the mother and father (Chatterjee, 1990: 84-6). Rashida Islam's 'Torn Pages from Two Diaries' conveys the sadness and pride of the mother thinking of her scientist daughter in Britain and its counterpart in the daughter's regrets that she could not convince her mother, now dead, that the westernisation her mother noticed was very superficial:

I have not changed at all, Maa. It is my destiny that has changed. Thinking of the future and the wellbeing of my own child has meant that I have had to harden myself. (Chatterjee, 1990: 19)

The link with the mother connects love of ancestral land and ancestral culture, for the woman is the main transmitter of tradition, custom and ritual through songs, stories and domestic rites. These concerns are evident in Ravinder Randhawa's first novel, *A Wicked Old Woman* (1987), which depicts the many facets and complexities of hybridisation in the lives of Asian women. The narrative pursues several threads of the immigrant story: conflict between the heroine Kulwant and her family over her fondness for an English boy, the conformity of an arranged marriage, and the later dissent that leads to divorce. Kulwant's life is dominated by her political and social radicalism, and yet throughout she maintains an internal dialogue with her mother – symbol of self knowledge, a character securely fixed in the conviction of her Indian values:

> I have never lost my anchor of certainty, this country has put you in one of its mixers and whirled you round till you can't tell your inside from your outside, your duty from your rights, your needs from your responsibilities. (Randhawa, 1987: 54)

Kulwant, in contrast, is divided. As a teenager she 'had wanted everything, wanted to be both Indian and English, wanted to choose for herself what she wanted out of both' (1987: 29).

The mother as the bearer of natal culture also figures in Randhawa's second novel, *Hari-jan*, a study in the creation of a hybrid Asian girl of seventeen who defies her mother over most of the ethnic cultural details that the mother hopes her daughter will learn in order to be a 'proper' Punjabi. When the mother chooses beautiful Punjabi clothes, the daughter spoils the effect by wearing heavy trainers; she deliberately distorts her given name; she comes home late. Yet the one thing the girl wants from her parents, especially her mother, she does not receive:

> But India was the unknown part of me, the unfulfilled, lonely, aching part: That's a major grievance with my parents, so busy making money, they couldn't be bothered to take me to the place that mattered. (1992: 69).

Her mother, laying down rules and regulations, could not give her the experience that really mattered.

The actress and comedian Meera Syal had her first novel, *Anita and Me* published in 1996. Its first person narrator is a little Indian girl on the verge of puberty, growing up in a West Midlands village where her middle class parents have bought a house. She is very different from the heroines of other Asian women writers of Syal's generation because she likes being British and aspires to be even more like her school mate Anita, a white working class girl. Although she follows her mother to the gurudwara (Sikh temple) and enjoys the family gatherings where friends and relations sing and recite poetry in Punjabi or Urdu, one is aware of her being an outsider until her grandmother, her Nanima, arrives on a visit. The grandmother becomes the key that unlocks the treasury of stories, legends, family anecdotes and, above all, the Punjabi language. The child had already begun to be stirred by her father's singing which 'unleashed emotions which were unfamiliar and instinctive at the same time, in a language I could not recognise but felt I could speak in my sleep' (Syal, 1996: 112). Her grandmother, ignorant of English, opens more doors into family and community history and fills the child with excitement, with the result that, 'for the first time I desperately wanted to visit India and claim some of this magic as mine' (1996: 211).

The diasporic displaced and dislocated seek a firm identity. The motherland, as interpreted by the mother and the maternal line, provides one anchor. Leena Dhingra, another actress who is also an accomplished writer, describes the confusion of her heroine in *Amritvela*, her first novel:

> The non-stop flight to New Delhi is now halfway. But only my watch informs me of that. Through the window we appear quite immobile, suspended over a vast expanse of curdling clouds. If, as I have often said, I feel myself to be suspended between two cultures, then this is where I belong, the half-way mark. Here in the middle of nowhere, up in the atmosphere, is my space – the halfway point between East and West. (Dhingra, 1988: 1)

By going back to her Indian family of aunts and great aunts the narrator who, like Dhingra, has spent more years in Europe and Britain than in India, is able to resolve her divided self. Dhingra, like other Asians, is very concerned with the capacity of British racism, both overt and concealed, to create categories and manifestations of otherness. The Asian, like the West Indian or African, is labelled and classified. Dhingra's much anthologised piece, 'Breaking Out of the Labels' describes the many ways in which she has been rendered other in Britain. She has been at times 'a girl from India, an Indian girl, a coloured, a Paki, a black wog, an Asian, and [has] recently graduated to becoming a member of an ethnic minority' (Cobham, 1987: 107).

Dhingra's politicised world-view is reflected in her current work – a play about her great uncle, Madanlal Dhingra, who was hanged in Pentonville prison for killing a British officer during the rise of militant Indian nationalism in the early years of the twentieth century. She is not atypical in her political concerns. Several of the writers being discussed are political sophisticates whose feminism reflects wider macro-political objectives, rather than the purely personal concern with subjectivity seen to be characteristic of Western feminism (Jayawardena, 1986). A recent history of the women's movement in India by Radha Kumar shows the 'growing interest within the femininst movement about the administration and organization of society' (Kumar, 1993: 194). The annual women's liberation conferences held in India engage with electoral representation, wages, civil rights, sex, violence towards women, reproductive rights and a wide variety of national and international issues. Arising from such engagement is criticism of western feminists for their preoccupation with individualism and their privileging of sexuality as the determining factor within women's lives (1993: 195).

As mentioned earlier, differences between Anglo-American, Black American and Third World feminisms have given rise to separate discourses. Asian women in Britain, caught in the midst of culture changes that affect them with great severity do make common cause with women of other races, particularly when patriarchal authority in the family or community restricts their freedom and subjects them to violence. Southall Black Sisters, founded in 1979, is composed of Asian and African-Caribbean women whose main target is domestic violence and providing assistance to the women who seek help.[5] When religious fundamentalism became an issue in the late 1980s, women from different races and religions came together to form Women Against Fundamentalism (Sahgal, 1992). Both organisations share common ground in helping women who are the victims of violence and coercion in the name of ethnic and religious tradition. They reflect the societal direction of Asian women's changing lives and their actions confound the stereotypes of passivity that so often characterise representations of Asian women. Strikes at Imperial Typewriters in Leicester, at Grunwicks in Brent, at Hillingdon Hospital in West London, the campaign for the release of Kiranjit Ahluwalia, imprisoned for killing her violent husband – all these actions parallel the activities of women's liberation movements in India, Pakistan, Bangladesh and Sri Lanka, where women fight for their rights as part of the broader field of democratic and economic struggles.

Asian women's writing in Britain reflects these wider political concerns, and the subjectivity revealed in the imaginative work surveyed nonetheless goes far beyond the purely personal. The introduction to the second collection from the Asian Women's Writers Collective states their literary credo. In the first collection *Right of Way*, the need was felt for 'positive but realistic images of Asian women' (1988: 31) and attitudes that were opposed to racism, religious fundamentalism, class bias and homophobia. The second book, *Flaming Spirit*, goes further in its political orientation, having to tackle divisions within the Asian communities as the growth of a substantial Asian bourgeoisie has resulted in the hardening of class divisions, while religious bigotry has intensified across the spectrum. The editors recognise that the Collective's political agenda 'carries its own cost and distances us from our communities, where so many of the cherished ideals and beliefs are embedded in religion and tradition' (Rukhsana, 1994: xv).

The notion that a woman realises her full potential and asserts her individuality within a social reality that acknowledges her role as daughter, wife and mother as well as a person in her own right, is embedded in much of the writing of Asian women. From the very beginnings of Asian women's writing in Britain, there has been a characteristic interweaving of a specifically female consciousness with an understanding of political contexts and changes. Attia Hosain and Kamala Markandaya are typical of the older generation of diasporic writers, and their work exhibits a particularly thought provoking biculturality. Hosain's small oeuvre – a collection of short stories, *Phoenix Fled* (1953) and a single novel, *Sunlight on a Broken Column* (1961) – might have been forgotten, had not the feminist publishers Virago selected them for the Modern Classics series. Republished in 1988, these bicultural texts were rediscovered by second generation Asian women in Britain.

Hosain's works centered on her North Indian Muslim background, and the changes wrought in the life of a young Muslim woman growing up in a family where Urdu and Islamic education at home were counterbalanced by English education at the local Loreto Convent and American Methodist college during the years immediately preceding and following Indian independence. The price paid for Partition and the departure of many Muslim families to create the new state of Pakistan, are among the social upheavals Hosain experienced and could utilise in her delineation of strong women who could withstand the disruption and even the disintegration of their families. Her own long stay in London which she regarded almost as exile, stimulated her to create characters such as Laila, her novel's narrator and central character, whose evolving consciousness and sense of self are accompanied by a recognition of the political and social forces around her. The book became required reading for many young Muslim women in Britain, who identified with Laila and found her odyssey comparable with theirs.

The work of Kamala Markandaya, although contrasting in style, also exhibits the characteristics of biculturality. Markandaya has lived in Britain for almost fifty years and yet regards herself not as an immigrant but as an Indian expatriate. Her gaze in most of her 10 novels to date has been backwards to her native South India on the eve of independence and since. She creates women drawn from diverse social classes – from the landed aristocracy to landless peasants. She also depicts British women characters interacting with Indians, generally in an Indian location, but occasionally in London. For a novelist of romantic fiction, Markandaya is remarkably concerned with socio-economic issues, such as the unequal ownership of land, the plight of the urban artisan, and the fate of women who have been seduced and abandoned. Without claiming to be a feminist she creates women, both Indian and British, who are neither subservient to male dominance nor overwhelmed by adversity. Her best known book, *Nectar in a Sieve*, first published in 1954 and reprinted eleven times, is the story of the hardships that befall a landless peasant woman and her family. Markandaya's fiction tends towards the romantic, and in *Nectar in a Sieve* this dimension is apparent in the attraction of a British doctor for an Indian woman who nonetheless remains loyal to her family – an episode that typifies the pattern of discrete worlds colliding, but not changing.

These bicultural narratives, then, are in distinct contrast to the narratives of cultural hybridity or fusion. As suggested earlier, it is difficult to distinguish exactly between these two categories, but fusion might be seen as the opposite of biculturality's rigidly maintained boundaries. Fusion recognises cultural differences which are then positioned to connect in the production of something new: a concept familiar to the poet Debjani Chatterjee. Her writing is directly engaged with Asian women's subordination under the twin oppressions of patriarchy and racism, but these political concerns are embodied in a poetry with a remarkably eclectic range of reference. Her verse encompasses everything from Cervantes and Edward Lear to the Sanskrit philosophers and Gandhi. Poems such as 'I was that Woman' cross historical and cultural boundaries to unite the mythical figures of Pandora, Sita and Eve, while other verses enage more directly with topical issues. In 'Primary Purpose' Chatterjee uses her astringent wit to challenge the iniquitous policies of British immigration law, which in the

1970s and 1980s resorted to virginity tests to establish the authenticity of Asian women's marital status. Describing an encounter between an Asian wife and an immigration officer, Chatterjee parodies the official line:

Those whom the immigration law has kept apart
Let no one join together.
Primary purpose of marriage – immigration
Is forever the Home Office incantation.

(Chatterjee, 1989: 22)

Asian women are then, both victims and makers of their own destiny. Both these aspects are described in some of the most interesting works of cultural fusion – fictions that radically undermine stereotypical expectations of Asian subjectivity. Rukhsana Ahmad's play, 'Song for a Sanctuary' is based on the actual murder of a Punjabi woman in a refuge. While the theme is tragic she creates characters of grit and courage in the sanctuary (George, 1993). Similarly, in Tanika Gupta's film script *Flight*, the tyrannical Hindu father who punishes his daughter for her alleged transgression – a sexual relationship with a Muslim boy – is undermined by the mother, who helps her daughter find shelter in a London home.[6]

The work of Suniti Namjoshi, acclaimed fabulist and poet, might also be regarded as an example of cultural fusion. Writing from a lesbian standpoint, she tackles the taboos of Asian society, while retaining her own sense of connection to her Indian roots. Through the irony and gentle ridicule of her witty fables, she has succeeded in exposing prejudices surrounding both race and gender.

The Asian diaspora in Britain faces change, although there is uncertainty as to its direction. Will the indistinct boundary between hybridity and fusion remain, or will it be further blurred as a way of life emerges in which disparate cultural strands are organically fused? The work of two contemporary writers suggests that the conception of Asian diasporic subjectivities, as embodied in women's writing, is increasingly one of fusion. Home land and new land are no longer clearly differentiated entities, and the focus of these writers can no longer be contained within the categories of expatriate or immigrant. *The Red Box* (1991), the first novel by Farhana Sheikh, of Pakistani origins, is set in the world of Muslim immigrants in London. Through a complex narrative involving three Muslim women from different class backgrounds who must make their lives in Britain, Sheikh introduces an ambivalence towards the British environment. Raisa, affluent, middle class and secular, is conducting research into the Islamic identity of Nasreen and Tahira, two working class Muslim girls in their final year in a London comprehensive school. The teenage girls express contradictory views of their Islamic faith, while the middle class researcher comes to question her place in British society through her encounters with both the girls and their working class mothers, and through the discovery that her own mother had also toiled in a sweat shop to augment the family income – a fact that had probably caused her death. The book is a positive contribution to the usual demonisation of Islam as a reactionary force in British society. By relating belief within the lives of women, some married, some divorced, some on the margins of Muslim life having been assimilated into westernised ways, and placing such questions in the context of the crass exploitation of women's labour and the racist bullying endemic in British schools, Sheikh is able to position Asian Muslim women's lives outside the stereotypes of purdah and seclusion.

Atima Srivastava, of Indian Hindu origins, who has lived in Britain since childhood, provides a final example. Srivastava attempts incursions into territory generally ignored by Asian writers – that of white working class life. Her story, 'Dragons in E8' is narrated by an English girl, a drug addict, who may not have long to live. She is devoid of self pity, planning a future with optimistic courage (Srivastava, 1995). Srivastava's first novel, *Transmission* (1992), takes place in the world of television and film, in which commercialism overrides humanity. The narrative focuses on the tension generated when an Indian film editor falls in love with an English working class man she had known in school, and who is now HIV positive. The novel's very title, *Transmission*, suggests the new world of shrinking boundaries, electronic communication and global infection. Written by a woman whose favourite painter in Edward Hopper, archetypal depictor of urban isolation, the South Asian writer has taken a great leap forward from the nostalgic gaze of the expatriate and from the immigrant focus of most writers. She is now a resident in the jungle of the metropolis, often alone – as Asian women tend to postpone marriage, whether arranged or of their own choice – left in a cultural limbo to find her own solutions to the tensions and conflicts that assail her. That this space is as likely to be debilitating as enabling is perhaps inevitable in a Britain still uncomfortable with its new multicultural identity.

Notes

[1] This article has selected material from my unpublished report, *South Asian Women Writing in Britain*, (University of Warwick, 1994).

[2] The critique of cultural imperialism presented by these critics is well known, but attention is drawn in particular to Spivak, 1988; Trinh, 1989 and Mohanty et al., 1991.

[3] A recent example of writing that exhibits these patterns is *Untold Words: Poems with translations by British Bangladeshis* (1996) Hyde: BICA-ACA Books.

[4] A typical example might be Rukhsana Ahmed's 1996 novel *The Hope Chest*, in which a series of parallel narratives focus on the mother-daughter bond in a Pakistani upper class family, a Pakistani domestic servant's home and a white middle class London couple.

[5] As documented in the 1990 publication *Against the Grain: A Celebration of Survival and Struggle*, London: Southall Black Sisters.

[6] Gupta's script has not been published, although the film *Flight* was shown at the 1996 London Film festival. (Alex Pillai, Hindi Picture Production for BBC TV)

References

Ahmad, Rukhansa, 1996, *The Hope Chest*, London: Virago.

Ahmad, Rukhsana and Gupta, Rahila (eds.) 1994, *Flaming Spirit*, London: Virago.

Asian Women Writers' Workshop (AWWW), 1988, *Right of Way: Prose and Poetry*, London: The Women's Press.

Ara, Safuran and Dolly Mandal, 1994, *Kobitanjali*, Sheffield: Bengali Women's Support Group. (Text in Bengali)

Bhabha, Homi K., 1994, *The Location of Culture*, London: Routledge.

Chatterjee, Debjani, 1989, *I Was That Woman*, Frome: Hippopotamus Press.

Chatterjee, Debjani and Rashida Islam (eds.), 1990, *Barbed Lines*, Castleford: Yorkshire Art Circus. (Bilingual text - Bengali/English)

Chatterjee, Debjani et al (eds.), 1993, *Sweet and Sour*, Sheffield: Bengali Women's Support Group. (Bilingual text - Bengali/English)

Cobham, R and Collins, M (eds.) 1987 *Watchers and Seekers*, London: The Women's Press.

Dhingra, L., 1988, *Amritvela*, London: The Womens Press.

Ebron, Paulla and A. L. Tsing, (1995) 'From Allegories of Identity to Sites of Dialogue', *Diaspora*, 4: 125-57

George, Kadija (ed.) (1993), *Six Plays by Black and Asian Women Writers*, London: Aurora Metro Press.

Grewal, S. et al (eds.), 1988, *Charting the Journey: Writings by Black and Third World Women*, London: Sheba Feminist Publishers.

Humm, Maggie, 1994, *Contemporary Feminist Literary Criticism*, Hemel Hempstead, Harvester Wheatsheaf.

Jayawardena, Kumari, 1986, *Feminism and Nationalism in the Third World*, London: Zed Books.

Kumar, Radha, 1993, *The History of Doing: An Illustrated Account of Movements for Women's Rights and Feminism in India, 1800-1990*, London: Verso.

Markandaya, Kamala, 1954/1982, *Nectar in a Sieve*, London: Virago.

Mohanty, C. T., A. Russo and L. Torres (eds.) 1991, *Third World Women and Politics of Feminism*, Bloomington: Indiana University Press.

Mukherjee, Arun, 1994, *Oppositional Aesthetics*, Toronto: TSAR.

Namjoshi, Suniti, 1989, *Because of India: Selected Poems and Fables*, London: Only Women Press.

Nasta, Susheila (ed.), 1991, *Motherlands: Black Women's Writing from Africa, the Caribbean and South Asia*, London: The Women's Press.

Randhawa, Ravinder, 1987, *A Wicked Old Woman*, London: Women's Press.

_____, 1992, *Hari-jan*, London: Mantra Books.

Raychaudhuri, Sibani and Rukhsana Ahmed (eds.), 1990, *Daughters of the East*, Newcastle upon Tyne: The Common Trust.

Sahgal, Gita and Nira Y. Davis, (eds.) 1992, *Refusing Holy Orders: Women and Fundamentalism in Britain*, London: Virago.

Sheikh, Farhana, 1991, *The Red Box*, London: The Women's Press.

Southall Black Sisters, 1990, *Against the Grain: A Celebration of Survival and Struggle*, London: Southall Black Sisters.

Spivak, Gayatri Chakravorty, 1988, *In Other Worlds*, London: Routledge.
Srivastava, Atima, 1992, *Transmission*, London: Serpents Tail
_____, 1995, 'Dragons in E' 8 in *Kunapipi*, XVII: 59-68.
Syal, Meera, 1996, *Anita and Me*, London: Flamingo.
Trinh, T. Minh-ha, 1989, *Woman, Native, Other*, Bloomington: Indiana University Press.
Women of South Asian Descent Collective, The (WSADC), 1993, *Our Feet Walk the Sky*, San Fransisco: Aunt Lute Books.

'She has been undone' – the Construction of New Zealand National Identity and the Containment of White Female Sexuality in *Desperate Remedies*

Ling-Yen Chua

Earlier in this book, Sophie Nield explored some of the ways in which women have been represented in discourses of nationalism. Nield argues that the representation of white women's sexualities in discourses of war and nationalism has been essentially binary in character – women are either passively maternal or virginally chaste. This article, like that of So-Hee Lee which follows later in the volume, engages with the work of contemporary post-colonial and feminist critics who examine the relationship between representations of women, discourses of race, and the construction of new national identities. Anne McClintock (1995), Felicity Nussbaum (1995), and Anne Stoller (1995) have argued that the regulation of white female sexuality is integral to the expansion of the British empire, especially in the new colonies. Stoller puts the case succinctly:

> the 'fate of the race and the nation' were also tied in colonial discourses to individual sexual practices in Africa, Asia, and the Americas . . . Male sexual anxiety focused on more than suitable Christian marriage partners for European women and on the transmission of property, but on the unmanaged desires of women themselves . . . In both the Dutch and British accounts, the sexual choices of white women were at issue; they are desired objects, but unruly desiring subjects as well.
>
> (Stoller, 1995 :41)

I want here to look at the 1994 New Zealand film *Desperate Remedies* with the aim of examining the close relationship between discourses of race, gender, sexuality and national identity. I will illustrate that the sexual containment of the film's central protagonist, Dorothea Brooke, plays an important role in the construction of pakeha New Zealand identity.[1] I suggest that Dorothea Brooke is depicted as dangerously sexually 'excessive' because she does not behave as a 'proper' sexually restrained English woman should do in the 'colonies'. By being involved in an illicit interracial heterosexual liaison with Fraser and a homosexual liaison with another English woman, Anne Cooper, Dorothea transgresses both the prohibitions against homosexuality and interracial relationships.

The film's representation of Dorothea's sexual transgressions suggests that the threat posed by white female homosexuality is similar to that posed by white women who engage in heterosexual interracial liaisons. This leads me to the conclusion that the unexpected ending of the supposedly pro-gay film, Dorothea's expulsion from 'Hope' (as New Zealand is called in the film), indicates that defiantly sexually transgressive white women have no place in the new British colony of New Zealand.

This brings me to an explanation of my use of the terms 'white', 'non-white' and 'mixed race'. Unlike the racial terms 'black' and 'people of colour', the terms 'white', 'non-white' and 'mixed race' are perceived as more 'offensive' for a variety of reasons. For instance, when I first presented this as a conference paper at the 1996 Women's Studies conference, I was questioned by some members of the audience as to why I use the term 'white'. After I was made to explain why as a Chinese woman, I am interested in discussing the representation of white female sexuality in a New Zealand film, (I explained that I grew up in New Zealand, where my family still live), it was suggested to me that a 'white person' does not exist, since the term 'white' disavows one's ethnic and racial specificity, such as being 'Welsh', 'English' or 'Scottish'.

Since my paper is about the New Zealand film *Desperate Remedies*, an easy solution to the question of terminology is to replace the contested term 'white' with the less politically loaded Maori term 'Pakeha'. After all, 'pakeha' is considered an acceptable alternative both in New Zealand and at British Women's Studies Conferences, since it supposedly avoids the connotations of supremacy that the term 'white' carries. However, as Dyson (1995) accurately points out, although 'pakeha' was originally a Maori term meaning 'outsiders' or non-Maori people, it has come to refer exclusively to people of a white ethnic identity. I thus suggest that although it is true that the term 'white' disavows one's racial, ethnic and national specificity, the real issue behind the discomfort of certain members of the audience with my referring to *Desperate Remedies*'s heroine Dorothea Brooke as 'white' has little to do with 'incorrect naming'. Instead, I posit, it is related to what Dyer calls the 'nothingness' of 'whiteness':

This property of whiteness, to be everything and nothing, is the source of its representational power . . . On the other hand, if the invisibility of whiteness colonizes the definition of other norms – class, gender, heterosexuality, nationality and so on – it also masks whiteness itself as a category.

(Dyer, 1993: 143)

Consequently, for the same reasons that Dyson continues to use the term 'white', the replacement of the term 'white' with the term 'pakeha' in this paper, would simply be 'window-dressing'. This brings me to my use of the terms 'non-white' and 'mixed race'. At the same conference, prior to my own presentation, I had attended an earlier session where the terms 'black' and 'people of colour' were used extensively by the speakers and members of the audience without inciting the same reaction as my use of the term 'white'. Yet one can similarly point out that these terms also do not acknowledge one's racial specificity. After all, in both North America and Britain, 'black' and 'people of colour' are widely accepted terms generally used to refer to all 'non-white' people, ranging from East and South Asians, and people of African descent, to 'mixed race' people.

Amongst the many valid, often political, reasons for the use of the terms 'people of colour' and 'black', is the claim that the alternative term 'non-white' uncritically sets up 'whiteness' as a norm against which all other races are defined. In this paper, it is for this precise reason – to clearly identify that the 'non-white' characters in *Desperate Remedies*, otherwise known as 'people of colour', have been depicted as the negative binaristic opposite of the white characters – that I persist in the continued use of the term 'non-white'. Similarly, I also use the term 'mixed race' in this paper to describe how certain other characters in the film are depicted racially. Instead of offensively suggesting that there exists something akin to 'pure' race, I use the term 'mixed race' to describe the character Fraser and his offspring because their specific racial identity is never revealed. We only know that Fraser calls himself 'half caste' in the film. Finally, in the context of current racial unease in New Zealand between Pakeha and Maori people, between Pakeha and Asian people, between Pakeha and people from the Pacific Islands, I suggest that films such as *Desperate Remedies* that are currently emerging from New Zealand, have to be examined in relation to how Pakeha New Zealand national identity is being reshaped by the presence of 'non-white' people living in New Zealand.

At this point, I wish to note that although sharing the same name as the heroine of George Eliot's *Middlemarch*, and although the film and the novel share a slim thematic similarity, (both Dorothea Brookes have bad first marriages before ending up with a partner they love), there is otherwise little similarity between the two Dorothea Brookes. Dorothea in *Middlemarch* is an idealist out to save people, whilst her counterpart in *Desperate Remedies* is depicted as more calculating and concerned with the fulfilment of her own desires, since she has to struggle with the isolation of being a pioneering woman in the new colony of 'Hope'. Given the very different characterisation of Dorothea Brooke and the negligible thematic relationship to *Middlemarch*, I will not further engage in a comparison between *Desperate Remedies* and *Middlemarch*. Instead, I wish to emphasise that the analysis of female sexuality through the representation of Dorothea Brooke in *Desperate Remedies* must be contextualized in relation to the construction of New Zealand national identity. After all, this is truly a New Zealand film – funded, written, produced, directed and acted entirely by New Zealanders.

Desperate Remedies did not receive a wide general release in North America and Britain, but it was enthusiastically promoted in both New Zealand and Australia. It was written and directed by the established New Zealand film-makers, Stewart Main and Peter Wells, who also both happen to be 'out' gay men. It was also released in 1994, around the same time as two more popular New Zealand films – the much discussed Jane Campion film *The Piano* (NZ, 1993)[2] and Peter Jackson's *Heavenly Creatures* (NZ, 1994). Like *Desperate Remedies*, *The Piano* and *Heavenly Creatures* both feature Pakeha women struggling to adapt to life in the new British colony. In *The Piano*, we follow Ada as she discovers her sexuality and negotiates her position as an English woman newly arrived in New Zealand. In *Heavenly Creatures*, Juliet, also recently arrived in New Zealand from

England, struggles unsuccessfully to find a place within heterosexual New Zealand society as she becomes sexually involved with her Pakeha girlfriend, Pauline.

Besides the three above-mentioned films, the subsequent two years saw the release of other New Zealand films such as *Once Were Warriors* (NZ, 1995), *The Cinema of Unease* (NZ, 1995) and *Broken English* (NZ, 1996). Although these three later films are not as explicitly concerned with the representation of Pakeha female sexuality, they are all preoccupied with an interrogation of pakeha New Zealand identity, both past and present. One of *Desperate Remedies'* film-makers, Stewart Main, also subsequently directed a short film called *Te Keremutunga o Nga Atua* (NZ, 1995), translated as *Twilight of the Gods*. The film tells the story of a tense camaraderie which develops between a toa (Maori warrior) and his Pakeha enemy during the historic land wars which took place before the creation of present day Pakeha New Zealand society. *Te Keremutunga o Nga Atua* explicitly foregrounds what is more subtly hinted at in *Desperate Remedies's* characterisation of Dorothea Brooke – that homosexual and interracial sexuality is unacceptable to the Pakeha soldiers who eventually won the war which marked the establishment of present day New Zealand society.

It is also worth noting that *The Cinema of Unease*, the New Zealand actor Sam Neil's production for the centenary of cinema, met with criticism within New Zealand even though it was enthusiastically received outside New Zealand. Since *The Cinema of Unease* is a documentary tracing how transgressive elements of a repressed heterosexual Pakeha New Zealand society emerges in New Zealand films such as *Heavenly Creatures*, *The Piano* and *Desperate Remedies*, I suggest that the New Zealand audience's reactions to *The Cinema of Unease*, combined with the type of films emerging from New Zealand in the last few years, reflect a moment of crisis in New Zealand national identity. I thus return to the character Dorothea Brooke in *Desperate Remedies*, and posit that the representation of her transgressive sexuality plays out the difficulty that New Zealand society has in positioning racial, gender and sexual difference.

Desperate Remedies

At the beginning of the film, right after the opening credits, the words 'a distant point of Empire, in a land called Hope', fill the screen. I suggest that this opening scene and other references later in the film, firmly identify this fantasy place called 'Hope' as New Zealand. First of all, the opening scene at the docks retells the history of the arrival of English settlers to the colonies. Then, in order to distinguish this place 'Hope' from other British colonies, there are several shots of people with Maori tattoos, identifying 'Hope' as New Zealand. Finally, the many pointed references to Sydney and later snide remarks about 'Australian aristocracy' situate the film firmly in the antipodes, and make it possible to read it explicitly as a story about the creation of Pakeha New Zealand society.

Lyden (1997) has suggested that ships and docks play an important role in New Zealand films since it is historically a settler nation. It is significant that *Desperate Remedies'* opening and closing scenes are set at the docks, with long shots, medium shots and close-ups of ships. We are also first introduced to Dorothea Brooke in this opening dockside scene. Dressed in a rich red period costume, Dorothea sweeps into view accompanied by an equally dramatic soundtrack. Her sumptuous appearance is highlighted by its marked contrast with the other more poorly dressed characters. In addition to her spectacular dress, Dorothea's social difference is emphasised as the scene ends with a close-up of her business card introducing her as a 'draper of distinction'.

This opening scene is also marked by an extended sequence of shot-reverse shots between Dorothea and the white hero, Lawrence Haste. I suggest that this heterosexual exchange of looks hints that Dorothea's social respectability is based on the presumption that she is a heterosexual woman whose sexual interest is directed towards socially acceptable white Englishmen. However, by the last scene, when Dorothea again returns to the dock, this time to flee the country, her social status has been tarnished. From being an economically successful entrepreneur and the upwardly mobile wife of a Minister of Parliament, Dorothea has fallen as a direct result of her transgression of the two prohibitions against miscegenation and homosexuality – to become a transgressive white woman who has to be expelled from 'Hope'.

Although it can be argued that her leaving the country is presented as a happy ending, the fact that she has no choice but to leave 'Hope' for some unknown place renders this optimistic reading problematic. This returns me to my argument that a white English woman's social position in the new British colony is never secure unless she also behaves in a sexually 'proper' manner. I will now examine Dorothea's transgression of the first taboo against interracial relationships.

Miscegenation

Before the prohibition against miscegenation can be discussed, cinematic representations of racial difference need to be examined. The different characters in *Desperate Remedies* are represented along marked racial lines, whereby the moral and social differences distinguishing the white characters from the non-white characters are established not only through narrative, but also through the use of costumes and soundtrack.

I return again to the first scene in the film. There is a shot of a placard in this scene saying 'Natives no problem'. The use of the term 'natives' indicates that the immigrants are arriving in a land where a racial discourse separating white people from the indigenous 'native' people has already been established. By stating that 'natives are not a problem', it also indicates that white people are already in control of the distribution of land and not the indigenous people. It reveals that white people are already making the rules about who is or is not a problem. Hence, the dynamics of white and non-white relations are already established in this first scene of the film.

Besides the sign clearly spelling out that the white English immigrant subject is already firmly located as the 'centre' and 'law-maker' of 'Hope', the difference in the dress of the characters further emphasises their racially dependant social position. As is the case in *The Piano*, the costumes of the various characters in *Desperate Remedies* are important indicators of their social status. Alongside the well-dressed white central characters, there exist some poorly dressed white characters – but even when these poor white characters resort to debauched sexual acts, they are depicted as victims of circumstances beyond their control. On the other hand, none of the few non-white characters are dressed in a 'civilised' manner. Just as the rich dress of the white characters, such as Dorothea Brooke, Lawrence Haste, Anne Cooper and even William Poyser, reflects their respectable social status and/or sexual desirability, so the dress of the non-white characters reflects their social and moral degradation. All the non-white characters in the film are depicted as evil seducers, opium distributors or servants. They are also regarded as sexual threats – and this threat is made explicit by costumes that reinforce the binary racial divide.

Said (1978) has argued that it is through the maintenance of racial stereotypes that the non-white subject is persistently reduced to the position of 'other'. Western film texts have frequently produced negative stereotypical images of non-white people that constantly emphasise their foreignness, alien sexuality and relatively low cultural or social skills. Young (1990) also explains that the West uses the 'non-West' as a signifier of all that is alien, perverse and 'other' in order to detract attention from its own 'perversity', which is disguised by the protective aura of whiteness.

The first non-white person depicted in *Desperate Remedies* is a Maori man with chains around his neck. This stereotypical representation of Maori people as savages that need to be tamed is continued throughout the film. In one of the last scenes, after the subtitle telling us that two years had passed, the camera zooms in to eroticize a shot of a man's naked buttock. Maori tattoos on this man's exposed bottom identify his ethnicity. Although he is shown serving a white guest food and drink, his face is never revealed. In contrast to the other people in this scene who are shown wearing trousers or dresses, the Maori servant is blatantly offered as a sexualized object of scrutiny.

Besides the Maori man in chains and the Maori man servant, there is also a Chinese character in the film. Again, old stereotypes about the Chinese being degenerate evil business people who profit from the distribution of illegal drugs are drawn upon. The Chinese woman works in the opium house, a place that thrives on the exploitation of masses of evil, laughing, pasty-looking, sick addicts wrapped in cocoons. She wears skin-tight sexy clothes, the type of clothing commonly worn by prostitutes in Western films. Besides being portrayed as an evil opium supplier, the Chinese woman, like the Maori characters, is transformed by her costume into a sexualised object.

Finally and most importantly, there is the racial representation of Fraser, the only non-white central character in *Desperate Remedies*. We are first introduced to a sexualized Fraser when Dorothea returns to her house after her visit to the docks. Fraser is shown topless, wearing only a pair of black leather trousers that cling to his lower body in a devilish sexual way. Other than the Maori man in chains, there have so far not been any bared torsos in the film. Later in the film, there are shots of another character, the white

Englishman Lawrence, in various states of undress. However, Lawrence is framed in a manner that suggests healthy desirable masculinity. The scenes in which Lawrence appear are accompanied by a soundtrack consisting of romantic music or happy laughter. In marked contrast, when Fraser is seen in similar states of undress, spooky music is played to suggest that something bad is happening. This only further emphasises the contrasting sexualization of Lawrence and Fraser. The negative sexualization of Fraser (through the aid of an appropriately atmospheric soundtrack) is remarkably similar to that of the other non-white characters in the film, suggesting that there is something threatening about non-white sexuality.

This leads me to the prohibition against miscegenation, the first sexual taboo which Dorothea transgresses. In a dramatic confession, we discover that her illicit sexual liaison with Fraser during her youth produced an illegitimate mixed race child. This revelation places Dorothea in the same position as her sister, Rose, who is described as having been 'undone' because of her interracial sexual liaison with Fraser. Miscegenation is deeply frowned upon in this film. Lawrence, who is set up as the representative voice of normative white heterosexuality, reacts negatively when he discovers that Rose and Dorothea were involved in interracial liaisons. With a sneer on his face, he tells Dorothea that 'the situation does not flatter you'. Clearly, despite the sign in the opening scene saying 'Natives No Problem', the reaction of the white characters suggest that 'natives' and all non-white people are actually a problem because they represent the ever present racial threat embodied by heterosexual miscegenation.

Young (1995) writes that white paranoia about non-white 'limitless fertility' is related to the fear that interracial reproductive sex will result in the creation of mixed race offspring who confuse the racial boundaries of black and white. It is thus not surprising that Dorothea is considered 'undone' because of her participation in interracial liaisons. Stoller (1995) further argues that the desire for the maintenance of racial boundaries and the fear of miscegenation is related to white fears about the instability of their own racial identity:

In contrast to the stereotype of the fixity of the racial other, bourgeois white identities, both child and adult, were more vulnerable, unstable and susceptible to change. Protection from this fear demanded a rerouting of desires, a displacement of eroticism, an externalization of arousal to a native or mixed-blood surrogate self.

(Stoller, 1995: 163-4)

By engaging in an interracial mixed race relationship, Dorothea's position as a respectable white woman is compromised. Just as Lawrence's discovery that his bride to be, Rose, has had an interracial liaison with Fraser is conflated with the revelation that his step-child will be 'half-caste'; the revelation of Dorothea's own interracial past also occurs simultaneously with her confession that she bore a mixed race child. I thus posit that the conflation of interracial relationships and the production of mixed-race children indicates that the prohibition of white women's interracial liaisons with non-white men is directly related to reproduction and the creation of socially unacceptable mixed race children.

Significantly, all the mixed race people (Fraser, Dorothea's child and Rose's child) in *Desperate Remedies* are illegitimate. The illegitimacy of these mixed race characters harkens back to old colonialist laws against miscegenation, which prohibit the legal recognition of marriages between people of different races. Lawrence's obviously negative reaction when he discovers that his step child (Fraser's child) is going to be 'half-caste', reaffirms *Desperate Remedies* unproblematised employment of racist discourses. The film's racial representation suggests that all mixed race people are inherently illegitimate, because they pervert the natural purity of the white race, through the transgression of racial boundaries.

Fraser, both the product and producer of illegitimate mixed race liaisons, has to be eliminated before the film's narrative can be resolved. The negative representation of his sexual history with the white heroine Dorothea and her sister Rose, suggests that Fraser is consistently presented as a dangerous sexual threat as long as he is alive. Even Fraser's death is not enough. All remaining traces of racial impurity are also erased when his mixed race child is killed by cholera. However, it is not only mixed race people who are eliminated. The white women who participate in interracial liaisons are also removed from 'Hope'. I have already mentioned that the film's heroine, Dorothea, who was involved with Fraser, is expelled from 'Hope' at the end of the film. Rose, the other white woman, who transgresses the taboo of miscegenation, is also removed from 'Hope' when she is killed off by cholera. Stoller suggests that by becoming involved with a non-white man, a white woman's racial identity is threatened in a more fundamental way than a white man who is interracially involved with a non-white woman.

> Europeanness was not only class-specific but gender coded. A European man could live with or marry an Asian woman without necessarily losing rank, but this was never true for a European woman who might make a similar choice to live with or marry a non-European. Thus in the legal debates on mixed-marriage in 1887, a European woman who has married a native man was dismissively accorded native legal status on the grounds that her very choice of sexual and conjugal partner showed that she has 'already sunk so deep socially and morally that it does not result in any ruin . . . [but rather] serves to consolidate her situation.'
>
> (Stoller, 1995 :115)

Therefore, having already jeopardised her social status through her involvement in an interracial relationship with Fraser, Dorothea's later lesbianism comes as no surprise, since she is already perceived by Lawrence and the Pakeha New Zealand society of 'Hope' as being a sexually transgressive woman. This leads me to the second taboo, the prohibition against homosexuality, which Dorothea also breaks.

White female homosexuality

In most mainstream films, the predominant representation of the lesbian and gay person is generally a depressingly negative one. Some common (and almost always sexualized) stereotypes include the effeminate gay man, the man-hating butch lesbian, the depressed, perverse and immoral homosexual. Without actually listing all the commonly used stereotypes, it suffices to say that these sexualized stereotypes are employed effectively to emphasise the difference of homosexuals from more socially 'normal' heterosexuals:

> Our culture routinely demands an explanation of our desires, presumed in advance to be abnormal, deviant, aberrant, even pathological. Even in current theories of representation, where identity, subjectivity, and sexual difference figure prominently, *homo*sexual identities, subjectivities, and differences are frequently overlooked, disavowed, or otherwise declared irrelevant.
>
> (Bad Object Choices, 1991: 12-13)

However, unlike most mainstream films, *Desperate Remedies* does not stereotype Dorothea negatively because of her homosexuality. In fact, *Desperate Remedies* is constructed around the 'heroic' struggle that Dorothea and Anne have to undergo in order to dispose of Fraser before they can live together as lovers. The audience is invited to identify and sympathise with the two lesbians. However, despite portraying the lesbians sympathetically, the film ends by indicating that there is no place where they can be together in the new British colony of 'Hope'. Just as Dorothea had to hide her socially prohibited interracial relationship with Fraser, so she also had to hide her homosexual relationship with Anne. Homosexual liaisons are thus depicted as being as socially unacceptable as interracial ones.

Elleray (1997) has argued that the lesbianism of Juliet and Pauline in *Heavenly Creatures* questions and unsettles the identity of the 1950s community of Christchurch, New Zealand, because as a new settler community, New Zealand national identity is still insecure. Although *Heavenly Creatures* is based on a real-life event whilst *Desperate Remedies* is fictional, I suggest that Elleray's remarks can also be applied to the representation of lesbianism in *Desperate Remedies*, where Dorothea and Anne are expelled from 'Hope' because their lesbianism represents a transgressive challenge to Pakeha New Zealand identity. After all, the film's narrative posits that Dorothea becomes a social outcast because of her transgressive homosexual desire for Anne. Even though Dorothea manages to hide her transgressive interracial liaison with Fraser for many years, her uncontainable homosexual desire for Anne eventually leads to her exposure as *both* racially and homosexually transgressive.

I would also suggest that by the end of the film Dorothea and Anne's illicit homosexual desire for each other has rendered them remarkably similar to the villain, Fraser. At the beginning of the film, Anne and Dorothea remind each other 'don't forget why we are doing this'. By the end of the film, we find out that their homosexual desire for each other has led to the creation of a complicated plot which results in the deaths of Rose, Fraser and their son. Their homosexual desires are thus implicated as negatively destructive, and not dissimilar to Fraser's destructive mixed race sexuality which led to the social expulsion and moral demise of two white women. Jennifer Terry (1995) has suggested that there is a similar reason why both homosexuality and interracial sexuality are often considered to be negatively transgressive:

> In the larger social context, some of the same logic applied to homosexuals that applied to those whose relationships crossed racial and class boundaries: sexual contact of an 'unnatural' sort would corrupt the population and lead to further social disorder. Panic about miscegenation was deeply tied to eugenic fears about ensuring proper rates of reproduction among the desirable (i.e., white) members of society.
>
> (Terry, 1995 :139)

I have already indicated that non-white people, like homosexuals, have frequently been marginalized through the use of negative stereotypes in Western cinematic discourse. Non-white people are perceived as different because of their racial identity, whilst homosexuals are coded as 'perverse' because of their sexual difference. However, although they are superficially minoritised for different reasons, the fact that the strategy of racist discourse, like homophobic discourse, often relies on extreme negative *sexual* stereotypes, suggests that both non-white people and homosexuals are cinematically represented in negative sexual terms because of their threatening reproductive power. As Terry suggests, whilst homosexuals are depicted as being sexually perverse because of their failure to reproduce the 'proper' heirs, non-white people are depicted as sexually perverse because of the fear of miscegenation – that is, their potential to reproduce '*im*proper' heirs.

This leads me to posit that it is not homosexual practices in general which are transgressive. In a film such as *Desperate Remedies* which engages with Western discourses of race, sexuality and nationality, only *white* homosexual relationships are transgressive. Non-white homosexuality is not threatening to the interests of the expanding British empire. Lynda Hart (1994: 116) writes that 'the lesbian enters representation . . . in response to the demands of white supremacy. This lesbian has thus entered representational histories *as* white'. She further explains that the white lesbian is seen as 'the enemy *within*' because she does not assist in the maintenance of the white race through engaging in reproductive heterosexual relations. *Desperate Remedies* is structured around a heterosexual versus homosexual romantic conflict, embodied in Anne and Lawrence's pursuit of Dorothea; and by choosing an unreproductive homosexual relationship, Dorothea simultaneously rejects her proper role as an English woman – namely the furtherance of the heterosexual reproduction of white English settlers which would be achieved by setting up home with Lawrence Haste in New Zealand.

The Construction of White Heterosexual New Zealand Society: 'The Land of Milk and Honey'

Hence, by participating in both interracial and homosexual relationships, Dorothea doubly undermines the British Empire's aim of constructing a racially secure white heterosexual society in the colony 'Hope'. Through her interracial relationship with Fraser, Dorothea becomes a transgressive white woman who 'betrays the (white) race' by producing the racially 'wrong' children. Similarly, by engaging in a non-productive white homosexual relationship, she again 'betrays the (white) race' because she does *not* reproduce, and does *not* assist in maintaining the heterosexual nuclear family by reproducing the right heirs.

Therefore, it is not coincidental that the celebration of winning the war takes place when Dorothea Brook flees the country with Anne Cooper. I suggest that by ending the film at this stage – where the war has been won, the white lesbians expelled, the mixed race Fraser, his racially transgressive white lover Rose and their mixed race child all dead – the film suggests that the creation of an acceptable Pakeha New Zealand society is only possible with the exclusion of these sexually and racially transgressive characters.

In a scene in Dorothea's living room, William Poyser, Member of Parliament, declares: 'We will build a land of milk and honey' (*Desperate Remedies*). As a member of parliament, William Poyser is in a position to shape the construction of the new society. However, in that same scene, we also see that William's vision of an ideal society is received with discomfort by Dorothea. The camera first pans from William's beaming face to a close-up of Dorothea's uncomfortable expression. The camera then pans from Dorothea's worried upturned face to the living quarters upstairs, where Rose is suffering from being involved in an interracial relationship with Fraser and Anne is hiding her homosexual relationship with Dorothea. I suggest that this scene clearly illustrates Dorothea's awareness that as a white woman who has sexually transgressed the prohibitions against both homosexuality and interracial involvement, she does not have a place in the world of William Poyser, nor in 'Hope', nor in the 'land of milk and honey' which is also New Zealand.

Notes

1. 'Pakeha' is a Maori word, now commonly used to refer to white New Zealanders of European descent.
2. For instance, *Screen* journal Vol. 36 No. 3, Autumn 1995, features a special debate on *The Piano*, which in turn led to further articles in other *Screen* journals about the representation of white female sexuality in the same film.

References

Bad Object Choices (ed.), 1991, *How Do I Look? Queer Film and Video*, Seattle: Bay Press.

Dyer, Richard, 1993, *The Matter of Images: essays on representations*, London: Routledge.

Dyson, Lynda, 1995, 'The return of the repressed? Whiteness, femininity and colonialism in *The Piano*', *Screen* 36 (3), pp. 267–276.

Elleray, Michelle, 1997, '"Impressions of exotic lands": settler space in *Heavenly Creatures*', in Hanson, Ellis (eds.) *Out Takes: Essays on Queer Theory and Film*, North Carolina: Duke University Press.

Hart, Lynda, 1994, *Fatal Women: lesbian sexuality and the mark of aggression*, London: Routledge.

Lyden, Anne, 1997, 'Dockside Amour: Sexualized Spaces in *Desperate Remedies*', presentation at The Sixth Annual Cultural Studies Symposium, Kansas State University, Manhattan Kansas, March 1997.

McClintock, Anne, 1995, *Imperial Leather: race, gender and sexuality in the colonial contest*, London: Routledge.

Nussbaum, Felicity A., 1995, *Torrid Zones: Maternity, Sexuality and Empire in Eighteenth Century English Narrative*, USA: John Hopkins University Press.

Said, Edward, 1978, *Orientalism*, London: Penguin.

Stoller, Ann Laura, 1995, *Race and the Education of Desire*, London: Duke University Press.

Terry, Jennifer, 1995, 'Anxious Slippages between "Us" and "Them": A Brief History of the Scientific Search for Homosexual Bodies' in Jennifer Terry and Jacqueline Urla (eds.) *Deviant Bodies*, Bloomington: Indiana University Press, pp. 129–169.

Young, Robert, 1990, *White Mythologies*, London: Routledge.

Young, Robert, 1995, *Colonial Desire*, London: Routledge.

Nationality, Territoriality, and Communication:
Korean Context/Canadian Text

So-Hee Lee

> It (expressing yourself) is opening yourself, discarding your *self*, so that the language and the world may be evoked through you. *Evocation* is quite different from *expression* . . . Maybe the writer *expresses*; but *evocation*, calling up, is what writing does for the reader.
> Margaret Atwood, 'An End to Audience?' (Emphasis mine)

At the Intersection: A Canadian Writer meets Korean Readers

In his provocative article, 'What is an author?', Michel Foucault calls into question the unique relationship between an author and a text, suggesting that writing creates 'a space into which the writing subject constantly disappears' (Foucault 1969/1988: 198). For him, discourse as the social function of meaning becomes a substitute for the traditional concept of the author. Writing is redefined as the interplay between the author as an individual and the author-function as a discourse, because the author's name represents a particular mode of existence of a specific discourse, while the author-function implies and reflects the existence, circulation, and manner of certain discourses within a specific socio-historical context.

Margaret Atwood, as a Canadian author, provides one of the best examples of Foucault's ideas on author-function and transgressive history in terms of a concept of 'national consciousness',[1] and this paper aims to explore the circulation of her writing within the specific socio-historic context of contemporary Korea. In Margaret Atwood's writing, her national identity as a Canadian is even stronger than her sexual identity as a woman. While Elizabeth Barrett Browning, the English woman poet, sought to find a literary grandmother, Margaret Atwood, the 'Canadian' 'woman' writer, began to look at first for 'Canadian' writers, rather than 'woman' writers in Canada. This is a conspicuous factor among major women writers in English-speaking countries. In her witty autobiographical forward entitled 'Great Unexpectations', Margaret Atwood described the situation in 1960 when she was looking for Canadian writers: 'For one thing, I was Canadian, and the prospects for being a Canadian and a writer, both at the same time, in 1960, were dim . . . Canadian writers, it was assumed – by my professors, my contemporaries, and myself – were a freak of nature, like duck-billed platypyses' (Atwood, 1988: xiii). In those days, for Atwood, being a Canadian was a much more serious issue than being a writer. Even the awakening consciousness of being a Canadian was a revolutionary act: 'It was at Harvard then that I first began to think seriously about Canada. Even the idea of thinking seriously about Canada had something shocking about it: seriousness and Canada just didn't seem to go together. It was almost revolutionary' (Atwood, 1982: 384). At last, by the time she was about 21, Atwood had both found and helped to found a tradition of Canadian writers. In other words, she is a producer as well as product of 1960s and 1970s literary nationalism in Canada. For instance, Atwood's 1972 publication *Survival* symbolizes the systematic pattern of a Canadian national literature and announces a simple statement, 'We exist'. Since then, 'survival' has been the main theme in Atwood's major writings. In *The Handmaid's Tale*, she is evidently concerned with this theme, which persists as a focus throughout her experiments in style, genre and narration.

The debate about national consciousness is now emerging as a pioneering field in the area of cultural studies – its relevance heightened by the technological developments that have broken down national, cultural, physical and geographical boundaries, creating an era of globalization. Homi K. Bhabha was among the first to comment upon these borderline non-signified spaces and he has proposed the terms *inter*national and 'in-between' space to facilitate analysis within this field. He raises the issue in *Nation and Narration*, where most essays are concerned with aspects of the British national consciousness. He questions 'What kind of a cultural space is the nation with its transgressive boundaries and its 'interruptive' interiority?' (Bhabha, 1990: 5). His interpretation of national consciousness as a cultural space leads us to a new conception of the *inter*national space as incomplete signification:

> The 'locality' of national culture is neither unified nor unitary in relation to itself, nor must it be seen simply as 'other' in relation to what is outside or beyond it. The boundary is Janus-faced and the problem of outside/inside must always itself be a process of hybridity, incorporating new 'people' in relation to the body politic, generating other sites of meaning and, inevitably, in the political process, producing unmanned sites of political antagonism and unpredictable forces for political representation.
>
> (Bhabha, 1990: 4)

In his recent book, *The Location of Culture*, Bhabha develops this idea of *inter*national and 'in-between' space, focusing not on the duration or end product, but on moments or processes that are produced in the articulation of cultural differences:

> These 'in-between' spaces provide the terrain for elaborating strategies of selfhood – singular or communal – that initiate new signs of identity, and innovative sites of collaboration, and contestation, in the act of defining the idea of society itself.
>
> (Bhabha, 1994: 1-2)

However, this 'newness' that emerges from the borderline work in 'in-between' space does not mean that a continuum can be established between the past and the present, nor does it suggest the dominance of a particular side. Rather, 'it creates a sense of the new as an insurgent act of cultural translation' (1994: 7). In 'The Commitment to Theory' first published in 1989, Bhabha has already argued the importance of a Third Space, which later gives way to his concepts of *inter*national and 'in-between' space. He insists, 'The production of meaning requires that these two places be mobilised in the passage through a Third Space, which represents both the general conditions of language and the specific implication of the utterance in a performative and institutional strategy of which it cannot "in itself" be conscious' (Bhabha, 1994: 36). By emphasizing the importance of language and utterance in a Third Space, he summarizes this unconscious relation as an ambivalence in the act of interpretation (36). Like Michel Foucault, he also considers 'it's a problem of verbalisation' (1990: 8).

Therefore, the purpose of my paper is to explore Bhabha's Third Space, through a verbalisation of the cultural communication between a group of Korean readers and a Canadian writer. By focusing on the intersection of two national consciousnesses in the process of reading literature, it becomes possible to map out otherwise hidden psychological dimensions. In order to do this, the positionality of my *localized* discourse is one of standing between Korea and Canada on the borderline of an *inter*national and 'in-between' space.

Cultural Communication : Korean Readers' Responses to *The Handmaid's Tale*

For the purpose of this research, since 1994, I had looked within Korean academic institutions for a postgraduate group which would be well prepared for a productive discussion on female sexuality. There were not many candidates for my purposes.[2] After contacting several groups, the 'Public Culture & Feminism' course in the Sociology department at Yonsei University in Seoul was chosen. The number of students was around 10–13. Most of them were first-year postgraduates from 23 to 28 years old. Only one of them was over 30, a married Ph.D. candidate, and the group also contained a Japanese postgraduate majoring in Sociology at Yonsei University. Exceptionally, during this term, all the students were women. That was an unusual case even in a course on feminism. The discussion on *The Handmaid's Tale* was held on the 26th of April, 1994 as a Canadian example of foreign public cultures, located between *Orlando*, the British/European film, and *Three Colours: Blue*, the French/European film. The translated text was used for the class discussion[3] and we watched the film in order to make a genre comparison.

The most prominent and common response was an uncomfortable feeling. The students did not enjoy reading it at all. Nor was it pleasurable. Most of them were irritated by the story and the narrative style. One of them who could not bear Atwood's 'violent' writing[4] went back to the last part of the text, 'The Historical Notes', after reading several early chapters, because she was looking for a commentary to aid her understanding. However, unfortunately, she was much more confused after reading it, because this epilogue provides perhaps the best example of Atwood's violent writing throughout the text, subverting the female persona's first-person narrative through the male academic's patriarchal interpretation. Another student

149

confessed that she would like to avoid reading the text, if possible, because she had known the story from watching the film several years ago. But, this time, while she was reading the text, she developed an ambivalent feeling about Atwood's writing that she found very difficult to articulate:

> During my reading of the text, I have had an ambivalent feeling. That is, I am very much struck by Atwood's highly elaborated and delicate writing, while I am feeling a chill creep over myself. The text says too many things, but I can't grasp what they are, in detail. I have felt a complicated feeling, but I can't describe what it is. Now, I can see myself hesitating and wavering still about my position, because I can't find any language to analyze my feeling which implies that something wrong has been said and defined, related to the term 'female sexuality'.
>
> (Choung-Rhan Cho 1)

This writing shows well the reader's paradoxical involvement with distance from the text, which can be the ambivalent counterpart of Atwood's violent writing.

Female sexuality in the Canadian written text and in the Korean socio-historical context gradually emerged as the main topic of the students' discussion. All of them pointed out the 'Ceremony' section as the most awful and terrifying part of the whole story. None of them had ever imagined such a mechanical act of fertilization, where love, passion, tenderness, any kind of human communication, even sexual desire was forbidden. They said it was very disturbing and shocking, especially this paragraph:

> My red skirt hitched up to my waist, though no higher. Below it the Commander is fucking. What he is fucking is the lower part of my body. I do not say making love, because this is not what he's doing. Copulating too would be inaccurate, because it would imply two people and only one is involved. Nor does rape cover it : Nothing is going on here that I haven't signed up for. There wasn't a lot of choice but there was some, and this is what I chose.
>
> (Atwood, 1985/1987: 104–105)

In very cautious mood, an opinion was suggested that this 'Ceremony' scene was reminiscent of the use of Korean Military Sexual Slavery Women by the Japanese state power during the Japanese colonial period from 1910 to 1945. The situation of these women was quite similar to structures described in Atwood's text. The students referred to the Handmaid's dutiful 'work' as a sexual slavery, and thoroughly discussed the colonization of female sexuality by state power. For Korean women readers, Offred's story was not a future tense but a past history. This mechanical fucking, as a collective act, constituted the repetition of a historical patterning from the 1920s and 1930s in Korean history.[5] While Gilead state power put a small tattoo on the fertile female body to indicate it was a national resource before allocating it to the Commanders in the text, so Korean women were sent to battle fields outside Korea as sexual commodities for Japanese male sexual desire, labelled as a 'present from the Great Japanese Emperor'. In an interview for the Canadian Broadcasting Corporation, Atwood had already remarked that every event in the text was now happening or had already happened somewhere in the world: 'I clipped articles out of newspapers. I now have a large clipping file of stories supporting the contents of the book' (Kolodny, 1990: 97). Moreover, this scene confirmed that *The Handmaid's Tale* could be classified as what Linda Hutcheon terms 'historiographic metafiction'. But this definition depends not only upon the writer's input, but also upon the reader's output. For Korean women readers, it seemed that *The Handmaid's Tale* traced 'the processing of events into facts, exploiting and then undermining the conventions of both novelistic realism and historiographic reference'(Hutcheon, 1989: 78). The Gileadean Handmaids must perform this mechanical act of fertilization once a month as 'two legged wombs, sacred vessels, ambulatory chalices' (Atwood, 1985/1987: 146) for the 'white' species in the name of Gilead. But Korean Military Sexual Slavery Women had to suffer this mechanical act of penetration many times in a day, normally 30 or 40 times and even over 80 times.[6] In both cases, women were exchangeable sexual commodities. In an interview with Cathy Davidson for *MS* magazine, Atwood remarked 'I didn't invent a lot' (1986: 26) in *The Handmaid's Tale*: 'I transposed to a different time and place, but the motifs are all historical motifs' (1986: 24), confirming again that everything in the text had already occurred in some society. What is implied here is the crucial issue of how we have chosen to construct history. Offred imagines that 'From the point of future history . . . we'll be invisible' (Atwood, 1985/1987: 240). And Atwood's text explores the evils of a society based upon hierarchical dichotomies, while forcing her readers to 'recognise their blindness and responsibility' in a specific socio-historical context (Grace, 1983: 13). However, although Korean Military Sexual Slavery Women were rendered invisible by Japanese history, their existence was prominently and clearly imprinted upon the record of Korean history. On the other hand, several students expressed objections to reading the text in terms of 'blindness and responsibility'. To them such a reading translated into a definition of Korean women as other – as the object of sensationalised western discourse about the non-western world. These concerns gave rise to some tension during the discussion of the 'Ceremony' section, before the group moved on to consider the power relationship between husband and wife, especially at the moment of sexual intercourse.

Female sexuality in Offred's story was colonized not only by state power but also by economic power in everyday life. In the Republic of Gilead, women were not allowed to have any financial property or hold a job. However, even in the pre-Gilead days, when 'the narrator'[7] realized that she would no longer be allowed to hold a job, or property, or even her own 'Compucount', she was filled with rage, anxiety, and humiliation: 'Desperation alone should have driven me. But I still felt numbed. I could hardly even feel his hands on me' (Atwood, 1985/1987: 191). She felt that the loss of financial power meant sexual colonization. She could not make love as usual and her body began to be stiff.

I felt shrunken, so that when he put his arms around me, gathering me up, I was small as a doll. I felt love going forward without me.

He doesn't mind this, I thought. He doesn't mind it at all. Maybe he even likes it. We are not each other's, any more. Instead, I am his.

(Atwood, 1985/1987: 191)

This episode prompted the Korean women readers to discuss a newly coined metaphor for female bodies circulating in contemporary Korean society, 'the washing board'.[8] This image suggests that the wife's body must be ready in the name of the marriage whenever the husband needed it. This kind of power relationship in terms of sexuality was in many cases paralleled by the wife's economic disability in capitalist patriarchal Korean society. A student described her feeling after looking at the Gileadean society as follows:

While watching such a strange and unthinkable society, I began to think that we also may live such a strange and unthinkable society if someone outside of our social system and cultural value is watching our society. In addition, if this story shows the extreme of our social discourse around female sexuality, it also may imply that we are living in a closed society, subordinating our female selves to the patriarchal social system and cultural value in our society.

(Ji-Yeon Lee 2)

Now, she began to look at herself from a certain distance within the Korean context, defamiliarizing her own socio-historical context. Therefore, the theme of female sexuality in *The Handmaid's Tale* has stimulated these Korean women readers to recognize the positionality of their national and sexual identities within contemporary Korean society.

Most of the students commented upon the fragmented writing style, tricky genre, and scattered nature of Offred's narratives. Their impression was that the future tense in the text had, in effect, become the present tense, because they felt that this whole story was happening in contemporary Korean society. It was a very frightening story. But nobody denied that it was a part of contemporary Korean society. The students had mostly admired Atwood's 'persistent' style of writing, and this opened up another important discussion about the text. Why were this writer's perceptions of patriarchy and sexual politics so different from those of other British and American women writers? Even though the translated text was used for this discussion, they noticed that Atwood's writing style was very different from their other reading texts, whether written in Korean or translated into Korean. One of them suggested that someone who had never been marginalized could not have this kind of point of view and maybe could not persist so tenaciously with such a fragmented style, unless the writing was emerging from her own experience. During that discussion, it was also said that men could not understand women's marginalized experience and the colonizer could not know how the colonized had been repressed and exploited throughout their everyday lives. But, they did not mention racial issues at all, because Korean society had never witnessed racial conflict until 1990, when foreign workers from South East Asia began to come to Korea. Of course, whether the characteristics of Atwood's writing could be Canadian or not was also discussed, and was followed by further discussion about the difference between the novel and the film. The women regretted that there was no strong tension in the film, which most of them considered as the most manifest characteristic of the text. They suggested that the reasons why the film was so disappointing compared with the novel were, firstly, because the director was not a woman and, secondly, not a Canadian. It was also said that the film was a non-Canadian product, except the initiating imagination. For me, this response was quite exciting if we considered that Atwood had defined herself at first as a Canadian and then as a woman. To Korean women readers, it was the writer's sexual identity rather than her national identity that had appealed to them as an influencing factor in her creative imagination, emphasizing their better understanding of women's communal experiences.

Their responses to 'The Historical Section' also expressed an ambivalent duality. On one hand, they felt happy that the Republic of Gilead had disappeared and the new society had emerged where people could talk about the Handmaids in the public domain. But, on the other hand, they were very disappointed about the way in which the male historian, Pieixoto, had treated Offred's story, because they considered it Offred's silent screaming to publicize her 'survival', saying 'I exist here as a woman'. When they were describing this sentence, I was secretly very much surprised at the exact coincidence of vocabulary, because they had never read any informative articles about the 'survival' theme in Margaret Atwood. Furthermore, one of them described Offred's narrative as her substitute for her life, dangerously continued in desperate circumstances. At the last stage of their discussion, they were reaching a secure agreement that it was another kind of repression, to ignore anyone's effort to preserve her self in an urgent situation, which they had never thought of before, even if it was looked on by others as trivial. Nobody could accuse the others of this triviality because no one could fully understand the whole situation of *the other*. Their last response to 'The Historical Section' is instead the violent question, 'How can we expect that Pieixoto as a male academic could understand how desperate Offred's life was as a Handmaid in Gilead?'

The Handmaid's Tale as a postmodern text did work successfully to expand these readers' reading from the text itself to their own living context. It had wonderfully *evoked* and *called up*, as Margeret Atwood said, the Korean readers' way of looking at themselves in a Korean context with a new point of view. One of the students said that *The Handmaid's Tale* forced her to contemplate two issues: One was her sexual identity in Korean society, that is, how different her situation was from women in the Republic of Gilead. The other was how the patriarchal ideology about child-bearing and rearing had dehumanized women's lives with an incredibly forceful power and influence. By this reading act, they illustrated that they were the writers as well as the readers of the postmodern text, *The Handmaid's Tale*. At the same time, they also proposed that texts were not fixed at all, but

153

always waiting for the subjective as well as the creative interpretation. These students' responses to *The Handmaid's Tale* showed the reading process to be capable of stimulating a self-conscious awakening to an awareness of differences and commonalities through cultural communication.

In the *Inter*national and 'In-between' Territory : Reading Korean Context from/on Canadian Text

Since Roland Barthes's 'The Death of the Author' (1968) and Wolfgang Iser's 'The Reading Process: a Phenomenological Approach'(1972), the relationship between the text and the reader has been conceptualised as more of a socialization process. However, there is an absence in the work of Barthes and Iser. Terry Eagleton points out that both Barthes and Iser ignore *'the position of the reader in history'*, namely the specific socio-historical context:

> If Iser offers us a grimly 'normative' model which reins in the unbounded potential of language, Barthes presents us with a private, asocial, essentially anarchic experience which is perhaps no more than the flip-side of the first. Both critics betray a liberal distaste for systematic thought; both in their different ways ignore the position of the reader in history. For readers do not of course encounter texts in a void: all readers are socially and historically positioned, and how they interpret literary works will be deeply shaped by this fact.
>
> (Eagleton, 1983: 83)

This discussion of *'the position of the reader in history'* is directly linked to arguments on postcolonialism in the 1990s, because the reader's self-conscious reading becomes the starting point for self-representation by producing a subjective, specific and autonomous discourse. Hae-Joang Cho, working on postcolonialism and Gender Studies in Korea, defines from her position the term *'colonial'* as the counterpart of *'postcolonial'*:

> In my writing, I call *'colonial'* society the society which does not have its own discourse to explain its own problems, which cannot produce its own autonomous theory to analyse its social phenomena. Here, the term, *'colonial'* means the phenomena of disconnection between the knowledge and the life in that society, rather than the concrete colonized historical fact of that society.
>
> (Cho, 1992: 22)

Korean women readers' responses to *The Handmaid's Tale* have both illustrated the kind of social discourse that has been conducted around female sexuality at the public level within Korean society and suggested the possibility of a postcolonial discourse on the subject.

Because of its socio-historical heritage of Confucianism,[9] Korean society has only recently allowed discussion of female sexuality in public domains, such as the classroom within an academic institution. Owing to the Korean women's movement and the democratization of Korean society in the 1980s, social awareness regarding sexuality and sexual politics has dramatically increased through the 1990s.[10] In particular, the generation born in the late 1960s and early 1970s, when Korea was achieving a certain level of economic development, are now beginning to shake this Confucian cultural heritage.[11] However, this generation now stands on the borderline between the globalizing social process of westernization and the Korean web of strong Confucian tradition. Their sceptical response to traditional concept of female sexuality at the private level as 'the washing board' reflects their recognition that the wife's sexuality has been socially defined as subordinate to her husband. However, most women have stopped at the level of awakening and have not yet gone further to discuss their own subjective female sexuality. This means that the social discourse around female sexuality in Korean society is still not an easy topic to discuss and debate is not yet as sophisticated and diversified as in western European societies. Rather, Korean women have come to understand sexual intercourse within the marriage as a power-game between two sexes.

Nonetheless, the debate about female sexuality at the public level illustrates the impact of Korean women's history upon the national consciousness. Discussion has circulated widely in contemporary Korean society since Hak-Sun Kim in her late 60s became the first former Korean Military Sexual Slavery Women to tell her experience at the church group's office in Seoul on 14 August 1990.[12] This is why the 'Ceremony' scene has become for them the best example of what Wolfgang Iser terms *gestalt* – that is, the meeting point where the intersubjective interaction happens between historical reality and the reader's imagination.

> This *gestalt* must inevitably be colored by our own characteristic selection process. For it is not given by the text itself; it arises from the meeting between the written text and the individual mind of the reader with its own particular history of experience, its own consciousness, its own outlook.
>
> (Iser, 1972/1988: 219)

In this case, the *gestalt* arises from the meeting between the Canadian text, *The Handmaid's Tale*, and the individual mind of the Korean reader, drawing on its own particular 'collective' experience from history. The emergence of national and sexual identities from the nebulous territory of the national consciousness facilitates readers' simultaneous involvement in and distance from the text. In addition, their ambivalence to this *gestalt* substantiates Bhabha's argument about the national consciousness as a cultural space rather than a definite entity.

This act of reading a text from another culture from a feminist point of view can question and answer at the same time the universality of gender oppression and the homogeneity of national consciousness, which still remains in many western feminist discourses. By this experience of a reading act, I can say that historicizing and locating the reader's response can provide an essential alternative to formulations based on universality and homogeneity. As Chandra Talpade Mohanty insists in her article, 'Feminist Encounters: Locating the Politics of Experience', the crucial questions in the 1990s concern the construction, examination and, more significantly, the institutionalization of difference *within* feminist discourses (1992: 74). For her, working in American society, the universality of gender oppression is a problematic concept, based as it is on the assumption that the categories of race and class have to be invisible for gender to be visible (1992: 75). But, my experience working in 'English' Studies as a 'Korean' feminist critic has shown[13] that readers from one culture can respond to texts from another culture by creating their own subjective discourse without imposing a false 'universality' and a national 'homogeneity'. What is at issue here is rather a cross-cultural interaction in the *inter*national and 'in-between' territory where the postcolonial feminist critic can discover a *localized* gendered oppression within a *heterogeneous* national consciousness.

Notes

[1] For my argument on Margaret Atwood in the Canadian context, I prefer to use the term 'national consciousness', rather than 'nationalism' or 'nationality'. As Benedict Anderson defines the nation as 'an imagined political community' and shows the origins of national consciousness in late eighteenth and early nineteenth century Europe, so Margaret Atwood can be seen to provide a Canadian counterpart (cf. Benedict Anderson, 1983, 'The Origin of National Consciousness' in *Imagined Communities: Reflections on the Origin and Spread of Nationalism*, London: Verso, p. 15). Ernest Gellner has observed that 'Nationalism is not the awakening of nations to self-consciousness: it *invents* nations where they do not exist' (cf. Ernest Gellner, 1964, *Thought and Change*, Weidenfeld & Nicolson, p. 169). However, I would like to focus on the process of an individual's self-awakening to the concept of her national identity, and have selected the term 'national consciousness' as more appropriate for this focus.

[2] Since 1994, I have taught this text in several courses in English Studies and Women's Studies. In most cases at undergraduate level, the theme of female sexuality in the text would only superficially be mentioned. Undergraduates need more explanation than their own discussion. However, even in the postgraduate level English course, this text is considered too radical to discuss in the classroom because of its representation of female sexuality.

[3] This is another issue between language and literature that arises in the Korean context, where English is a foreign language. However, I think this methodology of using the Korean translation and discussing it in the Korean language in the classroom is the best way to figure out opinions on female sexuality in a specifically Korean context.

[4] Since Sherrill E. Grace (1980) suggested 'violent duality' as characteristic of Margaret Atwood's writing, surviving through 'violent

duality' has become a symbol for Atwood's concern with the process of overcoming the polarization of world and self, as well as the hierarchical power structures which such divisions produce.

[5] Approximately 100,000 to 200,000 Korean women were appropriated for this 'service', representing 80% of those placed in Asian Military Sexual Slavery Women by Japan.

[6] This is quoted from 'The Murmuring', a Korean documentary film about the former KMSSW. It was released for the first time at two commercial theatres and two university theatres in Seoul from 29 April to 13 May 1995. Later, its showing was extended for two months in Seoul and revived several times at various places. It was warmly and passionately welcomed by the younger generation of Koreans and won the Ogawa Shinske Prize at the 1995 Yamagata International Film Festival, the Jury Special Mention at the 1996 Amsterdam Amnesty International Film Festival as well as at the 1996 Munchen International Documentary Film Festival.

[7] Here, I use this term because, in another example of Atwood's linguistic games, we do not learn Offred's name in the pre-Gilead days.

[8] This term is used for describing a wife's passive and subordinate sexuality within marriage in the Korean film, 'A Story of Marriage' (1992). Another sexual metaphor for a married woman's position in that film was the bed in the bedroom. Since then, this metaphor 'the washing board' has gained wide circulation to indicate current attitudes to female sexuality among young Korean women.

[9] Since the Yi dynasty took Confucianism as the spirit of the national foundation in 1392, Confucianism has become Koreans' fundamental way of thinking and had a powerful influence on the Korean way of life. It emphasizes loyalty, filial piety, ancestor worship and, especially for women, fidelity and chastity. The basic idea of Confucianism is expressed by 'the three fundamental principles and the five moral disciplines' in human relationships. For instance, between sovereign and subject, justice and righteousness should mark the relationship; between father and son, there should be affection; between husband and wife, there should be the matrimonial etiquette which confirms the segregated gender roles; between the younger and the elder, precedence should be given to the elder; between friends, faith should reign over the relationship. Even if it is evident that it has been weakened by western cultural influence since the liberation from Japanese colonialism in 1945, the Confucian value system still strongly permeates everyday life in Korea.

[10] When I carried out my research on 'Women Characters in Victorian Novels' at the Faculty of English, Cambridge, in 1986, I was so embarrassed about what I heard during the lectures and seminars. Why were they talking about sexuality, masculinity, and femininity? What was the relationship between those terms and feminist literary criticism? In those days, we Koreans didn't have exact counterpart terms for sex, sexuality, sexual intercourse, and gender, and it can be imagined how confused I was in establishing the appropriate meanings. In Korean, one

term could be generally used for these four concepts, and its particular meaning depended on the speaking and listening context. Since language is the social vehicle for the specific meaning, this episode illustrates that those concepts were not diversified in Korean society in the mid 1980s. At the annual Korean Women's Studies Association Conference in 1989, this issue was raised and discussed. In recent days, amongst the four terms, the Korean counterpart of sexual intercourse has become widely used, accompanied by the frequent use of the Korean counterpart for sexual violence.

[11] From this point of view, the year of 1995 played an important role as a key period in the social discourse on female sexuality, because young Korean women in their late 20s began to speak about their sexual subjectivity in the form of popular culture, for example, the novel *The Pornography in My Mind* and the film *Mommy has a lover*. Both blatantly challenged and resisted female fidelity and chastity as symbolised by the silver knife in strict Confucian culture. In traditional Korean culture, when a woman, especially a married woman, was seen to be sexually unfaithful, she was expected to kill herself with the small silver knife which she always kept with her. However, the social discourse on female sexuality completely outside marriage has yet to be developed.

[12] For instance, at the annual Korean Women's Studies Association Conference held at Ewha Woman's University in Seoul, Korea in June 1994, Professor Hae-Shoo Shin delivered her paper 'Nationalism and Feminism: Their Reconciliation and Conflict in the Case of the Korean Military Sexual Slavery by Japan'. She demonstrated her own experience during the last two years, while working as the President of the International Co-operation Committee in Korea for the Military Sexual Slavery by Japan. Two years later, Young-Sook Shin and Hye-Ran Cho published the invaluable and widely researched article 'On the Characteristics and Special Nature of the Korean "Military Comfort Women" under Japanese Rule' in *Korea Journal*, Vol. 36, No. 1, Spring 1996, pp. 50–78. Now, the autobiographical testimonies of 19 Korean Military Sexual Slavery Women are also available in English translation, *True Stories of the Korean Comfort Women*, (ed.) Keith Howard (London: Cassell, 1995).

[13] For me, these two categories have formed a hostile contradiction, because both locate me in marginalised territory in terms of culture. If I was not doing English Studies but Korean Studies, my epistemological development would be quite different.

References

Atwood, Margaret, 1982, 'An End to Audience' in Atwood, M. (ed.) *Second Words*, Ontario: House of Anansi Press, pp. 334–357.
Atwood, Margaret, 1982, 'Canadian-American Relations: Surviving the Eighties' in Atwood, M. (ed.) *Second Words*, Ontario: House of Anansi Press, pp. 371–392.

Atwood, Margaret, 1985/1987, *The Handmaid's Tale*, London: Virago Press.

Atwood, Margaret (ed.), 1982, *Second Words*, Ontario: House of Anansi Press.

Atwood, Margaret, 1988, 'Great Unexpectations: An Autobiographical Forward' in Spanckeren, K. V. and Castro, J. G. (eds.) *Margaret Atwood: Visions and Forms*, Carbondale and Edwardville: Southern Illinois University Press, pp. xiii–xvi.

Bhabha, Homi K., 1989, 'The Commitment to Theory', in Bhabha, Homi K. *The Location of Culture* (1994), London and New York: Routledge, pp. 19–39.

Bhabha, Homi K. (ed.), 1990, *Nation and Narration*, London and New York: Routledge.

Bhabha, Homi K., 1994, *The Location of Culture*, London and New York: Routledge.

Cho, Choung-Rhan, 1994, 'Reading *The Handmaid's Tale*', short piece of solicited writing (in Korean; translated by So-Hee Lee).

Cho, Hae-Joang, 1992, *Here and Now, In the Classroom*, Vol. 1 of *Reading Books & Reading Lives*, 3 Vols. 1992–94, Seoul: The Alternative Culture Press (in Korean; translated by So-Hee Lee).

Davidson, Arnold E. (ed.), 1990, *Studies on Canadian Literature: Introductory and Critical Essays*, New York: The Modern Language Association of America.

Davidson, Cathy, 1986, 'Feminist 1984: Margaret Atwood talks about her exciting new novel', *MS*, 14, pp. 24–26.

Eagleton, Terry, 1983, *Literary Theory: An Introduction*, Oxford: Basil Blackwell.

Foucault, Michel, 1969/1988, 'What is an author?' in Lodge, D. (ed.), 1988, *Modern Criticism and Theory*, London & New York: Longman.

Foucault, Michel, 1990, 'The Minimalist Self' in Kritzman, Lawrence (ed.) *Michel Foucault: Politics, Philosophy, Culture, Interviews and Other Writings 1977–1984*, London and New York: Routledge, pp. 3–16.

Grace, Sherrill E., 1983, 'Articulating the "Space Between": Atwood's Untold and Fresh Beginnings' in Grace, Sherrill E. and Weir, Lorraine (eds.) *Margaret Atwood: Language, Text, and System*, Vancouver: University of British Columbia Press, pp. 1–15.

Grace, Sherrill E., 1980, *Violent Duality: A Study of Margaret Atwood*, Montreal: Vehicule Press.

Hutcheon, Linda, 1989, *The Politics of Postmodernism*, London & New York: Routledge.

Iser, Wolfgang, 1972/1988, 'The Reading Process; a Phenomenological Approach' in Lodge, D. (ed.) *Modern Criticism and Theory*, London & New York: Longman.

Kolodny, Annette, 1990, 'Margaret Atwood and the Politics of Narrative' in Davidson, Arnold E. (ed.) *Studies on Canadian Literature: Introductory and Critical Essays*, New York: The Modern Language Association of America, pp. 90–109.

Lee, Ji-Yeon, 1994, 'Reading *The Handmaid's Tale*', short piece of solicited writing (in Korean; translated by So-Hee Lee).

Lodge, D., (ed.), 1988, *Modern Criticism and Theory*, London & New York: Longman.

Mohanty, Chandra Talpade, 1992, 'Feminist Encounters: Locating the Politics of Experience' in Barrett, M. and Phillips, A. (eds.) *Destabilizing Theory*, Cambridge: Polity Press, pp. 74–92.

Conversions and Inversions:
Body Language in Nineteenth-century Welsh Women's Writing

Jane Aaron

During the second half of the nineteenth century, Welsh women were entrammeled in a particularly torturous version of the 'double bind' syndrome. In 1846 an English governmental inquiry was commissioned 'into the state of Education in the Principality of Wales, especially into the means afforded to the labouring classes of acquiring a knowledge of the English language' (quoted in Jones, 1992, 123). When the *Report* was published in 1847, it became apparent that its three Commissioners had gone way beyond their brief, and taken the opportunity to list in detail the 'sins' of the Welsh, from the English Victorian perspective. To Welsh horror, premarital 'want of chastity' in women was placed at the top of the list. Adultery, apparently, was not much practised in Wales in the nineteenth century, or, if it was, it escaped the attention of Her Majesty's commissioners. Nor did the commissioners attend to the fact that if women were heterosexually active pre-marriage then Welsh men cannot have been entirely passive either. For the *Report*, pre-marital female licentiousness was 'the giant sin of Wales', and one which accounted for all other characteristic Welsh iniquities, such as 'thefts, lying, cozening, every species of chicanery, drunkenness . . . and idleness' (*Report*, 1847, ii, 60 and 56). Summing up on the vices of that area of the Principality to which he had been allotted as judge and assessor (namely, the mid Wales counties of Breconshire, Radnorshire and Cardiganshire), Jelinger C. Symons alleged that:

> [W]ant of chastity in women . . . is sufficient to account for all other immoralities, for each generation will derive its moral tone in a great degree from the influences imparted by the mothers who reared them. Where these influences are corrupted at their very source, it is vain to expect virtues in the off-spring. The want of chastity results frequently from the practice of 'bundling' or courtship on beds, during the night – a practice still widely prevailing. It is also said to be much increased by night prayer-meetings, and the intercourse which ensues in returning home . . . These practices obtain in the classes immediately above as well as among the labouring people. (*Report*, ii, 56)

'Courtship on beds' refers to the socially accepted practice of acknowledged lovers getting to know one another better while lying, supposedly fully clothed, in the woman's bed: as an additional protection, the girl's mother might also lay a bolster between the two, or stitch the girl up in a bolster case, hence the appellation 'bundling'. For lack of any other private space during the winter months, the practice was common in other parts of rural Europe too before the mid century, but the Victorian morality of middle-class England, with its stress upon the sanctity of the marriage bed, was by now demanding a change in sexual mores. The *Report* represents 'bundling', however, not so much as a wide-spread practice of the labouring or working classes but rather as a failing pertaining to the Welsh as a nation. Welsh women's so-called licentiousness is represented as a racial rather than a class trait: it crosses class boundaries. Given the relative poverty of the vast majority of Welsh people during the nineteenth century, few individuals could claim to belong to a class higher than 'the classes immediately above . . . the labouring people.' Furthermore, the Report claims that 'courtship on beds' as a practice was positively encouraged by the religion of the Welsh, Calvinistic Nonconformity with its 'night prayer-meetings' or 'seiadau'. And it was a lapse of such magnitude as to condemn the whole nation, man, woman and child, to moral turpitude.

In order to refute the findings of the 1847 Report, outraged Welsh respectability required of its womenfolk a cultural representation of their manifest purity. It was not enough that Welsh men should defend them; women's voices needs must speak up and proclaim the innate purity of the Welsh female body. But this was to be accomplished during an era in which, according to gender ideology, it was barely proper for women to make themselves heard in the public sphere at all, and certainly most improper for them to speak of the female body. This contradiction, or double bind, resulted in the production of a number of characteristic women's texts which, I want to argue in this paper, obsessively encode the body and sexuality at the same time as they overtly deny their existence. I shall refer to both Welsh- and English-language texts in developing this argument and will focus in particular on the work of two Welsh-language poets, Elen Egryn and Cranogwen, and two English-language prose writers, the biographer and historian Jane Williams, Ysgafell, and the novelist Alis Mallt Williams.

The first public summons to Welsh women to give tongue to their own virtues and refute the 1847 report came from the editor of the first Welsh-language periodical for women, Ieuan Gwynedd. He launched *Y Gymraes* in 1850 with the overt intention of both asserting the manifest purity of the Welsh female character in the face of its late defamations, and of improving Welsh women. His two stated aims constitute a contradiction from the start: if Welsh women were pure, why all this effort to gild the lily? In his first editorial he asks women to contribute to his new journal: 'Permit us to hear your voices', he says 'for what voice can be sweeter than that which has its source in a woman's tender heart?' (Jones, 1850-1, i, 7). Yet some of the articles published in later numbers of his journal paradoxically advocate muteness as a necessary female virtue. 'I prefer to recognize the person of a young woman through the medium of the eye rather than that of the ear', says one of the journal's male contributors, listing 'humility' as his chief requisite in choosing a wife (Jones, 1850-1, i, 110). It is hardly surprising, therefore, that few women did respond to Ieuan Gwynedd's challenge, and contribute to a periodical which pleaded with them both to speak up and to shut up at the same time.

One female correspondent, who signs herself 'Martha', did, however, contribute to the periodical's attempts to rebuff the 1847 *Report*. In *Y Gymraes* and elsewhere Ieuan Gwynedd argued that if Welsh women had admittedly not yet reached a state of absolute perfection, then English women were still that much farther from the mark. Making detailed reference to contemporary census figures, he shows that the rate of illegitimate births were considerably higher in some of the rural counties of England that they were in Wales (Jones, 1850-1, i, 104-5). Furthermore, though the illegitimate birth percentage in Wales was 1% (but *only* 1%) higher than that of England as a whole, England's lower score was to be accounted for, Ieuan Gwynedd argued, by the relative paucity, or at least lack of record, of illegitimate births in major towns, like London and Manchester, where prostitution flourished on a scale unknown in Wales (though how English prostitutes managed to rid themselves of unwanted pregnancies is not a question *Y Gymraes* chooses to consider). This line of argument in effect inverts the findings of the *Report*: it is not Welsh customs and sexual mores which are truly degrading, but English ones. 'For Wales, see England', as reference books' indexes used to say. Martha's contribution to this retaliatory argument comes towards the close of an essay in which she is largely concerned with the importance of education for women. Yes, Welsh women do need more education, Martha says, in agreement with the *Report*, but they certainly do not need the type of English education, then in vogue with the middle-classes, which was already insidiously infiltrating the border counties of Wales:

Y mae llawer o ferched yn cael cam drwy gael rhith addysg. Addysg i beidio gwneud dim, addysg i wneud eu hunain yn *ddolis*, i anghofio eu hiaith, i ddynwared boneddigesau . . . Mae gormod o'r dosbarth hwn ar gael yn bresenol, yn enwedig yn ein gororau, y rhai a dybiant mai bod yn ddilafur a di-Gymraeg, yw bod yn foneddigaidd.

[Many women are cheated by a fake education. An education in doing nothing, in making of themselves dolls, in forgetting their language, and in imitating ladies . . . Too many of this type are to be found at present, particularly in our border counties, those who think that to be without work and without the Welsh language is to be ladylike.]

Martha develops her argument into a full-scale attack on the indolent luxuriousness and self-indulgence which she sees as encouraged in middle-class English woman, and which she contrasts to the healthy industriousness and self-denying puritanism of Welsh women. The physical image of these two contrasting types of femininity are central to her argument, yet the body itself barely figures in her account; rather, images of the English versus Welsh female body are conjured up for the reader by means of detailed contrasting descriptions of their respective material accoutrements, and of what they ingest and secrete:

Er na orchuddir ein gorweddfa gan leni sidan, na'n lloriau gan lawr-leni drudfawr, na'n heisteddleoedd gan glustogau melfed; er na feddwn na *drawing room*, na *sitting room*, na pharlawr, yn amgen na'r gegin; eto, ni fydd ein cydwybod yn llai tawel, na'n cân yn llai ffraeth. Er mai awel y bore ydyw y gwin sydd yn rhuddo ein gwynebau, a gwaith ydyw yr *Opium* sydd yn melysu ein cwsg; eto, ni fyddwn yn llai diwyd nac yn llai diwyr. Er ini fod yn anwybodus o'r disiau, a'r cardiau, a phob gwag ddifyrwch o'r cyffelyb. Er i ni fod yn anwybodus o ffug-chwedlau, coeg-foesau, a phob mursendod o'r fath; eto, ni fyddwn yn anwybodus o waith, nac o Feibl; efallai na bydd wedi ei rwymo mewn *morocco*, nai addurno a dalenau aur, ond addurnir ef a phethau llawer my gwerthfawr – *dagrau*. (Jones, 1850-1, i, 15-16)

[Though our beds are not covered by silken sheets, our floors by rich carpets, or our seats by velvet cushions; though we own neither a sitting-room, nor a drawing-room, nor a parlour; yet our conscience will not be less quiet, or our song less ready. Though the breeze of the morning is the wine which reddens our countenance, and work is the Opium which sweetens our sleep, yet we will not be less industrious or less steadfast. Though we be ignorant of dice, and cards, and of other such empty entertainments, though we may know nothing of novels, false refinements, and all such pretensions, yet we will not be ignorant of work, or of the Bible; perhaps it will not be bound in morocco, or decorated with gold leaf, but it will be adorned by things much more precious – *tears*.]

But the image of the English female body suggested here, as gambling, card-playing, and wine and opium-imbibing – as a Jezebel in other words – represents something of an anachronism in the mid-nineteenth century. It would have been more convincing had it referred to the eighteenth-century upper class English woman, of the Vauxhall pleasure gardens period, than to the Victorian gentlewoman, with her characteristic good works and strict propriety. If the idea of the English character in vogue in Wales at this time was generally as out-moded as this quotation would suggest, then it is no wonder that the 1847 Report came as so much of a shock to the Welsh. In a further essay from *Y Gymraes*, however, Ieuan Gwynedd similarly attempts to turn Welsh women's minds away from any desire to ape or admire their English neighbours by constructing an unappealing portrayal of the 'spirit of England' which is much more historically up-to-date. The English spirit is imperialistic, he says; it exploits the wealth and peoples of other nations, or, where it cannot do so, destroys them. He cites contemporary evidence such as the British army's 1849 massacres of so-called rebels in colonized India's Punjab region and in Borneo as support for his argument (Jones, 1850-1, i, 76).

But to convince Welsh woman that the English were covetous, exploitative, and not to be emulated was but a minor feature of *Y Gymraes*'s work; its major aim was to persuade its female readers to adopt as absolutely as possible the rigorous image of the 'chaste' Welsh woman, hard-working, pleasure-abstaining, religious and above all 'pure' of body. A woman who failed to fashion herself according to such a model was imperilling the honour and good name of her country and her religion, and was not worthy to be called a Welsh woman. 'Honourable they must be . . . in moral superiority, if they truly deserve to be called Welsh women of Wales,' proclaims another of *Y Gymraes*'s female contributors, and the journal's patron, Gwenynen Gwent, Lady Llanover (Jones, 1850-1, i, 8). With hysterical over-insistence Ieuan Gwynedd and his contributors repeatedly assert that the female Welsh body must be abstemious and disciplined: 'The purity and beauty of the Welshwoman's lips is too sacred to be tainted by the least drop of alcohol' according to 'Tydfelyn' of Merthyr (Jones, 1850-1, i, 166). A loud-mouthed, laughing woman is no Welsh woman for 'Brodor' in his very damning account of 'The Social and Moral State of the women of Cardiganshire'. Indeed, the actual behaviour of young Welsh women, as he witnessed it during rural fairs and other feast days, is in his eyes not human at all, but animal: 'screeching . . . our foolish girls . . . flock arm in arm, neighing on their way to the slaughter-house, and raving on their journey to extermination.' (Jones, 1850-1, i, 333). But this contributor too, when he formulates his ideal Welsh woman, like Martha disparages the English model of feminine gentility as inappropriate and artificial, and favours a more sturdy and robust home-made version, untainted by 'false refinements, and all such pretensions'.

To transform Welsh women as speedily as possible from animals to rough-hewn but still holy icons becomes *Y Gymraes*'s moral mission, a mission which was soon to receive fervent support from the massed and very influential powers of Welsh Nonconformity generally. But how does an icon give tongue to its own virtues, without discrediting them in the process? One way it can do so is through a 'pure' body language, the language of the 'speaking' pure body; hence the stress at the close of Martha's essay on '*tears*'. Tears shed over a Welsh-language Bible: they are the appropriate language of the Welsh female, and unequivocally repudiate the lies of 1847 *Report*. Another female contributor to *Y Gymraes*, and one whose first book, published in 1850, was much hyped by that periodical, was the poet Ellin Evans, or Elen Egryn, to give her her bardic name. In her poems too, female tears speak - literally. In her poem 'The Tear', her tears speak to the poet of the true depths of her inconsolable grief after the loss of her parents. And her poem 'Sigh' personifies, more strangely, another of the body's unwilled self-expressions. The speaker of this poem strives to present a cheerful face to the world, but her sigh belies her:

> Ochenaid, ai'th ddifyrwch yw
> > Datguddio briw fy mynwes?
> Er ymdrechiadau fwy na rhi',
> > Ti fyni ddewyd fy hanes.
> E lwyddodd ymdrechiadau gwych
> > I gadw'n sych fy nwyrudd,
> Ond ni all dim dy attal di
> > I daenu dy adenydd.
>
> . . . .

165

Wrth gwrdd â chyfaill yma a thraw,
        Er estyn llaw yn llawen,
Dy chwedl yma myni ddweyd,
        Er llwyr ddadwneud fy llonwên.

[Sigh, is it your pleasure
to reveal my breast's wound?
For all my numberless exertions
you insist on proclaiming my history.
Splendid exertions succeeded
in keeping my cheeks dry,
but nothing can stop you
from spreading your wings.

....

Meeting friends here and there,
though I shake hands cheerfully,
you your tale will utter,
to the complete undoing of my smile.]

The message of this poem accords closely with the gender ideology omnipresent in *Y Gymraes*: the speaker has been distanced from her own body, which speaks through the sigh, by a code of social manners and niceties. But the language of the body is a stronger and more truthful language, and will make itself heard: she may control her tears and manufacture smiles but the sigh triumphs. At the close of the poem, the speaker reconciles herself with this voice she has sought to repress; it is her friend as it speaks truly of her condition. She also acknowledges this language of the body to be purer and more religious – in closer direct contact with God – than the language of her conscious will. It is thus a consolation to her, even as it is also a distress, and she loves it as an 'Other', stronger than her self:

Ond er na fyni gelu'm brad,
        Wyd gufad i dy gofio
....
Ti ddygi beth o'm baich i'r lan
        Pan 'rwyf ry wan i'w gario.

Rho dy gymdeithas ym mhob ton,
        Mae 'nghalon yn dy garu;
Ti ydwyd unig eli'm cur...
        ....
Ond pan fo'm baich ry drwm i'w ddwyn,
        Caf roddi'm cwyn a'm trallod,
A'i anfon yn dy go'l i fan
        Lle na cha'r gwan ei wrthod. (Evans, 1850, 23-4)

[But though my treachery you won't hide
yet your remembrance is dear

....

You bear part of my burden ashore
when I'm too weak to carry it.

Give me your company in each wave,
my heart loves you;
you are my pain's only ointment.

....

When my burden's too heavy to bear,
my complaints and tribulations I can
send in your embrace to a place
where the weak are not refused.]

The poem is interesting as a secularization of Calvinistic Methodism, which held that the heart was stronger than the head, and that it was appropriate to give physical expression to one's feelings during religious worship, and make confession in a public prayer meeting of the deepest recesses of one's spiritual condition. The sigh valiantly attempts to perpetuate this tradition, while the mannered, and as it were anglicized conscious self betrays it. Yet what is most likely to strike the contemporary reader of this poem is the degree of alienation between this speaker and her own body: her 'I' and the 'you' of the sigh never become one, not even in the closing lines, though there they do embrace. She does not own her own body, which appears to be given up to undisclosed, and perhaps unconscious, mortifications of which the sigh hints. But she loves that sigh, she loves that pain: in Freudian terms, one might say that she is entrammeled in the seductions of a narcissistic type of masochism, in which her sigh serves as an hysterical symptom of repressed conflict. And of course Freud would say that the betrayal revealed by the sigh is the betrayal of desire: the desires of the animal body, repressed not only by anglicized manners but also by the prescribed rigours of the Welsh female role model. The speaker of the poem has converted that pain into a perverse and hysteric satisfaction.

Yet this is, I suggest, a very physical poem; the body speaks in it with more gusto – literally gusts of expression – than it would in most English poems of the period. The extremity of physical repression to which Welsh women were most abruptly required to habituate themselves after 1847 not unnaturally produces a preoccupation with that which was meant to be, and indeed was, at the overt level, denied – the animal body and its pleasure-seeking desires. The English-language novels of a later nineteenth-century Welsh woman, Alis Mallt Williams, provide a somewhat cruder and less complex expression of the same type of compensatory activity. There is absolutely no suggestion of approved of physical contact in Williams' two novels, for all the frequently acclaimed desirability of her heroines. In the second novel, *A Maid of Cymru*, the heroine, on the eve of a marriage long-delayed due to her qualms about forsaking her maidenhood, is very suddenly and shockingly trampled to death by a herd of stampeding Welsh mountain ponies: but better that end, presumably, than to go the way of all flesh. Similarly, Gwyneth Gwyllt, the virginal heroine of Williams' first novel, *One of the Royal Celts*, takes it into her perverse head, as her long-awaited marriage nears, to holiday in the Sudan during the Mahdi uprising. Abducted by the 'dusky foe' she manages to escape into the desert, but cannot avoid her fate:

> Gwyneth lay out all alone in the desert - the gentle, delicately brought up Welsh girl – alone in the foeman's country, surrounded by wild animals and dusky tribes . . . like a broken, fragile lily . . .When at last she opens her eyes, they fall tremblingly on the figure of a dusky warrior who stands watching her . . . Drawing away the small white hands, he lifted the slight, shrinking, struggling girlish figure, and . . . galloped into the desert, further and further, deeper and deeper, into the very heart of the African desert, where British foot had never penetrated. Fair, sweet, gentle Gwyneth Gwyllt, it rends my heart to think of your cruel fate. (Williams, 1889, 385-6)

For all the author's protestations to the contrary, a distinct sense of gratified physical desire imbues both these brutal ends. In Gwyneth Gwyllt's case in particular, the images of deep penetration which accompany the description of her final abduction – 'deeper and deeper, further and further, where British foot had never penetrated' – suggest intense masochistic satisfaction. The ideal of the inviolate and spiritualized Welsh female body is roughly and, surely, pleasurably shattered at the sensationally physical climaxes of these novels, in what seems a very clear case of the gleeful if traumatic return of repressed animality.

But for all her insistence on retaining a pure virginity, it is unlikely that *Y Gymraes*'s contributors would have approved of the inappropriately named Gwyneth Gwyllt ('gwyllt' means 'wild' in Welsh). Her lily-like gentleness and delicacy, her small white hands and shrinking figure, suggest ladylike qualities quite antipathetic to their image of the true-blooded Welsh woman. Alis Mallt William's general endorsement in her novel of nineteenth-century England's imperialist mission, and the identification with 'Britain' rather than Wales suggested at the close of the quotation I've just cited, comes as no surprise given the anglicized middle-class characteristics of her heroine. To be feminine, in the Gwyneth Gwyllt manner, was not to be truly Welsh. There is no word in the Welsh language for 'feminine' as distinct from 'female': it is still not a naturalized Welsh concept. For all its insistence on chastity, the nineteenth-century Welsh female ideal in some respects allowed women more freedom than the English Angel in the House model, and is to my mind quite distinct from it. Both the Welsh Mam and the ideal Welsh maiden are more self-reliant and more robust – more butch, one might say – than the English model, largely, of course, because they emerge from a predominantly working-class culture.

At any rate, few real-life female figures can have been physically more at variance with the Angel in the House ideal than that of the redoubtable

Cranogwen, or Sarah Jane Rees, who according to her biographers spoke and looked like a man, and yet who pursued with great success a varied public career as sailor, teacher, poet, preacher, lecturer, journalist and Temperance leader in mid and late nineteenth century Wales. Venerated in a number of bardic eulogies as the purest of pure women, anecdotal evidence suggests that she did indeed make short shrift of any male advances (see Jones, n.d.), yet her culture allowed her to give expression to her actual physical and emotional gratifications to a degree which seems surprising, in view of English attitudes at this time. Although her poem to 'My Friend' is obviously making use of the cultural acceptance of the so-called 'Romantic' single-sex friendship, yet it would appear to represent a more blatant celebration of homosexual love than could have been publicly acceptable from the pen of an English Victorian poet:

> Ah! annwyl chwaer, r'wyt ti i mi,
>> Fel lloer i'r lli', yn gyson;
> Dy ddilyn heb orphwyso wna
>> Serchiadau pura'm calon
>
> ....
>
> I seren dêg dy wyneb di
>> Ni welaf fi un gymhar...
> Mae miloedd eraill, sêr o fri,
>> Yn gloewi y ffurfafen;
> Edmygaf hwy, ond caraf di,
>> Fy Ngwener gu, fy 'Ogwen'.
>
> ....
>
> A phleser cu fy mywyd i
>> Fydd syllu arni'n mhobman. (Rees, 1870, 74-5)

> [Ah! dear sister, you are to me
> as the moon to the sea, constantly;
> following you restlessly are
> my heart's purest affections
>
> ....
>
> To the fair star of your face
> I see no equal...
> A thousand other stars of distinction
> brighten the firmament;
> I admire them, but I love you,
> My beloved Venus, my 'Ogwen'.
>
> ....
>
> And the dear pleasure of my life
> will be to gaze on her everywhere.]

Here, particularly with the reference to 'Ogwen', the female partner in a popular romantic ballad of the period, Cranogwen places herself unequivocally, and without any apparent embarrassment or self-consciousness, in the male lover's role. Of course, in an age when the royal head of state repudiated the possibility of its existence, lesbianism was barely an acknowledged concept. I'm not trying to argue here that Cranogwen was 'out' in the modern sense, and accepted as such in Victorian Wales, but her very public image certainly represented the apotheosis of the conventionally feminine, and yet, by all accounts, it was widely regarded with respect and affection.

Which is not to say that Welsh culture at this time was not homophobic: indeed, even today, Welsh literary history has not to my knowledge acknowledged the existence of any lesbian writer in its canon (of course, this is partly because there are remarkably few women writers in the mainstream Welsh canon). But it does suggest that even in the latter half of the nineteenth century, the Welsh construction of ideal womanhood did not enforce the adoption of any distinctively feminine traits apart from the all-important eschewal of premarital heterosexual contact. And it must be admitted that any researcher into nineteenth-century Welsh women's writing will find evidence of what we might now likely conjecture to be lesbian lifestyles. Jane Williams, Ysgafell, for example, when she died in London in 1885, left the bulk of her property to her life-long companion and maid, Mary Willey, and recorded formally in her will the great debt of love she owed to one who 'made the comfort of my daily life'. When Mary Willey died a scant three months after her friend, she was buried in her mistress's grave - a very unusual ending, given the strict social hierarchies of Victorian society (see Fraser, 1961, 105 and 113). And in her transcription of the *Autobiography of Betsy Cadwaladr*, orally delivered to her in a series of interviews with the book's subject, Jane Williams records with evident glee an incident of cross-dressing and same sex flirtation which befell the adventurous and never-married Betsy during a period of employment as a domestic in Paris. In this scene, the master and mistress of the household have just left to attend a state gathering:

> After the carriage was gone, the lady's-maid expressed to me her eager desire to go too, adding that nothing should prevent it, if she had but a proper man to accompany her. 'If that is all,' said I, 'you shall have one, for I will myself be your beau, and we will both go.' . . . I knew where our master's things were kept, went to his dressing-room, took out his Spanish uniform, put it on, and also his moustache and whiskers...and set off with Owen to St Cloud. We gained admission without difficulty, and I made my way through the crowd with an air of authority . . . I amused myself by flirting with some young ladies, who were evidently gratified by my attentions. (Williams, 1857, 29)

This scene makes a mockery of both gender and class difference, and represents both as a matter of play acting, clothing and disguise. The body's polymorphous potential cannot unintermittently be straightjacketed into prescribed roles of gender, class or sexuality. Nonconformist Wales's attempts to thrust upon women a role model potentially very severe in its restrictiveness seems in some incidences to have produced consequences inconceivable to the perpetrators of the new ideal, and yet seemingly inevitable. Forbid young women to conceive of their bodies as objects of masculine attention, segregate them much more rigorously than before from men, and yet encourage them to take pride in robustly physical lives of hard labour, in rural or early industrial environments, and what will you get? You'll get, in some cases, a female type which might well have proved more of a shock to the Victorian sensibilities of the commissioners of the 1847 *Report* than the practice of 'bundling'. For very many other nineteenth-century Welsh women, however, the consequences of the trauma of 1847 were an increased alienation from the female body as a receptacle of sin and poison, a disfigurement which could not be conceived of as a matter of play, and which took more than one generation to efface.

References

Evans, Ellin [Elen Egryn] (1850) *Telyn Egryn*, Dolgellau, Evan Jones.

Fraser, Maxwell (1961) 'Jane Williams (Ysgafell)', *Brycheiniog: Journal of the Brecknock Society*, vii, 95-114.

Jones, D. G. (n.d.) *Cofiant Cranogwen*, Caernarfon: Argraffdy'r Methodist-iaid Calfinaidd.

Jones, Evan [Ieuan Gwynedd] (ed.) (1850-1) *Y Gymraes*, Cardiff: William Owen.

Jones, Ieuan Gwynedd (1992) *Mid-Victorian Wales: The Observers and the Observed*, Cardiff: University of Wales Press.

Rees, Sarah Jane [Cranogwen] (n.d., 1870) *Caniadau Cranogwen*, Dol-gellau, R. O. Rees.

Report (1847) *Report of the Commissioners Appointed to Inquire into the State of Education in Wales*, London.

Williams, Alis Mallt [Y Dau Wynne] (1889) *One of the Royal Celts*, London, Spencer Blackett & Hallam.

Williams, Jane [Ysgafell] (ed.) (1857) *The Autobiography of Elizabeth Davis, Betsy Cadwaladr, A Balaclava Nurse*, reissued Cardiff: Honno Press, 1987.

Disfiguring the Mother (tongue): Erotic Readings of Kate Roberts

Francesca Rhydderch

So what is a mother? Someone who makes the stereotypical gestures she is told to make, who has no personal language and who has no identity. But how, as daughters, can we have a personal relationship with or construct a personal identity in relation to someone who is no more than a function?

In a sense we need to say goodbye to maternal omnipotence (the last refuge) and establish a woman-to-woman relationship of reciprocity with our mothers, in which they might possibly also feel themselves to be our daughters. In a word, liberate ourselves along with our mothers. That is an indispensable pre-condition for an emancipation from the authority of fathers.

Luce Irigaray, 'Women-mothers, the silent substratum'[1]

Born in 1891 in Rhosgadfan, a poor rural quarrying community in north Wales, Kate Roberts came to be respected in Welsh-language culture as the 'mother' of the short story and as the 'queen of our literature'.[2] By the time of her death in 1985 she had become something of a national monument. A consideration of Roberts's image as the Welsh 'mam' *par excellence*, in its relation to the discourses of the female body within which she was herself mothered, reveals the close interrelation of iconized representations of motherhood – disseminated through such media as popular magazines for women published during the second half of the nineteenth century – and the predominantly maternal images consistently projected onto the childless writer and her works. Channelled into one acceptable form, that of the mother's body, they are confined within the borders and boundaries of motherhood. Roberts's own representations of mother and daughter in her autobiography *Y Lôn Wen* [The White Lane] (1960) demonstrate the degree to which her text coincides with and reproduces dominant images of proper, upstanding Welsh maternity. If, however, French critic Roland Barthes's notion of pleasurable reading as a disrespectful playing with the mother tongue (a blissful 'disfiguration' both of language and of the mother's body) is read in the interstices of *Y Lôn Wen*, then the pleasure of the text emerges in Roberts's representations of the reading practices of mother and daughter. The qualification in her text of those pleasures as *generationally* and thus as historically and culturally specific does nevertheless question the assumptions of the universal mother-figure deployed by Barthes in *The Pleasure of the Text*. The forcefully bordered cultural site that is the Welsh-language text can therefore be profitably transgressed through the admission of criticism deriving from beyond those borders: that cultural site, however, simultaneously reveals the unarticulated boundaries of the self-professed master text.

One of the archetypal representations of Welsh motherhood which was developed during the latter half of the nineteenth century – and which, it has been argued, popularized restrictive representations of female sexuality – can be traced to the periodical *Y Gymraes* [The Welshwoman].[3] Launched in 1850 by Nonconformist minister Ieuan Gwynedd, *Y Gymraes* was in part a reaction to the damning assessments of a government survey published in 1847, the *Report of the Commissioners Appointed to Inquire into the State of Education in Wales*. The report associated the 'want of chastity in women' which it found in Wales with their provincial, uncivilized language, intimating that their inability to speak English left them undesirably alienated from the civilizing impetus of imperial advances being made by the British government in its colonies (Williams, 1991: 70). That *Y Gymraes* was founded as a national defence seems certain: it combined the adoption of a didactic tone towards its assumed female readers with staunch praise of the faultless *Cymraes*, an impeccable icon who served as an example for both young unmarried women, on whose chastity the reputation of Wales now depended, and married mothers, in whose wombs lay the state and fate of the nation. Expression of female sexuality was limited to the most confined terms, and this suppression was harnessed to and propagated by the spread of Nonconformity through the country during the period. The result was the alienation of the Welsh woman from her own sexually desiring body as anything other than the iconized vessel of future morally upright inheritors of the Welsh language and culture. An early contribution (by one W. Edwards) to *Y Gymraes* focuses solely on '[y] gair cysegredig *mam*' [the sacred word *mother*], stressing that:[4]

> *[m]ae mam yn bwysig yn nghadwen bodoliaeth.* Hebddi ni byddai na dyn nac anifail nac un creadur[.] Gweinidoges natur yw, wedi ei neillduo i'r gwaith pwysicaf [. . .] Hi a esgor ar feibion a merched, – o honi hi y tardda cenhedloedd lluosog – a chanddi y megir y cewri cedyrn, a phobl heb rifedi.

> *[t]he mother is important to the chain of existence.* Without her there would be neither man, beast nor creature[.] She is the Servant of nature, who has been reserved for the most important work [. . .] It is she who bears sons and daughters, from her there issue many generations – and she nurtures the stalwart giants and numberless people.

> (Edwards, 1850: 70, my translation)

Secondary, but only just, to her role as a seemingly omnipotent creator, is that of educator of the nation's children:

Fel y gwna y fam y gwna y plentyn, y ffordd a gerddodd hi a gerdda yntau. Un o'r pethau mwyaf effeithiol yw [e]siampl y fam. Mae yn wers fywiol a ddelir i'w sylw beunydd [. . .] *Mae addysg mam yn bwysig ac angenrheidiol.*

As the mother does, so does the child, the path which she has walked he too will walk. A mother's example is amongst the most effective of things. It is a living lesson to which he will attend daily [. . .] *Education by the mother is important and necessary.*

(Edwards, 1850: 71)

A living exemplar, the mother literally holds the future of the Welsh race in her hands: the author of the article emphasizes that '[h]i sydd yn ei ddysgu i siarad, gan roddi yn ei enau yr iaith a ddewisai' [[i]t is she who teaches [her child] to speak, placing in his [sic] mouth the language she chooses], thus linking the mother's virtuous example to the survival of the Welsh language (Edwards, 1850: 71). The mother, as constructed by the (usually male) contributors to *Y Gymraes*, rears offspring whose chastity and language together repudiate the *Blue Books*, as the 1847 report came to be called. Her children are chaste because they speak Welsh, and they speak Welsh because they are of a righteous race (they learn virtue from a Welsh-speaking mother). Siân Rhiannon Williams observes that the mother was 'the most important agent in the process of reform' instigated and developed by *Y Gymraes*, commenting that, 'although limited, her role would not be an entirely passive one, since it was through her influence that a new generation would be educated and trained' (Williams, 1991: 74–5). The pages of *Y Gymraes* are amply strewn with homilies and articles similar to that of W. Edwards, addressed emotively as it is to '[O] famau Cymru!' [the mothers of Wales!], and with personal memories and poems dedicated to and dominated by unmatched mothers (Edwards, 1850: 73).

It seems however that many of the readers of *Y Gymraes*, by the editor's own admission, were not mothers, or even women. In the final issue of the periodical, published in 1851 shortly before its amalgamation with *Y Trysorydd* [The Treasurer], the editor insists that, although *Y Gymraes* is a publication aimed particularly at women, it was never supported by '[F]erched Cymru' [the Women of Wales], and that, since it was read primarily by men, articles had become more literary and general than was initially intended (Gwynedd, 1851: 365). Nevertheless, it is not the shadowy presence of a predominantly male audience and the attendant absence of the female reader which explains the inclusion of such columns as 'Gwersi Amaethyddol' [Agricultural Lessons]. Women worked out of doors like the men during this period: agricultural lessons were therefore of as great a relevance to them as were the cookery columns which featured regularly in the magazine. In one unsigned contribution to the periodical, written in November 1850, which records the 'cyflwr cymdeithasol a moesol merched swydd Aberteifi' [the social and moral condition of the women of Cardiganshire], the author refers directly to women's work in the fields:

Mae llawer o honynt allan haf a gauaf, oerni a gwres, gwlaw a hindda, nes yn ugain a phump ar ugain oed [. . .] Cymdeithasant â'r gaib a'r rhaw, yr aradr, a'r ogau, yn lle â'r nodwydd a'r gwebin, y llaethdy a'r gegin [.]

175

Many of them are out of doors come summer and winter, cold and warmth, rain and shine, until they turn forty-five [. . .] They keep company with the dungflies and the shovel, the plough and harrows, rather than with the needle or the mirror, the dairy or the kitchen.[5]

The image created of a hardworking wife and mother who tills the soil in order to feed her family suggests a particularly rural, working-class and Welsh femininity, far removed from that of the 'Angel in the House' which so dominates English discourses of Victorian femininity. The fragility of the Angel in the House was not for the *Gymraes*: the latter's body and body image were shaped by hard and heavy labour.[6] The boundaries between femininity and masculinity evidently vary both from class to class and from culture to culture: in a predominantly rural or early industrial working-class culture such as Wales during the nineteenth century, the class and national markers of femininity coincide. The moulded 'manliness' of a hardworking and hardworked female body may appear masculine in comparison with the appealing vulnerability of the Angel in the House. In terms of *Y Gymraes*, however, such a body image was economically and morally desirable in the years following the publication of the *Blue Books*. The 'unfeminine' beauty of Cardiganshire women attracts a warmly expressed admiration from one contributor:

Mae eu cyfansoddiad naturiol yn wrol a chadarn: yn gyffredin maent yn fyrion a thewion, yn gochion ac iachus eu hymddangosiad. Nid ydynt fel llawer o ferched ein gweithfaoedd a'n trefydd mawrion, fel pe buasent wedi tyfu dan lestr, heb weled goleuni y dydd, teimlo gwres yr haul, na mwynhau awyr bur ac iachus erioed, nes maent mor llwydion â chanwyllau, mor feinion â brwyn, ac more weinion ag ewyn.

They are of a naturally brave and strong constitution: generally, they are short and fat, red and healthy in appearance. They are not like many of the women in our workshops and large towns, who look as if they had grown under glass without ever seeing the light of day, feeling the warmth of the sun, or enjoying the fresh and healthy air, so that they are as grey as candles, as thin as rushes, and as feeble as foam.

(*Y Gymraes* 11, 1850: 329)

Notably, this author emphasises the connection between *place* and the Cardiganshire woman's masculine and attractive beauty, an emphasis which is created through reference to the rural woman's 'negative' counterpart, the female town dweller. Such discourse stresses the differences between femininities as they were constructed in the rural bastions of Welsh-speaking Welshness and the anglicised, early industrial towns, thus asserting a geographically specific Welsh norm of femininity in contrast to the urban Angel in the House. However, the author of the same article simultaneously criticizes Cardiganshire women for *not* matching up to English norms of femininity. Cardiganshire women spend so much time working out of doors that they cannot be good housewives: 'yna pa fodd y gallant fod yn ddefnyddiol a glanwedd mewn tŷ?' [and so how can they be useful or clean in the home?] (1850: 329). The effect which outdoor work has upon their femininity relates not only to the housework (or the lack of it) which defines that femininity, but also to the physical attributes which express that femininity:

[O] ganlyniad maent nid yn unig heb amser at orchwylion o'r fath, ond collant eu harchwaeth atynt yn hollol. Mae yr arferiad farbaraidd hon yn sychu eu teimladau tyner, yn difwyno eu tegwch merchaidd, yn lladd eu gwylder benywaidd, ac yn dinystrio eu defnyddioldeb teuluaidd. Nid ydym yn anfoddlon iddynt fyned allan ar amserau nodedig, megis y cynhauaf gwair ac ŷd, ond eu danfon allan ar draul esgeuluso i mewn sydd goll gwarthus yn Nghymru[.]

[A]s a result they are not only without the time for such tasks, but completely lose their appetite for them. This barbarous custom dries their tender sentiments, spoils their girlish fairness, kills their feminine modesty, and destroys their familial usefulness. We are not unwilling for them to go out [into the fields] at specified times, for the hay and corn harvests, for example, but to send them out at the expense of the hearth is a disgraceful defect in Wales.

(*Y Gymraes* 11, 1850: 330)

It is difficult to reconcile this image of dried up womanhood with the fertile *Gymraes*-mother, and yet the contradiction expressed by the coexistence of both such images in *Y Gymraes* reflects a tension which was fundamental to a periodical which both sought to defend Welsh womanhood to the English, and thus to refute the word of the *Blue Books*, and yet at the same time strove to educate Welsh women in order to make them more morally upright, and thus more like their 'angelic' English counterparts. This tension is indicative of the internalization of English norms by nineteenth-century patriotic Welsh cultural commentators, in this instance in the form of a particular construction of a socially acceptable femininity.

As one of the daughters mothered by such contradictory discourses of maternal and 'macho' femininity, Kate Roberts (who occupies the unique position of female icon of twentieth-century literature in Welsh) has often been read as the *Gymraes* projected in the texts of nineteenth-century cultural commentators and moralists. While she became a figure of great literary stature during her own lifetime, it was as a writer fiercely defensive of rich, literary, idiomatic Welsh, as a journalist and active Plaid Cymru [Welsh Nationalist Party] member determined to further the cause of a political party committed to resisting the continued oppression of Wales under British government, as a dutiful wife and chapel-goer, and as a regular contributor to the cookery column in the newspaper *Y Faner* [The Banner]: in short, as the archetypal *Cymraes*. Prevalent readings of her work seem to support this image. Kate Roberts is seen as the stable, unchanging representative and reproducer of the Welsh nation and its language: Bobi Jones, for example, praises the 'consistency linking all her works,' laying particular emphasis upon the uniformly high standard of her writing (Jones,

1967: 306). The focus of many of Kate Roberts's short stories and novels on the female voice and on the sensual (if not sexual) experiences of women, both inside and outside marriage[7] is displaced and stabilised into the socio-sexual category of the archetypal Welsh Mam. Emyr Humphreys, for example, compares one of Kate Roberts's most famous heroines, Jane Gruffydd, with the heroes of Homeric verse:

> Fel yr oedd gwŷr arfog Homer yn byw i ryfela, felly y mae merched *Traed Mewn Cyffion* yn byw i'r ymdrech ddyddiol o gadw tŷ, cynnal cartref a magu teulu.

> As Homer's armed men lived to wage war, so the women of *Feet in Chains* live to make the daily effort of keeping house, running a household and bringing up a family.
>
> (Humphreys, 1969: 59–60)

The childless writer is 'validated' as the mother of her texts, which like the hypothetical children of the ideal mother projected by *Y Gymraes*, are held up as models of Welsh national and literary identity. Like the *Gymraes*-mother, she is typically strong and heroic, and yet her nurturing qualities are only enhanced by her physical strength. Dewi Lloyd Jones, writes that, before Kate Roberts:

> [B]aban gwan iawn ydoedd [y stori fer] a thyfodd yn fenyw eiddil, heb wybod yn iawn sut i wisgo. Kate Roberts a ddysgodd iddi sut i wisgo. Hi a wnaeth wraig ohoni.

> [I]t [the short story] was a very weak baby which grew to a fragile womanhood, without really knowing how to dress. Kate Roberts taught her how to dress. She made a woman of her.
>
> (Adler, 1983: 27)

In their intimate association with the images of strong femininity constructed by *Y Gymraes*, the inclusion in critical discourse on Roberts of both typically masculine and feminine stereotypes is no contradiction: both reflect the mothering qualities typical to a particular culture, class and community. Curiously (or rather, predictably) evident in both discourses – the discourses of femininity represented here by *Y Gymraes* and the critical discourse clustered around Kate Roberts's work – is the voice of the male commentator and critic. Both are discourses written by men about women: while this does not mean that they are deliberately directed at men, the silencing of female voices thereby incurred is remarkable.

If the female critic turns to one of Kate Roberts's own *self*-representations, specifically to her autobiography, *Y Lôn Wen* [The White Lane], she finds that Roberts devotes an entire chapter to her mother – 'Fy Mam' [My Mother] – which focuses particularly on the exhausting and tedious routine of Catrin Roberts's life, spent maintaining a quarry worker's cottage, smallholding and family of seven children (Roberts, 1960: 98–118).

Roberts tells her reader how her mother used to sew and knit for all the family, bake nine large loaves for them three times a week and make butter. A painstaking description of her mother's butter-making exemplifies the extremely demanding physical work required daily of Catrin Roberts:

> Rhoid y llaeth i gyd felly yn y corddwr i'w gorddi, a gwaith trwm oedd, troi'r handlen am dri chwarter awr o amser nes iddo droi'n fenyn. Nidd oedd wiw ychwanegu mwy o ddŵr nag oedd yn angenrheidiol, er mwyn ei frysio (gwnâi rhai hynny) neu fe fyddai'r menyn yn wyn ac yn anodd ei drin. Wedyn, tri chwarter awr arall neu fwy i drin y menyn, er mwyn cael y dŵr i gyd allan ohono, a'i gael yn bwysi solet i'w rhoi ar y llechen gron.

> Thus she put all the milk into the churn to churn it, which was heavy work, turning the handle for three quarters of an hour until the milk turned into butter. It was careless to add more water than was necessary, just to rush things (there were some women who did this), because the butter would be white and difficult to treat. Next, it would take another three quarters of an hour to treat the butter, to drain all the water from it and to divide it into good solid pound weights, which would be put on the round slate.

> (Roberts, 1960: 101–2)

Roberts's emphasis on the arduous physical labour undertaken by her mother reminds the reader that the Welsh woman typified by *Y Gymraes* was no Angel in the House: her body was moulded by heavy physical work. In winter, for example, Roberts's mother had to tackle many extra tasks out of doors on the smallholding, as night would have fallen by the time her husband arrived home from a day's work at the quarry (Roberts, 1960: 100). The pride with which Roberts recounts her mother's conscientious completion of each task echoes the images of virtuous and strong femininity generated and iconized by Ieuan ap Gwynedd and his like in the pages of *Y Gymraes* (and, notably, reproduces the pattern of example evident in the periodical whereby the virtuous Welsh woman was frequently constructed against her negative counterpart, the fallen woman or slothful mother: Roberts stresses that *her* mother never rushed her butter-making, although 'there were some women who did [this]'). Her physical strength does not, however, detract from Catrin's mothering qualities: Roberts relates anecdotes of her mother's work as a gentle and caring midwife and nurse, which depict her as an angelic figure in the careworn community, who brings a little cheer to households and individuals beset by illness. She recounts one young woman's admiration of Catrin Roberts: "'Bron na theimlwn," meddai, "y byddai'n beth braf fod yn sâl, er mwyn i'ch mam fy nghodi yn ei breichiau" ["I almost felt," she said, "that it would be pleasant to be ill just so that your mother would hold me in her arms"'] (1960: 103). Catrin Roberts here becomes the mother not only of her own family but also of the whole community: a heroic character, she represents perfect Welsh femininity, preserving and reproducing a Welsh race 'uncontaminated' by English values. Kate Roberts's description of Rhosgadfan cemetery stands as an epitaph to her mother as representative of the Welsh language and culture:

Ni welsom erioed gyfoeth, ond cawsom gyfoeth na all neb ei ddwyn oddi arnom, cyfoeth iaith a diwylliant. Ar yr aelwyd gartref y cawsom ef, a'r aelwyd honno yn rhan o'r gymdeithas a ddisgrifiais ar y cychwyn. Yn y fynwent yn Rhosgadfan mae'n gorwedd gymdeithas o bobl a fu'n magu plant yr un pryd â'm rhieni innau, ac yn ymdrechu'r un mor galed. Cymry uniaith oeddent i gyd, a chwith oedd gennyf weld pa ddydd, fod ambell garreg fedd Saesneg [. . .] wedi ymwthio i'r ardd honno.

We never knew riches, but we had a wealth which no-one could steal from us, a wealth of language and culture. It was handed down to us on our own fireside, a hearth which was part of the community which I described at the beginning [of the book]. In the cemetery at Rhosghadfan there lies a whole community of people who reared children at the same time as my parents, and who worked just as hard. They were all monolingual Welsh speakers, and I was sorry to see the day when the occasional English gravestone had pushed its way into that garden [.]

(Roberts, 1960: 117–8)

Figurative of all mothers of the Welsh community, Catrin Roberts has propagated Welsh values and preserved the Welsh language in the face of an English cultural invasion. The cemetery in Rhosgadfan is portrayed as a Garden of Eden: the Fall, of course, being represented as the influx of the English language into Wales.

Roberts's portrayal of her own mother, therefore, representing her as the ideal *Gymraes*, seems to conform to dominant discourses of Welsh femininity, and thus to support the similarly 'maternal' readings of her own role as writer and cultural icon generated by (male) Welsh critics. Her paean to Welsh motherhood culminates in an emotionally weighted anecdote which lays stress once more on Catrin Roberts's devotion to duty:

Dyma un o'r pethau a ddywedodd fy mam wrthyf yn ei chystudd olaf. 'Rydw i wedi cael oes faith a helbulus, ac mi fydda' i'n dyfaru am lot o betha heddiw. Mi fydda' i'n dyfaru na baswn i wedi canu mwy i chi, a deud mwy o straeon wrthoch chi pan oeddech chi'n blant, ond 'roedd gin i gimint o waith.' Mae hynna yn symio ei brwydr bob amser rhwng ei phleser a'i dyletswydd.

One of the last things which my mother said to me during her last illness was: 'I have had a long and troubled life, but I regret a lot of things today. I regret that I didn't sing to you more, and tell you more stories when you were little, but I had so much work to do.' This sums up her constant struggle between pleasure and duty.

(Roberts, 1960: 118)

And yet, while Roberts emphasizes the tortuous distance which lies between pleasure and duty for the conscientious *Gymraes*, her portrayal of

180

Catrin Roberts has focused a great deal more on duty than it has on pleasure. Indeed, Kate Roberts has insisted that her mother, 'thought that it was sinful to enjoy herself too much'. For this reason, Roberts says, even had there been the opportunity to see plays or films in Rhosgadfan during her mother's lifetime, her mother would never have indulged in such activities: 'Yr oedd yn well ganddi aros gartref a darllen, a byw ar ei dychmygion ei hun' [she preferred to sit at home reading, living on her own fancies] (Roberts, 1960: 110). Reading is the epitomy of virtuous activity for the diligent *Gymraes*, it seems, and it is as such that Roberts introduces her description of her mother's reading practice. If there was nothing else for Catrin to read – in a household which could not afford many magazines, and sometimes also had difficulty in obtaining new volumes – then she would turn to her Bible: 'Pan âi yn big arni am ddim i'w ddarllen, ail ddechreuai ddarllen ei Beibl o'i gwrr' [When she was desperate for something to read, she would pick up her Bible and read it from beginning to end] (1960: 114). She thereby enacts the response solicited by *Y Gymraes* contributors through the admonishment to '[c]ymeryd y B[e]ibl ac edrych' [take and contemplate the Bible] (*Y Gymraes* 11, 1851: 353). Where, then, is the 'pleasure' against which Catrin Roberts 'struggled' to be found in this seemingly impeccable text of iconized motherhood which is 'Fy Mam'?

In a French text published fifteen years after Roberts's autobiography, Roland Barthes argues that the text is like a body, in that it can be stimulated to orgasm (*jouissance*) through reading and writing. In fact, the text for Barthes is another body:

> Apparently Arab scholars, when speaking of the text, use this admirable expression: *the certain body*. What body? We have several of them; the body of anatomists and physiologists, the one science sees or discusses: this is the text of grammarians, critics, commentators, philologists (the pheno-text). But we also have a body of bliss consisting solely of erotic relations, utterly distinct from the first body: it is another contour, another nomination; thus with the text: it is no more than the open list of the fires of language [. . .] Does the text have human form, is it a figure, an anagram of the body? Yes, but of our erotic body. The pleasure of the text is irreducible to physical need.
>
> (Barthes, 1976: 16–17)

While the text is not a reproduction of the body, it can be read as a body, erotically: Barthes lauds 'language lined with flesh, a text where we can hear the grain of the throat' and challenges the 'objective', 'frigid' academic to come (on) to the text (Barthes, 1976: 66). He interprets reading as an essentially erotic activity, a meeting of bodies – the body of the reader and the body of the text – and thus an erotic textual intercourse. The text is irreducible to physical need, according to Barthes: its pleasure lies beyond a purely physical orgasm. It is in this irreducibility that the pleasure of 'Fy Mam' – if read erotically – can be found.

Kate Roberts inscribes a more adventurous image of her pleasure-seeking mother in-between texts, in the seams of the text(s) in which Barthes finds bliss, in-between text and subtext for example, and also in-between the texts of the Welsh novels read by Kate and Catrin Roberts. While Kate Roberts stresses that her mother, the archetypal *Gymraes*, chooses to sit at home reading rather than seek pleasure outside the four walls of her family home, her text simultaneously indicates how reading would yet permit Catrin Roberts to escape the containment of those four walls by allowing her to 'live on her own fancies'. The pleasure obtained by Catrin Roberts from reading novels provides the ideal site from which she can let her imagination run riot and where she can inhabit a fantasy world which is *not* that of *Y Gymraes*:

> Meddwl rhamantus a oedd ganddi. Yr oedd yn ddigon bodlon edrych ar fywyd hollol fel yr oedd bob dydd, ac ni chaeai ei llygaid i'w bethau annymunol. Ond mewn stori yr oedd arni eisiau gweld bywyd fel y dymunai hi iddo fod ac nid fel yr oedd.

> Hers was a romantic temperament. Willing enough to contemplate life as it was every day, she did not close her eyes to unpleasant things. But in a story she wanted to see life as she wished it to be and not as it was.
>
> (Roberts, 1960: 114)

Although Catrin Roberts sits reading in the virtuous enclosure that is her home, she nevertheless seeks and obtains a dubious (illegitimate) pleasure through the activities of reading and writing.

Firstly, she experiences the reading pleasure of the text in all its erotic materiality: 'Ei dull hi o ddarllen nofel oedd ei darllen yn frysiog i'r diwedd i weld beth oedd wedi digwydd, ac yna ei hail ddarllen i'w mwynhau' [Her way of reading a novel was to read it hurriedly to the end to find out what had happened, and then to read it again in order to enjoy it] (Roberts, 1960: 115). Barthes elevates such reading to the realm, of 'bliss', postulating that 'the interstice of bliss occurs [. . .] in the uttering, not in the sequence of utterances: not to devour, to gobble, but to gaze, to browse scrupulously, to rediscover [. . .] the leisure of bygone readings' (Barthes, 1976: 13). The *Gymraes* obtains pleasure in the *leisure* of reading: in contrast to her work in the kitchen, dairy, garden and field, it makes no task-driven physical demands on her. In effect, it does quite the opposite; it results in a physical relaxation, an easing of the muscles which in turn facilitates a pleasurable relationship with the text.

Secondly, Catrin Roberts rewrites the texts of the Welsh 'modern' literary canon, such as Daniel Owen's novel *Gwen Tomos* (1894):

> Yr oedd Daniel Owen wedi difetha Gwen Tomos iddi drwy wneud iddo ddiweddu yn anhapus. 'I beth oedd eisio iddo fo fynd â hi i'r Merica', meddai, 'yn lle gorffan pan gawson nhw'r pres yn y cwpwrdd?' Wel, ie wir. Gwn mai meddwl ei dymuniad o gael diwedd hapus yr oedd fy mam.

> Daniel Owen had ruined *Gwen Tomos* for her by making it end unhappily. 'What did he want to take her off to America for,' she said, 'instead of bringing things to an end when they had money in the

cupboard?' Well, yes indeed. I know that what my mother meant was her wish for a happy ending.

(Roberts, 1960: 114–5)

This mother who has been represented in 'universal', or rather, national, terms as the upholder of Welsh-language culture reveals a rebellious streak: rewriting a 'master text' of that culture, a book by the 'father' of the novel, she fulfils her reading desires; stimulating and altering the text to her satisfaction, she seeks and obtains pleasure from it.

Writing, for Roland Barthes – and, by intimation, reading – is not so much a playful intercourse with language, but rather a more specifically aggressive intercourse with the mother tongue, and, thereby, with the body of the mother:

> No object is in a constant relationship with pleasure (Lacan, apropos of [de] Sade). For the writer, however, this object exists: it is not the language, it is the *mother tongue*. The writer is someone who plays with his mother's body [. . .] in order to glorify it, to embellish it, or in order to dismember it, to take it to take bliss in the disfiguration of the language, and opinion will strenuously object, since it opposes 'disfiguring nature'.

(Barthes, 1976: 37)

Each time Catrin rereads and rewrites Daniel Owen's text, she is dismembering the mother culture which the mother's body, the body of *Y Gymraes*, typifies; each time, she goes beyond pleasure to 'take bliss' (*jouissance*) in the disfiguration of that body. In disruption lies 'bliss' (*jouissance*), according to Barthes: disruptive reading releases Catrin Roberts from the constraining mould of the perfect *Cymraes*. Kate Roberts's representation of her mother, therefore, can be seen both to refigure Catrin Roberts in terms complicit with those of *Y Gymraes* and to 'disfigure' her, to destroy her iconic status, thereby releasing her from its constraints. However, for Barthes as a male, the aggressive act of disfiguring the mother's body does not carry the same echoes of self-mutilation as it does for the daughter who, of course, shares the sex of her mother. As a French speaker, writing from Paris, the very heart of the French Empire, Barthes can also afford expansively to validate the equally aggressive act of disfiguring the mother tongue, which, in the restrictive terms of *Y Gymraes*, is purely representative of an endangered Welsh culture.

Reading and writing are activities so deeply conditioned by the cultures within which they take place that it is not possible to for the critic to undertake a reading of 'Fy Mam' which assumes pleasure and *jouissance* to be concepts which translate without difficulty from language to language and from culture to culture. One of the reasons for which Catrin reads and rereads her Bible, for example, and that an image of her as a diligent *Cymraes* is thereby created, is that there are simply not enough books available in her own language. Kate Roberts writes that '*Y gwaethaf ohoni oedd nad oedd digon o lyfrau Cymraeg i'w cael iddi*' [The worst of it was

that she just could not get hold of enough Welsh[-language] books]
(Roberts, 1960: 113). While this comment indicates the extent of Catrin's
enthusiasm for reading, it also refers to the material difficulties which
dogged the acquisition of new books, difficulties which were not entirely
financial. A contributor to *Y Gymraes* reflects upon the reasons for the lack
of books available in Welsh in 1850:

> Os nag oes llyfrau ar y gyfraith yn y Gymraeg, dylid cofio mai nid yn yr
> hen iaith y gweinyddir hi. Os ydym heb lyfrau meddygol, cofier nid yn y
> Gymraeg yr addysgir ein meddygon. Os ydym heb lyfrau ar beirianwaith
> a chelfyddydau cywrain, byddai yn fuddiol ystyried nad yw y dosparth y
> perthynant iddynt yn ddigon lluosog yn Nghymru i'w prynu. Rhaid cael
> darllenwyr cyn y bydd galwad am lyfrau, ac os na bydd eisiau llyfrau ni
> bydd darllenwyr.[8]

> It should be remembered that, if there are not enough books in Welsh on
> the law, this is because the law is not administrated in the old language.
> Remember that, if we are without medical books, this is because our
> doctors are not trained through the medium of Welsh. If we are without
> books on machinery and fine art, it would be worth considering that the
> members of the class which can afford to buy such things are not
> numerous enough in Wales. One must have readers before one calls for
> books, and if there is no call for books, there will be no readers.
>
> (*Y Gymraes* 3, 1850: 74)

In Wales, languages were (and are) not working side by side. As the
above comment on printed literature intimates, Welsh was being wiped out
by English (the 'official' language). Reading Catrin Roberts's
reading/writing practices in conjunction with Barthes's conception of
pleasure, uncovers the pleasure inherent in her textual engagements, but it
also reveals the universalism presumed by Barthes's mother tongue – French,
a widely and yet not a universally spoken language. It shows how the
material and linguistic conditions of reading temper the pleasure of the text.
It also reveals the universalism assumed by Barthes's mother tongue in his
text to be mirrored by the universalism of the mother's body in his text. An
interpretation of Catrin's reading undermines this assumption. *Y Gymraes*,
the 'universal' mother's body which her reading pleasure disfigures, is a
body which exists within extremely specific cultural, historical, linguistic and
geographical parameters.

Kate Roberts's representations of her own reading practices renders the
notion of the mother's body, and that of the role of the daughter reading and
writing that body through the medium of the mother tongue of her text, to be
even more specific. Commenting on Catrin's desire to rewrite Daniel
Owen's *Gwen Tomos*, Roberts, it may be remembered, adds, 'Well, yes
indeed. I know that what my mother meant was her own desire to have a happy
ending.' This final interpretation ('I know [that] what my mother meant')
shows that the pleasure of Catrin's reading is uncovered by the daughter's
rereading of her mother's speech-text. It also draws the daughter into a

complicit relationship with her mother's pleasure, suggesting that she too desires a happy ending. However, when Kate Roberts does disclose her own response to *Gwen Tomos*, her reaction is couched in terms which differ vastly from those deployed by her mother. '[O] safbwynt technegol, credaf y byddai *Gwen Tomos* yn well fel nofel pe gorffenasid hi yn y fan yna,' she writes [From a technical point of view, I think that *Gwen Tomos* would be a better novel if it had finished there [when they had money in the cupboard].] (Roberts, 1960: 115). Although Roberts is complicit with pleasurable, desirable reading when writing about her mother's reading practices, when she describes her own, she de-eroticizes the process of reading completely: this contradiction implies how repressive a control is being wielded by the spectre of the *Gymraes* over her own text. Roberts seems to flee before her own female pleasure into the 'masculinity' of textual authority. And yet, her desire is ultimately similar to that of her mother: to see *Gwen Tomos* end happily. The difference in expression and fulfilment of that desire lies in the way in which it is legitimated by Roberts. Articulating her urge to read a happy ending through the medium of the technicalities of writing has the effect of de-eroticizing the materiality of the text: it becomes more a sum of completely analysable and controllable parts than a living, breathing, sensual body. The critical discourse by means of which Roberts distances herself from her mother also indicates the daughter's superior education and her authorial career, and thus the very specific historical circumstances which dictate the differing relationships of mother and daughter to the mother tongue/text. Kate Roberts's mother went into service at the age of ten. Kate Roberts herself, however, was a child of the Welsh Education Act of 1870, and thus remained in education until the age of twenty one, when she qualified as a teacher.[9] Her response to the texts which she reads is clearly more educated than that of Catrin Roberts, a point which she strives to convey to the reader by glossing her mother's reading from a position of assumed omniscience ('I know [that] what my mother meant').

Such a deliberately controlled critical discourse emerges more clearly at an equally crucial, that is, potentially erotic, point in the text. Referring to the publication of Saunders Lewis's novel, *Monica*, in 1938, Roberts describes her apprehensions as to how her mother would react to the book in terms of a morally defined generation gap between mother and daughter:

Pan oeddwn yn byw yn y De byddwn fel arfer yn anfon pob llyfr diddorol a ddôi allan o'r wasg Gymraeg i'm cartref. Pan gyhoeddwyd Monica, ni wyddai fy ngŵr a minnau yn iawn beth i'w wneud. Yr oedd fy mam yn bur eang ei bryd, ond gwyddem fod llawer o'r Piwritan ynddi yn y bôn, ac anodd oedd penderfynu sut y cymerai hi *Monica*. Pernderfynasom beidio â'i anfon iddi.

When I lived in the South I used to send home a copy of any interesting books published by the Welsh[-language] press. When *Monica* was published, my husband and I did not quite know what to do. My mother was perfectly broad-minded, but we knew that there was a great deal of the Puritan in her deep down, and it was difficult to know how she would take *Monica*. We decided not to send it to her.

(Roberts, 1960: 115)

185

Finally, however, it emerges that another relative had given a copy of *Monica* to Catrin, and that she taken great pleasure in reading it. Discussing her mother's response to the novel, Roberts repeats Catrin's claim that 'Mi gafodd yr hen jadan bob dim oedd hi yn 'i haeddu' [The old hussy got everything she deserved] and compares it to the critical discourse of contemporary reviews, which asserted that 'yr hyn a heuo dyn, hynny hefyd a fêd efe' [what a man sows, this also he reaps], concluding that 'Fe ddywedodd fy mam yr un peth yn ei dull gwerinol ei hun' [My mother said the same thing in her own rustic way] (Roberts, 1960: 115). By identifying her mother's reading practices as 'gwerinol' [rustic, literally: peasant-like], Roberts distances herself from that reading practice, elevating herself to the position of critic and of educator (as she had in fact elevated herself socially from the *gwerin* class to the professions by means of her own education). *Monica*, however, also operates in Roberts's text as a trope for sexual knowledge and its acquisition, and is thus more revealing of her sexuality than her deliberately assumed critical discourse would have her reader believe: the fact that it is the site on which the only intercourse of any kind between Roberts and her husband is represented in *Y Lôn Wen* is profoundly significant (Morris Williams is hardly even mentioned in the autobiography as a whole), and indicates some kind of repression. The adoption of a purposefully pitched critical discourse at such potentially erotic points in the text suggests that such a discourse surfaces in Kate Roberts's textual self-representations as a defensive mask, covering any potential discussion of her own sexuality, or even of her own femininity as another *Gymraes*, daughter of peculiarly (that is, culturally specific) repressive discourses of femininity. The generational differences between the reading practices of mother and daughter cannot be read in purely progressive terms: Roberts's is certainly not a liberated representation of female sexuality.

Kate Roberts's representation of the reading practices of mother and daughter resonates with images of the *Gymraes* which dominated discourses of femininity in the latter half of the nineteenth century. If, however, those practices are themselves read erotically, the seamless incorruptibility of the text fractures, opening up the fissures of *Y Lôn Wen* to the pleasurable consideration of the reader. Roberts's iconic heroines (in 'Y Fam', those heroines are her mother and herself) can be transformed into sexually motivated individuals. Of heroism and the text, Roland Barthes comments:

Still far too much heroism in our languages; in the best – I am thinking of Bataille's – an erethism of certain experiences and finally a kind of *insidious heroism*. The pleasure of the text (the bliss of the text) is on the contrary like a sudden obliteration of the warrior *value*, a momentary desquamation of the writer's hackles, a suspension of the 'heart' (of courage).

(Barthes, 1976: 30)

When the hackles of this Welsh woman writer are obliterated—albeit fleetingly – by overlaying her autobiography with *The Pleasure of the Text*, the sexual desires of mother and daughter are allowed expression.

An exploration of the *Gymraes* does nevertheless reveal heroism itself to be a culturally as well as a sexually conditioned concept. It is also a necessary heroism, necessary for the survival of an embattled culture. The political act symbolized by the founding of *Y Gymraes* in 1850 intimates that in this particular culture, at that particular time, pleasurable reading or writing would have been the progenitors not of liberatory *jouissance*, but rather of political annihilation. If reading becomes too playful, too destructive of the master discourses of a threatened culture, which is represented by its mother tongue, then it may appear to be running the risk of a very real self-mutilation rather than a textually s(t)imulated *jouissance*. The white lane may certainly not be as white as it is painted in Roberts's autobiography: however, the repressive strain of the text which seeks to cover the stains of its sexuality reflects a tortuously experienced tension between pleasure and duty, between the expression of female sexual desire and political necessity.

Notes

1. Irigaray, L., 1991, 'Women-mothers, the silent substratum', in Whitford M., (ed.), *The Irigaray Reader*, pp. 47-52, Oxford: Basil Blackwell. Originally published as 'Les Femmes-mères, ce sous-sol muet de l'ordre social', in Irigaray, L., 1981, *Le Corps-à-corps avec la mère*, Montreal: Éditions de la pleine lune.

2. For further introductory information on the life and works of Kate Roberts, see Morgan, D. L., 1981, *Kate Roberts* [Bro a Bywyd series], Cardiff: Arts Council of Wales; Roberts, E. L., 1994, *Kate Roberts* [Llên y Llenor series], Caernarfon: Gwasg Pantycelyn (both in Welsh); Humphreys, E., 1988, *The Triple Net*, London: Channel Four Television; Morgan, D. L., 1974 (repr. 1991), *Kate Roberts* [Writers of Wales series], Cardiff: University of Wales Press (English language).

3. See Aaron, J., 1994, 'Finding a voice in two tongues: gender and colonization', in Aaron J., Rees, T., Betts, S. and Vincentelli, M. (eds.) *Our Sisters' Land: The Changing Identities of Women in Wales*, Cardiff: Cardiff University Press; and Williams, S., R., 1991, 'The True "Cymraes": Images of Women in Women's Nineteenth-Century Welsh Periodicals', in John, A. V. (ed.), *Our Mothers' Land: Chapters in Welsh Women's History 1830-1939*, Cardiff: Cardiff University Press.

4. All translations which follow are my own, unless otherwise stated.

5. 'Cyflwr Cymdeithasol a Moesol Merched Swydd Aberteifi' [The Moral and Social Condition of the Women of Cardiganshire], *Y Gymraes*, **11**, 328-334 (329-330).

6. See Aaron, J., 1999, 'Conversions and inversions: Body-language in nineteenth-century Welsh women's writing', in Atkinson, K., Oerton, S. and Plain, G. (eds.), *Feminisms on Edge: Politics, Discourses and National Identities*, Cardiff: Cardiff Academic Press.

7. Her stories 'Y Golled' [The Loss] and 'Rhigolau Bywyd' [The Ruts of Life], and her novels *Y Byw sy'n Cysgu* [The Living Sleep], and *Tywyll*

Heno [Dark Tonight] are some of the most obvious examples of such explorations of female experience.

8   The quotation is taken from an article tellingly entitled 'Saisaddoliaeth' [The Worship of Things English].

9   See Evans, W. Gareth, 1990, *Education and female emancipation: the Welsh experience 1847-1914*, Cardiff: Cardiff University Press.

References

Aaron J., Rees, T., Betts, S. and Vincentelli, M. (eds.) *Our Sisters' Land: The Changing Identities of Women in Wales*, Cardiff: Cardiff University Press.

Adler, H. U., 1983, 'Y Stori Fer Gymraeg 1913-1937' [The Welsh short story 1913–1937], unpublished M. A. dissertation, University of Wales.

Barthes, R., 1976, *The Pleasure of the Text*, trans. Richard Miller, London: Jonathan Cape, p. 37. Originally published as *Le plaisir du texte* in 1975, Paris: Éditions du Seuil.

Edwards, W., 1850, 'Y Fam' [The Mother], *Y Gymraes* [The Welshwoman], **3**, 70-74 (70).

Gwynedd, I., 1851, 'At Dderbynwyr *Y Gymraes*' [To those who receive *Y Gymraes*], *Y Gymraes*, **12**, (365).

Humphreys, Emyr, 'Traed Mewn Cyffion' [Feet in Chains], in Jones, R. M., (ed.), *Kate Roberts: Cyfrol Deyrnged* [Kate Roberts: A Volume of Tribute], Denbigh: Gwasg Gee, p. 53.

Jones, R. M., (ed.) 1969, *Kate Roberts: Cyfrol Deyrnged* [Kate Roberts: A Volume of Tribute], Denbigh: Gwasg Gee.

Jones, R. M., 1967, 'Rhyddiaith wedi'r Rhyfel: Nofelau Kate Roberts' [Post-War Prose: The Novels of Kate Roberts], *Barn* [Opinion], **60**.

Lloyd Jones, D., 1938, 'Kate Roberts', *Yr Eurgrawn* [The Magazine], quoted by Adler, H. U., 1983, 'Y Stori Fer Gymraeg 1913–1937' [The Welsh short story 1913–1937], unpublished M. A. dissertation, University of Wales.

Report of the Commissioners Appointed to Inquire into the State of Education in Wales, 1847 (870), XXVII, Part II, London. Quoted by Williams, S. R., 1991, p. 70.

Roberts, K., 1929, 'Rhigolau Bywyd' [The Ruts of Life] and 'Y Golled' [The Loss], in *'Rhigolau Bywyd' a storïau eraill* [The Ruts of Life and other stories], Aberystwyth: Gwasg Aberystwyth.

Roberts, K., 1956, *Y Byw sy'n Cysgu* [The Living Sleep], Denbigh: Gwasg Gee.

Roberts, K., 1960, *Y Lôn Wen* [The White Lane], Denbigh: Gwasg Gee.

Roberts, K., 1962, *Tywyll Heno* [Dark Tonight], Denbigh: Gwasg Gee.

Williams, S., R., 1991, 'The True "Cymraes": Images of Women in Women's Nineteenth-Century Welsh Periodicals', in John, A. V. (ed.), *Our Mothers' Land: Chapters in Welsh Women's History 1830-1939*, Cardiff: Cardiff University Press.

Rethinking the Body: Corporeality and Sexual Difference

Gill Jagger

'Culture produces nature as its fictional origin' (Elam 1994:51).[1]

'The body as much as the psyche or the subject is a cultural and historical product' (Grosz 1994:187).

Contemporary feminist theories of the body, (or perhaps I should say bodies), concerned with the problematic of sexual difference, address the problem of how to avoid fixity, and the danger of tying women to some sort of essential nature, rooted in biology or the psyche, whilst also insisting that subjectivity is irreducibly tied to the specificities of sexed bodies.[2] As Diane Elam puts it, 'The body must not be taken as the ground of thought, but nonetheless the body's inescapability must be affirmed' (Elam 1994:174). This involves rethinking corporeality and rethinking the materiality of that corporeality. The problem is how to do that.

Traditional phenomenological approaches to the body have without exception neglected the sexed/gendered specificity of bodies.[3] How then are we to rethink corporeality in order to take account of sexual difference? How are we to think the materiality of the always already sexed/gendered body? Furthermore, although this project involves an emphasis on sexual difference, it also serves to open up the question of sexual difference. It raises the question of how to think of sexual difference in non-oppositional, non-binary terms: as something other than simply a matter of two contrasting, identities, fixed as male and female. How to think of it as both essential, as in inescapable, yet not fixed, cultural rather than natural, yet also material? This involves rethinking the relation between the cultural and the natural, representation and the objects of representation.

Moreover all this impinges on the Irigarayan problematic of how to establish a speaking position for women and in particular what it means to say one is 'speaking as a woman'. Feminist critiques of recent attempts by male philosophers to revalue the philosophical 'feminine' by speaking as a woman (e.g. Deleuze and Derrida) demonstrate that speaking as a woman from a subject position that is in fact that of a man, is simply not the same as speaking as a woman from the subject position of a woman (see for example Braidotti, 1991, 1994). The question then becomes how to establish such a subject position and whether it requires an autonomous female sexuality as Irigaray suggests.

The earliest attempts to establish a speaking position for women (as opposed to just Woman) through 'writing the body' came of course from the *écriture féminine* camp, widely maligned, misunderstood and criticised, in particular on the grounds of its biological essentialism, as well as its apparent obscurity, abstruseness and political inadequacy. However as a result of this questioning, so-called 'French Feminism', especially the theories of Irigaray, has increasingly been re-evaluated by Anglo-American feminists and others, concerned with the social constitution of sexed embodiment, and the possibilities for change this both implies and denies. They attempt to accommodate two key points – the Freudian insight that subjectivity is always sexed and the Lacanian insight that sexed identifications are made through entry into the symbolic order – with phenomenological theories of the body, while also attempting to avoid the masculinism at the heart of these insights. They argue, for example, that underlying Lacan's account of the (albeit shifting) discursive positioning of sexed identifications is a male-female structure, a hierarchical gender dichotomy, which necessarily devalues and/or excludes the feminine perceived in phallic terms as merely a lack. The point is that sexuality, in Freudian terms, is *always* defined in terms of masculine sexuality. Hence the call for an autonomous sexuality for women. Moreover if these insights are linked to Foucauldian notions of the body and sexuality, disciplinary technologies, biopower etc, (adapted to feminist concerns and thereby cleansed of their androcentrism), feminist theory is pushed towards a move beyond the essentialism versus construction opposition. This move renders more appealing Irigaray's step of accepting the Freudian basic insight, but rejecting the accompanying definition of sexuality in masculine terms and therefore attempting to affirm the feminine in sexual difference. Indeed it is this that sets the context (implicitly if not explicitly) for more recent turns to the problematic of corporeality, or embodiment and sexual difference.

To reiterate then, the focus on corporeality is not simply an attempt to tie bodies to their biology. It rather marks an attempt to escape from what Elizabeth Grosz (1994) refers to as 'the mire of biologism'. It also marks a significant move for both Anglo-American feminism and philosophy in their attempts to rethink corporeality beyond sex/gender, essentialism/ construction, biology/culture binary oppositions.

Beyond the Essentialism versus Construction Opposition
Judith Butler (1993) grapples with the question of rethinking the body to include attention to sexual difference. In doing so she attracts the label 'Queer Theory'. Queer theory in this sense is not so much a minority discourse but rather a tool of epistemological critique (hence the title of Eve Kosofsky Sedgwick's seminal book *Epistemology of the Closet*). Homosexuality is conceived as part of an epstemic/ontological regime, a power/knowledge nexus in which the hetero/homosexual binary plays a significant organising role, structuring much of western life and thought. Butler's concern is to bring into question this epistemic/ontological regime. It is this, she argues, that produces gender categories as ontological categories, which, moreover support both gender hierarchies and compulsory heterosexuality. In other words she wants to expose the foundational categories of identity – sex, gender, the body – as effects of specific power/knowledge formations, (what she calls at one point the heterosexual matrix and later heterosexual hegemony), in order to reveal

them as the productions of institutions, practices and discourses, that have a naturalizing effect; and in so doing destabilize the defining institutions of pallogocentrism and compulsory heterosexuality.

Implicit in Butler's work is a Hegelian notion of subjectivity and an attempt to move beyond it; she assumes the interrelational, intersubjective nature of subjectivity while resisting the binary, negating, totalizing aspect of Hegel that posits the self-other relation in terms of identity and sameness. She builds on the insights of poststructuralism, adapted to feminist concerns, drawing *inter alia* both on Foucault, and on Derrida's notion of temporality and associated concepts of iteration and citation. She argues that sexed bodies are socially constructed, and in order to make this argument, develops the notion of construction beyond that implied in the essentialism versus construction divide.[4] Indeed she argues that the very concept of materiality (as in the materiality of bodies) is itself a construction.

From Construction to Materialization

In *Bodies that Matter* Butler reconsiders the materiality of the body in response to criticisms of the theory of the body that she had developed earlier in *Gender Trouble* where, following Nietzsche and Foucault, she developed a view of the body as a construction, a product of the effects of power; she was then criticised for neglecting what is deemed to be the materiality of the body. In *Bodies that Matter* she addresses this criticism. She argues that posing materiality and construction as oppositional serves to obscure the matrix of power that actually produces this particular view of construction.

Indeed Butler argues that thinking the materiality of the body requires avoiding the sex/gender distinction and rethinking the meaning of construction beyond that implied in the essentialism and/or materialism versus construction dichotomies. To this effect she links the materialization of the body to the performativity of gender. In order to do this she adds Derrida to Foucault, drawing on Derrida's notion of iterability (as in his argument with John Searle in 'Signature, Event, Context' (Derrida 1988)) to develop the notion of gender as performance that she introduced in *Gender Trouble*. Performance becomes citation and gender reiteration. Thus she no longer equates performativity simply with performance which seemed to imply some sort of everyday optionality and a humanist choosing subject. Performativity, she argues, 'cannot be understood outside of a process of iterability, a regularized and constrained repetition of norms' (p.95). Significantly for understanding this distinction, she goes on: 'And this repetition is not performed *by* a subject; this repetition is what *enables* a subject and constitutes the temporal condition for the subject' (p.95, my emphasis). Nor is performativity to be understood as a singular act, 'but rather the reiterative and citational practice by which discourse produces the effects that it names . . . the regulatory norms of "sex" work in a performative fashion to constitute the materiality of bodies and, more specifically, to materialize sexual difference in the service of the consolidation of the heterosexual matrix' (Butler 1993 : 22). Therefore performativity is not about a person bringing into being that which s/he names but rather it is about 'the reiterative power of discourse to produce the phenomena that it regulates and constrains' (ibid. p.2), in this case sexed and gendered bodies. Adopting bodily norms is not something undergone by a subject who is separate from it but is one of the processes through which an authorial "I" is formed at all.

Basically then she is arguing that gender is constructed through relations of power that are inherent in normative constraints that both produce and regulate bodily beings (in all their diversity – those that matter and those that do not) through a process of ritualised repetition. Construction in this sense does not imply artificiality or dispensability but rather becomes a matter of constitutive constraint. By this she means, 'having the character of that without which we could not think at all' (p.xi), without which there would be no 'I', no 'we'. Construction therefore is not an origin or cause but rather, 'a process of reiteration through which both "subjects" and "acts" come to appear at all' (Butler 1993 : 9). Note moreover that 'there is no power that acts, but only a reiterated acting that is power in its persistence and instability' (p.9). 'Crucially then, construction is neither a single nor a causal process initiated by a subject and culminating in a set of fixed effects. Construction not only takes place in time but is itself a temporal process which operates through the reiteration of norms; sex is both *produced and destabilized* in the course of this reiteration' (p.10).

As far as identification goes, identification is not posed as the activity of a conscious being but rather in terms of an assimilating passion through which an ego first emerges. Accepting the Freudian account of the ego as 'first and foremost a bodily ego', she argues that the imaginary morphology through which an ego emerges is neither presocial nor presymbolic, 'but is itself orchestrated through regulatory schemas that produce morphological possibilities' (Butler 1993 : 13-14). Significantly however, '[t]hese regulatory schemas are not timeless structures, but historically revisable criteria of intelligibility which produce and vanquish bodies that matter' (1993:14).

She stresses the role the heterosexual imperative plays in enabling certain sexed identifications and excluding others. (This is where her attachment to psychoanalysis becomes apparent.) She conceives of a realm of abject unintelligible bodies which 'don't matter' but that are the necessary constitutive outside to the domain of intelligible bodies that 'do matter'. This realm is not conceived as a reverse discourse in a Foucauldian sense but rather as an excluded realm that always presents the possibility of a return as in a psychoanalytic model. In this sense then, abjection and the possibility of the disruptive return of the abject provide the possibility of rearticulations and therefore the space for change. Understanding construction as constitutive constraint allows us to examine the relations between the intelligible and the abject. A crucial question for Butler then becomes: how to alter the terms that constitute the necessary domain of bodies and which render unintelligible and unlivable those that comprise the abject?

However I will not go into all the various morphological intricacies that Butler presents, but instead merely emphasise the point that in following

Foucault and moving beyond the sex/gender distinction, she goes beyond the Foucauldian claim that there is no prediscursive sex that founds the cultural construction of gender in order to 'examine and subvert the ways in which the materiality of sex is forcibly produced' (p.xi).

Political significance

Butler's concern is thus with the political significance of the production and regulation of the matter of bodies. She wants to deconstruct notions of the body and materiality in order 'to displace them from the contexts in which they have been deployed as instruments of oppressive power' (Butler 1993 : 17). So to pose the question in terms of discourse or construction versus materiality is to miss the critical point. Her critical/political point is that deconstructing the materiality of bodies provides the conditions for the possibility of alternative formulations. Hence to deconstruct the category of sex in this way is not to 'question the urgency or credibility of sex or violence as political issues, but rather show that the way their very materiality is circumscribed is fully political' (1992 : 19). Butler explains the political significance of this by referring to the legal restrictions on what does and does not count as rape, evidence and the effects of violence etc., and the role of the category of sex as a principle of production and regulation rather than merely one of representation. Therefore she advocates putting the categories of sex and violence into quotation marks in order to denaturalize them and indicate that they are sites of political debate.[5]

Materiality

In considering the materiality of the body, then, Butler focuses on the processes of the body's materialization. Matter is reconceived, 'not as a site or surface, but as *a process of materialization that stabilizes over time to produce the effect of boundary, fixity and surface we call matter*' (Butler 1993 : 9, original emphasis). The 'matter' of bodies becomes an effect of the dynamic of power, inseparable from the regulatory norms that orchestrate their materialization and their signification. Importantly then, this reconceptualization of materialization allows Butler to focus on the way the category of sex is not immutable but produced as a normative, but nevertheless constitutive, constraint through which bodies are materialized. Since matter is posed as an effect of power, it cannot be seen to pre-exist, or ground, discourses on sex. Nevertheless, Butler argues, this presumption of the materiality of sex as the irreducible point of departure for various cultural inscriptions underpins feminist epistemologies, ethics and various analyses of gender. This leads her to state, in typical poststructuralist style: 'in an effort to displace the terms of this debate, I want to ask how and why "materiality" has become a sign of irreducibility, that is, how it is that the materiality of sex is understood as that which only *bears* cultural constructions and therefore cannot be a construction' (Butler 1993:28, original emphasis).

Is materiality then a linguistic product?

Butler however is not arguing for some kind of linguistic monism. Her argument is not that the materiality of bodies is nothing but a linguistic product but rather that the concept of materiality is inescapably bound up with signification. This seems to be a very significant point to grasp for those struggling to engage with the insights of poststructuralism; on the other hand to those who are not it doesn't seem to be saying anything very profound at all! Butler's point on this matter is that: 'To posit by way of language a materiality outside of language is still to posit that materiality, and the materiality so posited will retain that positing as its constitutive condition' (Butler 1993 : 30).

Problem of reference

All this has implications for our understanding of reference. It challenges traditional understandings of the meaning of reference which are simply not complex enough. Indeed traditional understandings of reference and materiality have been generally undermined by poststructuralist insights into meaning and knowing, truth and knowledge. Thus Butler, for example, argues on this point in the context of the body: 'To claim that discourse is formative is not to claim that it originates, causes or exhaustively composes that which it concedes; rather it is to claim that there is no reference to a pure body which is not at the same time further *formation* of that body. In this sense the linguistic capacity to refer to sexed bodies is not denied, but the very meaning of "referentiality" is altered. In philosophical terms the constative claim is always to some degree performative' (Butler 1993 : 10-11).

Hence Butler argues that the claim that she does not take account of the materiality of the body rests on the assumption of a metaphysical opposition between materialism and idealism which is undermined in a poststructuralist understanding of the performativity of discourse, in particular in this case, as it operates in the materialization of sex. Moreover she insists that she is not defending constructivism per sé but rather examining the omissions and the exclusions that constitute its limits (again a typical poststructuralist move). What she is doing then, she argues, is questioning materiality as a presupposition. Thus she is not so much disputing the materiality of the body as providing a genealogy of the 'normative conditions under which the materiality of the body is framed and formed, and, in particular how it is formed through differential categories of sex' (p.17).

Derrida on reference

Derridean deconstruction and in particular *différance* provide a view of reference and materiality that avoids the separation of text and extra-textual real. Deconstruction renders problematic the concept of materiality but this does not entail an incipient idealism or denial of the material. Indeed again the point is that the material is rendered problematic in the sense that the view of meaning and the productivity of language within deconstruction undermines the binary opposition (as indeed all binary oppositions) between the real and the ideal, the material and its representation, while insisting on the materiality of representation (or in more technical terms 'the signifier').

The point is that representation produces rather than captures the real or the material and furthermore there is always an excess to representation. What this amounts to, as Derrida explains in *Positions,* is a rejection not so much of matter per se as a rejection of matter in the logocentric sense as foundational in the sense of presence, reality, or any kind of transcendental signified (Derrida 1981 : 65).[6] Therefore if we see the matter of bodies as itself a matter of production rather than as a predetermining given we can begin to think about what goes into the production of those bodies as male and female subjects, and the social institutions, practices and knowledges (such as biology) that produce sex and gender as *causes* rather than effects. We can deconstruct the processes, representations and symbolic framework that pervade the cultural imaginary, through which we are constituted and through which we constitute ourselves.[7]

Sexual Difference

This all has implications for the question of the status or nature of sexual difference. Rosi Braidotti (1991, 1994) argues that to be is to be either a man or a woman, yet, as others have pointed out, in phallogocentricism sexual difference is deemed derivative of human being. This then allows for the notion of an abstract gender-neutral human being which feminist analyses repeatedly reveal to be problematic, for that gender-neutral body is revealed on closer examination to be rather an idealized male body from which female bodies then become a deviation. It seems as though male bodies can somehow transcend their immanence in biology, 'nature' and their sexed specificity. So, it might seem as Grosz argues, that to insist instead that sexual difference is not derivative, that there simply is no neutral being from which to measure the yardstick of sexual difference, then becomes both an ontological question and an epistemological one. However does this mean to say then that sexual difference is ontological difference, as indeed Braidotti (1994) claims? And if so, *how* is this so? What does it mean to say that bodies are, in fact, sexually marked from the beginning? How can we think sexual difference as constitutive without being determining, unless we posit some essential form of sexual difference overlaid by culture? Indeed insisting on sexual difference as ontological difference entails such questions as: '[I]s sexual difference primary and sexual inscription a cultural overlay or rewriting of an ontologically prior differentiation? Or is sexual differentiation a product of the various forms of inscription of culturally specific bodies? Do inscriptions produce sexual differentiation? Or does sexual difference imply a differential mode of inscription?' (Grosz 1994 189).

However, as Grosz herself notes in a footnote, Derrida's notion of inscription or the trace pre-empts the question of whether or not sexual difference implies a differential mode of inscription. For the trace precedes nature and culture in that it is 'not more natural than cultural, not more physical than psychical, biological than spiritual. It is that starting from which a becoming unmotivated of the sign, and with it all the ulterior oppositions between *physis* and its other, is possible' (Derrida 1976 : 48 quoted in Grosz 1994 : 226).

Hence where for Grosz the question becomes: 'My question to Derrida, then, is whether the trace itself is marked by or the mark of sexual difference. What is the relation between the trace and sexual difference?' (Grosz 1994 : 226, fn 1), I would rather suggest that this question is simply undecidable. The ontological status of sexual difference is undecidable. However, the point is that sexual difference *functions* within logocentricism as an ontological category. Therefore I find I have to agree with Robyn Ferrell's pertinent point: 'The challenge that deconstruction puts to feminism is to show cause why it is not a condition of its theory that *the truth of sexual difference be declared found*' (Ferrell 1991 : 181, original emphaisis).

The question of sexual difference is not a metaphysical question because it need not involve speculating about what *is* in an essential sense or the actual nature of things beyond appearances etc., but rather asks about how sexual difference functions as ontological difference within phallogocentricism. The point is that while the former (essences etc.) are simply undecidable, deconstruction demonstrates that what can be got at are the forces in operation in creating the illusion of decidability. Deconstructing the conditions of possiblity in this way reveals the violence and exclusions upon which the binarized version of sexual difference is established and opens the space for the possibility of disruption and displacement – what Derrida might call sexual difference otherwise.

Biology

But what about biology? One of the problems with accepting this view of the body is the apparent self-evidence of biological facts. However if this view of the body is linked to contemporary critiques of the status of scientific knowledge in general and bio-medical knowledge in particular this apparent self-evidence is undermined. The basic argument is that scientific facts are not objectively given mirrors of nature. Nor are they mere representations; scientists are *creating* rather than discovering reality. In terms of the body, this means that to view scientific models and attendant metaphors as mere representations of a natural body that can somehow dissociate itself from them is inadequate. As Diprose (1994) puts it these models do more than merely inform the way we represent our bodies to ourselves, they inform how we *live* our bodies. To understand these effects as simply superimposed on a natural body which could stand apart from them involves an atomistic view of the body as a discrete object in the world separate from the 'self' which owns and controls it.[8] The naturalistic body, then, is actually created by scientists as the object of scientific investigation and feminists critiques focus in particular on the role of gender in this process and the salience of sexual difference in the production of scientific 'facts' about the body. For example Nelly Oudshoorn in *Beyond the Natural Body* focuses on the construction of the hormonal body (which has currently become one of the main ways of thinking about sex differences). She undertakes an archaeology of the development of the concept of sex hormones concentrating in particular on 'how the "facts" about hormones came into existence' (Oudshoorn 1994, p.9). She explores the processes through which scientific claims come to be interpreted, accepted, disseminated and eventually acheive the status of universal, natural facts. In so doing she demonstrates the ways in which these apparently objective "facts" are pervaded by cultural assumptions.

Oudshoorn charts the development of the contemporary view of bodies as complex technological communication systems and the accompanying development of the neurosciences and fields of endocrinology and immunology. The concept of 'female' and 'male' sex hormones as chemical messengers of feminity and masculinity, was developed in the field of endocrinology, as the chemical basis of sex differences. By examining the ideas and cultural frameworks of sex endocrinologists she shows how cultural ideas became incorporated into this research. For example she shows how prescientific assumptions about sexual duality (located in the gonads) structured the develpment of hypotheses in research on the function and origin of sex hormones. She also shows how, while attempting to locate the chemical cause of sex differences, scientists were finding that all organisms were androgenous (the female hormone was isolated in the urine of stallions) thereby challenging the notion that sex is an ahistorical attribute of the human body. Not only did this revolutionize thinking about sexual differentiation, the 'facts' undermined the idea of two stable opposite sexes and there was even a moment when sexual duality could have been replaced. However male and female terminology was retained even though its meaning was now transformed. Moreover it was the female body that came to be portrayed as controlled by hormones not the male body, as Oudshoorn notes, and she also charts the social and cultural factors that facilitated this development.

By examining the social dynamics of the production of knowledge, then, Oudshoorn demonstrates some of the ways in which the apparent naturalistic reality of the hormonal body is created by scientists rather than determined by nature. Biomedical sciences are portrayed as discursive technologies that simultaneously construct and reflect our understanding of the body. There simply is no unmediated natural truth about the body and there is nothing self-evident about biological 'facts'. She argues that neither bodies nor technologies, are unequivocally determined by nature, and that medical knowledges do not have to be the way they are.

Oudshoorn also stresses the materiality of knowledge production which, she argues, is a factor that is frequently overlooked in criticisms of science that concentrate on theories and texts alone. The construction of scientific meaning involves both langue, and practices of sex and the body, eg. experiments, diagnostic tools and examinations, relations of power, medical treatment, drugs, changes in forms and procedures of intervention. She concludes: 'Who knows what might have happened to the hormonally constructed body concept if there had existed an andrological clinic rather than a gynecological clinic? Imagine what might have happened in a world with different cultural and moral attitudes to gender and responsibilities for family planning and childcare. It is not beyond imagination that we could have ended up with a male contaceptive pill, a medical treatment for male menopause and a classification system of multiple sexes' (Oudshoorn 1994: 151)

Conclusion

As more and more research points to the productive rather that descriptive role of biology/science, while at the same time feminists insist on the facticity of sexed/gendered bodies, it becomes clear that rethinking the body invloves rethinking the material. Conceptualizing construction as something in opposition to esssentialism or extraneous to an object is simply not adequate. What is needed is a way of thinking the imbrication of the material with the symbolic, the politics of signification, and the imaginary (in the Lacanian sense). Recent turns to the problematic of embodiment, subjectivity and sexual difference attempt to do that. The broad aim is the reinscription and transformation of bodies based on a shared recognition of the salience of sexual difference, the bodily roots of subjectivity and the view that social transformation requires change at the level of the symbolic, in the Lacanian sense.

Acknowledgements

This paper is a revised version of 'Beyond Essentialism and Construction' in *New Writing By Women in Philosophy*, a special issue of *Women's Philosophy Review*, University of Nottingham, March 1996.

Notes

[1] Elam (1994) explains how this works in relation to sex/gender through the work of Suzanne Kessler (1990) on the 'Medical Construction of Gender'.

[2] For an overview of feminist thinking around the body see Grosz (1994 : 15-19). Grosz discerns three broad categories; egalitarian, social constructionist and sexual difference theorists. Irigaray, Cixous, Spivak, Gallop, Gatens, Kirby, Butler, Schor, Wittig are listed as examples of sexual difference theorists who move beyond the essentialism vs construction opposition and in various ways attempt to avoid the mind/body dualism.

[3] Grosz (1994) for example demonstrates this with reference to the work of Foucault, Merleau-Ponty, Lingis, and Deleuze and Guattari among others.

[4] For a reassessment of essentialism see Schor and Weed (1994), Vicky Kirby (1991b), Diana Fuss (1989).

[5] Butler demonstrates the use of poststructuralism for considering the violence to women's bodies in Butler and Scott ((eds.)) 1992, particularly p.17-19. See also Sharon Marcus, 'Fighting Bodies, Fighting Words: A Theory and Politics of Rape', to which Butler refers, (also in Butler and Scott ((eds.)) 1992).

[6] Derrida also discusses the problem of reference and rejects charges that deconstruction involves the suspension of reference; see the interview with Richard Kearney in Kearney, (ed) (1984) *Dialogues with*

Contemporary Continental Thinkers : The Phenomenological Heritage,
Manchester: Manchester University Press. Vicki Kirby (1991a, 1991b,)
and Robyn Ferrell (1991) also discuss the question of reference and
materiality in relation to Derrida.

7   For a discussion of the apparent neglect of embodiment in
deconstruction see Diprose (1994: 77-81).

8   Diprose is concerned with the problematic of ethics, embodiment and
sexual difference. She argues that injustice against women stems from
the ways in which social assumptions about sexual difference establish
women's embodied existence as a deviation from a primary, male norm.
She examines the way this works in relation to traditional views of ethics
and in particular bio-medical ethics, which she argues cannot
accommodate specifically female aspects of embodiment such as
pregnant embodiment or surrogacy.

References

Armstrong, D., 1987, 'Bodies of Knowledge: Foucault and the Problem of
Human Anatomy' in Scrambler, G. (ed.) *Sociological Theory and
Medical Sociology,* London: Tavistock.

Braidotti, R., 1994, *Nomadic Subjects: Embodiment and Sexual Difference,*
New York: Columbia University Press.

Braidotti, R., 1991, *Patterns of Dissonance,* New York: Routledge.

Butler, J., 1993, *Bodies that Matter: on the Discursive Limits of "Sex",* New
York and London: Routledge.

Butler, J., 1992, 'Contingent Foundations: Feminism and the Question of
Postmodernism' in Butler, J. and Scott, J. (eds.) *Feminists Theorize the
Political,* New York and London: Routledge.

Butler, J., 1990, *Gender Trouble: Feminism and the Subversion of Identity,*
New York and London: Routledge.

Butler, J. and Scott, J., (eds.) 1992, *Feminists Theorize the Political,* New
York and London: Routledge.

Derrida, J., 1981, *Positions,* London: Athlone Press. Tr. Alan Bass.

Derrida, J., 1988, 'Signature, Event, Context', in *Limited, Inc.,* Evanston:
Northwestern University Press. Tr. Samuel Weber and Jeffrey Mehlman.

Diprose, R., 1994, *The Bodies of Women: Ethics, Embodiment and Sexual
Difference,* New York and London: Routledge.

Diprose, R. and Ferrell, R. (eds.), 1991, *Cartographies: Poststructuralism
and the Mapping of Bodies and Spaces,* Sydney: Allen & Unwin.

Elam, D., 1994, *Feminism and Deconstruction,* New York and London:
Routledge.

Ferrell, R., 1991, 'The Passion of the Signifier and the Body in Theory',
Hypatia vol. 6, no 3, Fall, 172-184.

Fuss, D., 1989, *Essentially Speaking: Feminism, Nature and Difference,*
New York and London: Routledge.

Grosz, E., 1994,*Volatile Bodies: Toward a Corporeal Feminism,*
Bloomington and Indianapolis: Indiana University Press.

Grosz, E. (ed.), 1991, *Hypatia* Special Issue *Feminism and the Body* vol. 6, no. 3, Fall.

Kearney, R. (ed.), 1984, *Dialogues with Contemporary Continental Thinkers,* Manchester: Manchester University Press.

Kessler, S., 1990, 'The Medical Construction of Gender: Case Management of Intersexed Infants', *Signs*, 16, 1, 3-26.

Kirby, V. 1991a, 'Corpus delicti: the body at the scene of writing', in Diprose R. and Ferrell R. (eds.) *Cartographies: Poststructuralism and the Mapping of Bodies and Spaces*, Sydney: Allen & Unwin.

Kirby, V., 1991b, 'Corporeal: Habits: Addressing Essentialism Differently', *Hypatia* vol. 6, no. 3, Fall, 4-24.

Osborne, P. and Segal, L., 1994, 'Gender as Performance: An Interview with Judith Butler'. *Radical Philosophy* 67, Summer, 32-39.

Oudshoorn, N., 1994, *Beyond the Natural Body: An Archaeology of Sex Hormones,* New York and London: Routledge.

Schor, N. and Weed, E. (eds.), 1994, *The Essential Difference*, Bloomington and Indianapolis: Indiana University Press.

Theory and Practice: Ways Forward

Chris Weedon

This paper was presented at the conference in a session entitled 'Backlash and Beyond'. It looks both backwards and forwards in order to consider where we are now as feminist scholars and activists and where feminism and Women's Studies might go from here. Seventeen years of Conservative government have had profound effects on social policy in Britain and on a feminist agenda in particular. Susan Faludi, among others, makes a powerful polemical case about the 'Backlash' in her 1992 book of the same name.[1] Yet in considering feminism as a politics and Women's Studies as politicised intellectual work, we might prefer to think about our recent history in a more differentiated way in terms of uneven development in the many areas of feminist struggle.

The processes of feminist change and transformation may no longer seem as clear cut as in the early years of Second Wave feminism. Yet, if we have suffered many setbacks over the last two decades, we have also made much progress. Feminism, today, I would argue, is alive and well and much more diverse than in the 1970s. It includes many more varied groups of women and women of many different generations. It includes the political and intellectual work of many women who would be unwilling to identify with the label 'feminist'. Moreover, women's studies and feminist teaching and scholarship have expanded and diversified beyond recognition over the last 25 years.

Much has happened in British feminism since the early activism of the 1970s when the feminist movement, so strong at the turn of the century, gained a new impetus. The movement of what has come to be known as Second Wave feminism organised itself around consciousness raising and campaign groups and began to put a radical set of feminist demands on the mainstream agenda.[2] Many women will remember the National Women's Liberation conferences of those years at which a series of demands were hammered out and became the basis for a national feminist agenda. They included the rights to equal pay, education, free contraception and abortion, twenty-four hour nursery provision, freedom from domestic violence and the sexual violence of the pornography industry, the right to define one's own sexuality and an end to heterosexist oppression. In the years that followed issues to do with racism and colonialism gained increasing recognition as Black and Third World women pointed to the racism and Eurocentrism of the movement. In the 1980s questions of peace and anti-nuclear struggles found a focus at Greenham common and elsewhere, and since then there have been important developments in ecological feminism.

My own experience of the Women's Liberation Movement in Birmingham in the mid-to-late 1970s was of an extensive network of groups of all kinds that sent delegates to a monthly meeting which served as a city-wide forum and published a newsletter. Yet even in the 1970s – when ideas of sisterhood were still widely proclaimed – different interest groups and conflicts of interest between women were apparent. Even within the intimacy of consciousness raising groups, questions of heterosexism and racism quickly came to the fore. The last national WLM conference, which was held in Birmingham in 1978, saw many of these conflicts acted out as lesbian and Black women protested against the failure of the movement to take their needs and interests seriously. Black women had begun to articulate a radical critique of mainstream, predominantly White, middle-class feminism which would have profound and lasting effects. They had also begun to analyse the situation of Black and Asian women in Britain.[3]

The 1970s also saw the beginnings of Women's Studies. Since its earliest days, the contemporary Women's Movement has privileged education as a crucial dimension of consciousness raising. Many women gathered in informal groups to discuss key feminist texts and fiction dealing with women's experience. In the United States the institutional struggles in the late 1960s and early 1970s to establish Black Studies, which gained momentum with the assassination of Dr Martin Luther King, paved the way for the subsequent establishment of Women's Studies programmes. In Britain the story was different. Much early work in Women's Studies took place in the adult education sector. Feminists offered courses for the WEA and university extra-mural departments and this path offered the possibility of reaching a wider audience. When, in 1976, women at the Centre for Contemporary Cultural Studies, where I was a postgraduate student, began the internal fight to set up Women's Studies, our struggle was on at least two fronts. On the one hand we wished to see Women's Studies recognised as central to the intellectual and political agenda, both within the Centre for Contemporary Cultural Studies and in education everywhere. On the other hand, we were acutely aware of the hostility to theory within the broader Women's Movement outside of academia. In the Birmingham Centre the immediate task, as we perceived it at that time, was to transform a Marxist orthodoxy and we set out collectively to develop a Marxist-*feminist* theory. Yet we were also committed to keeping our work rooted in a feminist politics not only within the university context but in the wider Women's Liberation Movement.

The struggles in Birmingham to establish feminist questions as central to the intellectual and political agenda motivated the collective writing of the Marxist-feminist book *Women Take Issue*.[4] Such work was soon challenged by Black women for the exclusion of serious consideration of race.[5] Indeed, the 1970s agenda of producing general theories of patriarchy – be these radical feminist or Marxist feminist – seems quite naively ambitious from the perspective of the 1990s. The subsequent diversification of the Women's Movement, the growth and diversification of feminist scholarship and the impact of postmodernism on social and cultural theory have put into question the viability of general theories.

Since the 1970s, the voices of marginalised groups of women – Black women, women of Colour, lesbian women, and so-called 'Third World' women – have gained strength. Recognition of the centrality of power relations of class, heterosexism, race and colonialism have complexified the question of gender oppression. Women's experience, which has been so important to feminism since the 1970s, can no longer be seen as in any sense transparent. While it remains central to feminist analysis and politics, it is an experience shaped as much by differences as by shared forms of oppression.

The issues we now face as feminists are as many and complex as they have ever been. They include:

- the increasing class divisions between rich and poor;
- the reduction of the welfare state;
- reduced provision for education, especially at the adult education level, which was so important in the early years of Women's Studies in Britain;
- local and global environmental problems;
- the failure to address global relations of wealth and poverty and the development of a fortress Europe.

Racism, Eurocentrism and heterosexism continue to oppress particular groups of women and men. Yet, at the same time, many people talk of the present as a 'post-feminist' era. As feminist teachers, scholars, intellectuals and activists, we need to broaden our audience and to speak to more than just ourselves. We need to extend our roots and put down new ones outside academia and our beyond own feminist circles. We need to ensure that the teaching and research that we do addresses important issues and is made accessible to a wider public. What kinds of feminist theory, I would like to ask, can help realise this agenda?

At the heart of a productive and enabling feminism for the 1990s and beyond must surely be the recognition of difference, respect for difference and a willingness to take seriously the many issues that face specific groups of women in today's world. To understand difference and the power relations that structure it is the first step towards turning our differences from relations that divide us socially and politically into forms of strength.[6] Thanks to those groups of women, marginalised in early Second Wave feminism, difference has become a key concept in feminist theory and practice. How, we need to ask, might we mobilise it in productive ways, avoiding those superficial celebrations of difference so popular in some forms of postmodern discourse which tend to mask the power relations that create differences?

The question of difference is central in feminist theory and politics. It has long been a key term in feminist thought. From the 1700s onwards, liberal feminists struggled for the inclusion of women in the new order. At issue were the ways in which *anatomical* and *biological* differences between the sexes were used to justify and enforce *social* differences which restricted women's legal rights to equality, self-determination and access to power both within and outside the home. Whereas in the 1970s, early Second Wave feminism stressed the centrality and often primacy of gender oppression as the basis for a universal sisterhood, more recent feminism has stressed differences produced by class, race, ethnicity, sexual orientation, disability and age. Moreover, recent feminism has drawn on early radical feminist critiques of the mind/body split and the privileging of rationality within the liberal tradition to reinstate the importance of embodied subjectivity for women.[7]

The recognition of the diversity of women's experience and cultural production – shaped as it is by factors such as class, sexual orientation, race, religion and ethnicity – has led to a variety of approaches to the question of difference within contemporary feminism. One key response has been identity politics, the other, a postmodern challenge to 'woman' as a transparent category and a deconstruction of the meanings of subjectivity and experience.[8] While identity politics strive for alternative oppositional positive identities for specific oppressed groups of women, postmodern feminism sees subjectivity as fractured, contradictory and as discursively produced.

The development of Western feminist theory since 1968 has been marked by a critical engagement with postmodern theory. Attempting to go beyond the liberal feminist goal of extending rights to women, postmodern feminists, like many other feminists, have sought to theorise those areas of women's experience and oppression that elude liberal theory and politics. In doing so they have mobilised the postmodern critique of the authority and status of science, truth, history, power, knowledge and subjectivity, bringing a transformative gender dimension to postmodern theory and developing new conceptions of sexual difference.

From the perspective of postmodern feminism, it is no longer a question of replacing patriarchal discourses of gender, which claim to be true, with a single, alternative, feminist truth. It is rather a question of looking at the network of power relations which produce particular discourses of gender and at their implications for women's everyday lives. It is a question of understanding the fundamental assumptions on which particular theories are based in order to judge their political and social implications and to develop oppositional strategies for transformation. We need feminist theories and politics that do justice to the local and specific while understanding the role of more global assumptions and power relations in shaping local conditions for women. In the process our assumptions about women, made from our own localised experience, are likely to be challenged.

The most controversial aspects of forms of feminism influenced by a postmodern agenda are that they question the category 'women' and the possibility of an objective position outside of ideology from which to make truth claims and ground politics. Contemporary feminism was founded on a recognition of the importance of women's experience and the politics of the personal. Yet, as most feminists now realise, we do not, as women, all share the same experience and identities. Moreover, there is a hierarchy in the power relations that produce differences between women. Some forms of experience and identity appear in much feminist work as unmarked, transparent and normative, for example whiteness. Other experiences – those of women marginalised by power relations of race, class, Eurocentrism and heterosexism – are marked as different from this norm rather than plural and complex in their own right. If we want to move beyond the oppositions that both structure and fracture feminism, both sides of these oppositions must be put under the microscope, analysed and transformed. It is not marginalised identities and experiences that are the problem, but rather the unchallenged hegemonic identities and experiences which profit from the marginalisation of others and the power relations which structure their dominance. Challenging racism, for example, in our own work and in the broader society means problematising whiteness and the role it plays in the perpetuation of racism. It is an active engagement with racism that is required of White feminists, not guilt, nor the attitude that sees race as an exclusively Black problem.

Perhaps more than poststructuralist theory *per se*, it was the experience of feminist politics (interpreted, of course in the light of theory) that taught me that it is no longer possible to occupy a privileged objective position from which to ground apparently universally valid ideas of truth and morality or the politics that follow from them. Nor do we have a single position from which to write a history that is objectively true. Knowledge and power are integrally related.

We need to challenge conventional ideas of reason and the reasoning subject in the Western tradition of social thought. Far from being an objective faculty, able to transcend the limitations of a particular time and place and access true knowledge, reason is partial in the double sense of incomplete and interested. Feminist scholarship of recent years has learned much from the work of Foucault (however anti-feminist the content of his work may at times be). Several key feminist concerns figure centrally there: the body as a site of power central to the constitution of subjectivity, the dispersed, discursive nature of power and its links with knowledge. Foucauldian derived approaches to knowledge take issue with centralised models of power. Power is not reducible to any one source, it is a relationship which inheres in material discursive practices. Discourses create forms of subjectivity which are implicated in power relations. Yet power also creates resistance.

As many Third World feminists and feminists of Colour have argued, Western feminists – many of whom are also White and middle class – need to question our taken for granted universals. Rather than claiming either objectivity or the universality of our experience, we need to focus on the very criteria by which we legitimize our claims to knowledge, and avoid generalizing from the experiences of Western, white, heterosexual, middle-class women. We need to question all essences and relativise truth claims, creating a space for political perspectives and interests that have hitherto been marginalised. Moreover we need to question our own identities and the positions that we occupy. We need, I would argue, located theories and practices which acknowledge their partiality in both senses of the term, i.e. as both incomplete and interested.

As feminists we need to use theory strategically in the interests of understanding and transforming oppressive social relations. Our theories may no longer have any external guarantee in so-called objective 'truth' but what is important is what they can bring about, i.e. their material effectivity in the struggle for change. We no longer need a single metanarrative in order to develop and use theories in politically effective ways. We may use categories such as 'gender', 'race', 'class' and 'women' in our social and cultural analysis, but we must make explicit that their meaning in any context is historically and socially specific and likely to exclude. Above all we need to listen to those women whose lives are shaped by power relations of class, race, heterosexism and Eurocentrism in order better to understand and take account of these differences and our own implication in their perpetuation. Differences once recognised can become the basis for shared forms of struggle.

Notes

[1] Susan Faludi, *Backlash: The Undeclared War Against Women*, Vintage, 1992.

[2] For a sense of the range and diversity of Second Wave feminism see the anthologies *Conditions of Illusion*, Feminist Books, 1974; *No Turning Back*, Feminist Anthology Collective, 1981; and *Sweeping Statements*, The Women's Press, 1984. See also the monthly magazine *Spare Rib* published from 1972-1992.

[3] Early examples of this work include *The Heart of the Race: Black Women's Lives in Britain*, edited by Beverley Bryan, Stella Dadzie and Suzanne Scafe, Virago, 1985 and Amrit Wilson, *Finding a Voice: Asian Women in Britain*, Virago, 1978.

[4] *Women Take Issue*, Women's Studies Group, CCCS, Hutchinson, 1978.

[5] See, in particular, Hazel Carby, 'White woman listen! Black feminism and the boundaries of feminism' in *The Empire Strikes Back: Race and Racism in 70s Britain*, Centre for Contemporary Cultural Studies, Hutchinson, 1982, pp. 212-225.

[6] Among others this idea is powerfully articulated by the late Black American lesbian feminist poet and activist Audre Lorde in her collection of essays *Sister Outsider*, Crossing Press, 1984.

[7] Concern with embodied subjectivity is shared by both psychoanalytic feminism (especially the work of Luce Irigaray) and recent poststructuralist feminist theory. For more on this see for example Rosi Braidotti, *Patterns of Dissonance*, Polity, 1991; Judith Butler, *Bodies that Matter*, Routledge, 1993; and Elizabeth Grosz, *Space, Time and Perversion*, Routledge, 1995.

[8] See, for example, the discussions of identity politics and postmodern feminism in *Feminism/Postmodernism*, edited by Linda J. Nicholson, Routledge, 1990 and *Feminists Theorize the Political* edited by Judith Butler and Joan. W. Scott, Routledge, 1992.

Notes on Contributors

Jane Aaron is Professor of English in the School of Humanities and Social Sciences at the University of Glamorgan. She has published a number of articles on Welsh writing in English and English Romanticism, and is the author of two monographs, one on the Romantic essayists Charles and Mary Lamb, and the other - a Welsh-language volume - on Welsh women writers of the nineteenth century. She also co-edited two volumes of collected essays: *Out of the Margins: Women's Studies in the Nineties* (Falmer Press) and *Our Sisters' Land: The Changing Identities of Women in Wales* (University of Wales Press).

Cara Aitchison is Senior Research Fellow in the Leisure and Sport Research Unit at Cheltenham and Gloucester College of Higher Education. Her research interests include gender and sexuality in relation to: social and cultural geographies of leisure and tourism; the development of critical leisure theory and education; and the provision of leisure services. She is currently co-authoring *Leisure Landscapes* (Routledge) with Nikki MacLeod and Steve Shaw, and co-editing *Places Pleasures: Leisure geographies of gender and sexuality* with Gill Valentine.

Ranjana Sidhanta Ash is a freelance lecturer and writer on South Asian literature. She has been an Associate Fellow at the Centre for Research in Asian Migration at the University of Warwick and an Editor-Consultant for the Heinemann Asian Writers Series. She has edited *Short Stories from India, Pakistan and Bangladesh* (1980) and her articles include 'The Search for Freedom in Indian Women's Writing' in Nasta, S. (ed.) *Motherlands* (1991) and 'Writers of the South Asian Diaspora in Britain: Post war Fiction in English' in *Wasafiri* (1995).

Karen Atkinson is Senior Lecturer in Sociolinguistics at the University of Sunderland. She has researched and published in the fields of language, media and cultural studies, and was one of the co-editors of *Women's Studies: A Reader* (Harvester Wheatsheaf, 1993). Her current work (with Sarah Oerton) focuses on discourses of lone motherhood in the South Wales Valleys, and (with Shaun Moores) on the interactional dynamics of broadcast troubles talk.

Gail Chester has been actively involved in the Women's Liberation Movement since 1970, and has long been interested in how to record its histories. She is an expert in the history of the WLM, and feminist and radical publishing in Britain. She is a writer and editor, and a researcher in the History of the Book. At present she is juggling her roles as a PhD student at Royal Holloway College, University of London, a parent, a carer, and a political activist.

Ling-Yen Chua is currently completing a PhD thesis on the intersections of race, gender and sexual orientation in the Film Studies Department at the University of Warwick. She has previously lived and been published in New Zealand. This partially explains her interest in the New Zealand film *Desperate Remedies* (NZ, 1994).

Frances Connelly is an activist and campaigner and currently works for Abolition 2000 UK, part of an international movement to bring about nuclear disarmament. She is also involved in Women for a Nuclear Free and Independent Pacific and is on the steering group of the British National Women's Network for International Solidarity. She is a contributor to *Feminist Perspectives on Sustainable Development*.

Jane W. Grant has been closely involved in the women's movement since 1984. She was Director of the National Alliance of Women's Organisations for five years and is, or has been, an active member or trustee of a range of women's organisations. She now combines freelance consultancy on organisational development, mainly with women's groups, with research on the governance of women's organisations at the University of Kent, where she also teaches part-time.

Gill Jagger is Senior Lecturer in the School of Cultural Studies, Leeds Metropolitan University. Her research and publications focus on theorising gender and the body; performance and performativity, and feminism and deconstruction. She also co-edited (with Caroline Wright) *Changing Family Values* (Routledge, 1999).

Liz Kelly is a feminist researcher and activist, who has been involved in the Women's Liberation Movement for 25 years. This includes establishing and working in local services including a refuge and two rape crisis centres, and being part of local, regional and national networks. She is the author of *Surviving Sexual Violence* (Polity Press, 1988) many book chapters, journal articles and research reports. She has worked at the Child and Woman Abuse Studies Unit, University of North London, for eleven years, and also acts as an advisor and consultant to Oxfam and the British Council.

Steph Lawler is Lecturer in Sociology at the University of Durham. She has been researching the significance of concepts of self and subjectivity in the mother-daughter relationship, and is currently planning research into adolescents' conceptualisations of self. She is the author of *Mothering the Self: Mothers, Daughters, Subjectivities* (Routledge, 1999).

So-Hee Lee was educated at Seoul National University of Education; Duksung Women's University and Hanyang University in Seoul. She holds PhDs from Hanyang University and from the University of Hull, and has held Research Fellowships at Girton College, Cambridge and the University of Toronto. At present she is Associate Professor in the English Department, Hanyang Women's College. She is currently working on issues of the enunciation on the borderline from the perspective of postcolonisation and gender.

Sophie Nield lectures in Drama at Goldsmiths College, University of London. She has published on popular theatre and 19th century theatre architecture, and is co-editor of *Raymond Williams Now: Knowledge, Limits and the Future* (Macmillan, 1997). Her research interests include the relationship between space and theatricality; public ceremony and the construction of national identity; and aspects of film and theatre history.

Sarah Oerton teaches Sociology in the School of Humanities and Social Sciences at the University of Glamorgan. Her past research and publications have been on gender, work and organization; family, kinship and household labour; and sexuality. Her most recent book was *Beyond Hierarchy: Gender, Sexuality and the Social Economy* (Taylor and Francis, 1996). She is currently completing research (with Karen Atkinson) on discourses of lone motherhood in the South Wales Valleys and (with Joanna Phoenix) on discourses of women bodyworkers and women sex workers.

Gill Plain is a Lecturer in English at the University of St. Andrews. Her research interests include women's writing of the First and Second World Wars, and gender and popular fiction. Her book *Women's Fiction of the Second World War* is published by Edinburgh University Press and she is currently working on a new book entitled *Twentieth Century Crime Fiction: Gender, Sexuality and the Body*.

Akuba Quansah was born in London in the 1960s and raised by white foster parents in Essex. She attended a convent school in Ghana, her ancestral home, in 1965 for two years before returning to her natural parents in London. She achieved her graduate and postgraduate qualifications in sociology, anthropology and education, respectively, as a mature student, and currently teaches Cultural Studies with the Open University, London. She is researching black female hair signification as her PhD thesis at the University of Middlesex. Akuba has three sons and sees herself as a 'black sister' who is inextricably linked to women.

Jill Radford is a feminist activist and academic. She worked for ten years at Rights of Women, a feminist legal project in London and is a member of the campaigning group Justice for Women. She has taught women's studies and criminology at several universities, including the Open University and the University of Westminster. She is now a Reader in Women's Studies and Criminology at the University of Teeside.

Monika Reinfelder has been active in the international lesbian feminist movement for many years. She has lived and travelled in Latin America and Africa and has worked in higher education, the voluntary sector and local government. At present she works as an equalities advisor for a local authority in London. Her publications include *Amazon to Zami: Towards a Global Lesbian Feminism* (Cassell, 1996).

Francesca Rhydderch has a BA in Modern and Medieval Languages from the University of Cambridge and a MA in Women's Writing and Feminist Theory from Trinity College, Carmarthen. She is currently completing a Ph.D. on Virginia Woolf and Kate Roberts in the Department of English, University of Wales, Aberystwyth, where she also teaches courses in English and Modern Welsh Studies. In addition, she works for the cultural magazine *Planet: The Welsh Internationalist* and is a regular contributor to *Planet, Poetry Wales* and *New Welsh Review*.

Joan Scanlon has been involved in various feminist campaigns and projects, including the Cambridge Women's Resource Centre, Campaign Against Pornography, and Action Against Child Sexual Abuse. She is on the editorial collective of the radical feminist magazine *Trouble and Strife*. She also edited a collection of young women's autobiographies from the Thatcher years, *Surviving the Blues* (Virago). Joan works full-time at the London Contemporary Dance School as Dean of Academic Affairs, and has taught women's studies for various institutions, including the Open University.

Chris Weedon is Reader in Critical and Cultural Theory at the University of Wales, Cardiff. She teaches feminist and cultural theory and Women's Studies. Her books include *Feminist Practice, Poststructuralist Theory* (1987); *Cultural Politics: Class, Gender, Race and the Postmodern World* (with Glenn Jordan) (1995) and *Feminism, Theory and the Politics of Difference* (1999).